THE PRIEST AT THE ALTAR

THE PRIEST AT THE ALTAR

AN HISTORICAL, LITURGICAL AND DEVOTIONAL
EXPLANATION OF THE MASS ACCORDING
TO THE ROMAN MISSAL

BY
DOM ERNEST GRAF, OSB

The current edition is based upon the 1926 publication by
Joseph B. Wagner, Inc., New York.

This edition republished 2023 by Silverstream Priory
with the kind permission of Buckfast Abbey.

Design of this edition is © 2023 by Silverstream Priory

All rights reserved.
No part of this book may be reproduced or transmitted,
in any form or by any means, without permission.

D. BENEDICTUS GARIADOR, OSB
Ab. Gen.

D. HIERONYMUS HAULER, OSB
Cons. a Secr.

Nihil Obstat
ARTHUR J. SCANLAN, STD
Censor Librorum

Imprimatur
✠ PATRICK CARDINAL HAYES
Archbishop of New York

The Cenacle Press at Silverstream Priory
Silverstream Priory
Stamullen, County Meath, K32 T189, Ireland
www.cenaclepress.com

ISBN 978-1-915544-12-4

Book design by Kenneth Lieblich
Cover design by Michael Schrauzer

PREFACE

THE substance of this book first appeared in the pages of *The Homiletic and Pastoral Review* in 1922 and 1923. When the publishers of that valuable Monthly decided to give his contributions a more permanent form, the present writer gladly concurred. His purpose has been a strictly practical one. He is conscious that, had such been his intention, he would yet have lacked the ability to contribute, even in a small way, to our actual knowledge of liturgical origins. What scholarship there is in these unpretentious pages, serves merely as a background for piety. Devotion must have a solid basis, or else it is apt to evaporate like any other emotion. Though these notes have been compiled, in the first instance, for the benefit of priests, others than priests will perhaps find here, within a small compass, information that is available only in larger works, or in books less accessible. Should these pages help even one priest during the priceless half hour of his daily Mass, the writer would deem himself amply rewarded for his efforts. To his Fathers and Brethren in the priesthood he reverently dedicates his little book.

Buckfast Abbey, Devonshire

CONTENTS

I	The Liturgy	1
II	Liturgical Vestments	11
III	*Introibo ad Altare Dei*	25
IV	*Judica Me* and the *Confiteor*	33
V	The *Introit*	35
VI	*Kyrie Eleison*	41
VII	*Gloria in Excelsis Deo*	45
VIII	The Collect and Its Conclusion	49
IX	The Epistle and *Deo Gratias*	57
X	The Gradual, Tract and Sequence	63
XI	The Gospel and the Homily or Sermon	75
XII	The *Credo*	83
XIII	The Offertory	89
XIV	From the Preface to the *Sanctus*	111
XV	The Canon	119
XVI	The Consecration	133
XVII	The Prayers after the Consecration	147
XVIII	The *Memento* of the Dead	161
XIX	*Nobis Quoque Peccatoribus*	167
XX	From the *Pater Noster* to the *Fractio Panis*	173
XXI	From the *Agnus Dei* to the *Domine Non Sum Dignus*	185
XXII	The Communion of the Priest	193
XXIII	Conclusion of the Mass	201
XXIV	Thanksgiving after Mass	211
	Appendix: The Ordinary of the Mass	217

CHAPTER I

THE LITURGY

THE Liturgy of the Catholic Church is no mere external pageant, vaguely satisfying the emotional and religious instincts of the human heart. There is indeed a vast amount of outward pomp and display in the Church's worship, but these externals are only the symbols of interior acts by which we honor and glorify the King of the universe. Or, to vary the metaphor, if rites and ceremonies, music and vestments are the *body,* faith, hope, and charity—the worship and praise of mind and heart—constitute the soul of the Liturgy.

The word *Liturgy* signifies a holy, a divine work, a service of God—not merely personal, private, and based on the best instincts of our rational nature, but—organized by the Church and sanctioned by Christ, who inspired His Church to institute a solemn ceremonial of worship, in the same way as God had given a ritual or liturgical code to the Israelites of old. We find the word Liturgy in the inspired books of the New Testament, where any act performed in the discharge of their official duties by those who are appointed to the service of God, is a liturgical act. In the New Testament, however, that term would seem to be peculiarly reserved to designate the rites which accompany the Eucharistic Sacrifice. It is thus that we are to understand the text of the Acts of the Apostles, when they describe the call of Paul and Barnabas: "As they were ministering to the Lord[1] and fasting, the Holy Ghost said to them: Separate me Saul and Barnabas, for the work whereunto I have taken them."[2]

This text is an obvious allusion to a definitely organized form of

---

[1] The Greek word, which the Douai-Rheims Version translates as "ministering to the Lord," means literally "performing the liturgy."
[2] Acts, xiii. 2.

worship, because the same phraseology is used in Holy Scripture in connexion with the highly developed and divinely established services of the tabernacle of the Testament and the Temple of Jerusalem.

The Church was never without a formal Liturgy, however rudimentary we may conceive it to have been. The symbolic actions which accompanied the Last Supper and the institution of the Sacrifice of the New Law, form the nucleus—the mother-cell, as it were—of all the subsequent additions and developments which have made of the glorious ritual of the Mass the most sublime pageant that ever was, or ever shall be, outside heaven.

Here it will not be without interest to consider what may be called the liturgical instinct of humanity, as it has worked itself out in those ancient races who, though they lived side by side with the people of Israel, were yet bereft of any definite knowledge of the true God. By far the most striking feature of all organized worship of the deity—and there never was a people so barbarous as to be wholly without some such worship—is that it gravitates around a central notion of sacrifice. Both history and archeology bear witness to the universality of sacrificial practices in every age. A casual glance at the various religions (or rather superstitions), which have at different periods of history swayed the hearts, even more than the minds of men, will at first produce only a sense of bewildering diversity and contradiction. But, if we would arrive at some just estimate of the fundamental ideas which underlie the choice of what one can only call parodies of a divine Liturgy, "we must enquire whether the details of the different rituals present nothing but diversity, or whether there is any respect in which they show likeness or uniformity. There is one point in which they resemble one another; and, what is more, that point is the leading feature in all of them: they all center round sacrifice."[3]

If we bear in mind that all false religions are a deviation, or retrogression, from the primeval revelation made to man, we shall have no difficulty in accounting for this striking consensus of humanity in regard to sacrifice. Mankind began with a true, not a false religion, for ignorance, error, and idolatry are the consequence and punishment

---

3 F.B. Jevons, *The Idea of God in Early Religions*, p. 63.

of sin. But, just as human nature is essentially one, and all men have ultimately a common standard by which they measure right and wrong (to wit, their conscience), so did they preserve some few at least of the root ideas of all religion and organized worship. The idea of sacrifice is one of these root ideas. Wherever we find a people or race enjoying an appreciable measure of civilization, we also invariably find that the oblation of sacrifice to the deity forms the chief act of religion. With the growth and development of the tribe or people, the number and solemnity, the variety and significance of sacrificial offerings are likewise increased. Even the most primitive races will make offerings to the deity of the first fruits of all things. Anyone who is at all familiar with the classical writers of Greece and Rome, knows how sacrifices were offered on all manner of occasions: sacrifice marked a man's coming into the world and his leaving it; nothing was bought or sold, no new enterprise was undertaken, no war declared, no treaty of peace or alliance entered upon, without the transaction being ratified, as it were, by the oblation of victims to the deity. These nations did not know the true and living God; yet would they call upon their gods and make them the witnesses of the transaction. We see a beautiful instance of this in the twelfth book of the *Aeneid*, where the poet describes the sacred rites which marked the compact entered into between his hero (Aeneas) and the King of the Rutuli, Evander, and his son Turnus:

> *Praecedunt castris, puraque in veste sacerdos*
> *Setigeri fetum suis, intonsamque bidentem*
> *Attulit, admovitque pecus flagrantibus aris.*
> *Illi, ad surgentem conversi lumina solem,*
> *Dant fruges manibus salsas, et tempora ferro*
> *Summa notant pecudum, paterisque altaria libant.*[4]

4 Then to the hearth the white-robed priest
  Brings two-year sheep all richly fleeced
    And young of bristly swine;
  They turn them to the radiant east,
  With knives the victims' foreheads score,
  Strew cakes of salted meal, and pour
    The sacrificial wine.
  (*Aeneid*, xii, 169 sqq. Conington's translation.)

Verily, pagans put to shame our "after-Christians," who ignore God and enter upon alliances and conclude treaties without asking His approval, blessing and sanction.

With practical unanimity mankind looks upon sacrifice as the chief act of religion or worship, and as the supreme manifestation of the sentiments of dependence, fear, gratitude and supplication which crowd in upon the human heart whenever it gives itself a chance to pause and reflect upon fundamental facts and truths.

The universality of the idea of sacrifice is readily accounted for, when one remembers that it is necessarily a remnant of the primeval revelation which God gave to the father of the human race. The opening pages of the Bible, which are also the earliest authentic records of human history, show the oblation of sacrifices as part, and the chief part, of man's worship of God. "And it came to pass after many days that Cain offered of the fruits of the earth gifts to the Lord. Abel also offered of the firstlings of his flock, and of their fat: and the Lord had respect to Abel, and to his offerings."[5] No doubt, these sacrifices cannot be properly described as "liturgical" functions in the strict sense of the word, because they were rather in the nature of purely personal acts of devotion. The idea, however, of honoring God by the oblation and destruction of the fruits of the earth, or those lower creatures which minister to man's needs, has obviously been fully worked out in the minds of the sons of Adam. A little later we meet, for the first time in history, with an organized cult, for we read that "to Seth also was born a son, whom he called Enos: this man began to call upon the name of the Lord."[6]

Evidently the name of the Lord had been called upon by others prior to the time of Enos. What then is the meaning of the peculiar eulogy bestowed upon Enos? It seems natural to interpret it, as we interpret those other remarks of the inspired writer when he says, for instance, that Jubal was "the father of them that play upon the harp and the organs," and that Tubalcain was "a hammerer and artificer in every work of brass and iron."[7] Jubal and Tubalcain and their fellows were the first artists and craftsmen, the originators and first inventors

---

5 Gen., iv. 3, 4.   6 Gen., iv. ult.
7 Gen., iv. 21, 22.

of the varied and ever-increasing devices which tend to make life not merely possible, but agreeable. In like manner, Enos must be looked upon as the first liturgist, that is, the first author of some form of organized, public and solemn rites and ceremonies by which the world, as yet in its infancy, paid its debt of worship to the omnipotent Creator.

It is likewise noteworthy that the priestly class is contemporary with more elaborate rituals. Here again man feels the need of one who would approach the Deity on his behalf, for he is aware that a special commission is required if a man is to act as mediator between God and his fellow-men, as well as a special holiness and consecration. The priest is essentially an ambassador, or representative, who deals with God in behalf of man. But his chief function and ultimate *raison d'être* is the oblation of sacrifice.

From the very start the arts also are made subservient to religion; in fact they owe their greatest development to religion. Wherever we find an organized ritual (and we find it everywhere), it is invariably accompanied by gestures, sacred dances, chants, and the use of a ceremonial vesture. In a word, the service of God is meant to be *beautiful*, because a true instinct of man makes him realize, even when he is in a state of retrogression and barbarism, that all that is best and noblest must be made subservient to the worship of the Lord and Creator of all.

The observance of certain sacred times and days is likewise an adjunct to divine worship. So universal is this observance that here also we find ourselves in presence of a survival of former times, a reminiscence of the example given to man by God Himself, who made the world in six days and rested upon the seventh from all the works He had performed, even though His work had entailed no exertion, and He had no need of repose in order to repair an exhausted vitality.

A profound thought underlies the setting apart of certain days as sacred, and days of religious repose. The working day is man's day; the festival day, the day of rest, is God's day. Sacrifice and sacred rest are correlative. That which is sacrificed to God is taken from among our possessions, is something deliberately given up by man and presented to God. The holy day is a day on which man refrains from work—consequently from gain and profit—not chiefly for the sake of enjoying physical repose, but to honor God. Thus the holy day—the *otium* of the feast-day—is also in the nature of a sacrifice to the Divinity. We find these festive days and seasons among all peoples. The Greeks and Romans were strict observers of such days, and everybody knows how severe were the restrictions concerning the observance of the sacred repose of the Sabbath. Virgil describes his happy countryman observing the repose of the holy day:

> *Ipse dies agitat festos, fususque per herbam,*
> *Ignis ubi in medio, et socii cratera coronant,*
> *Te, libans, Lenae, vocat....*[8]

Our remarks on natural or pagan liturgies—parodies or caricatures, as they often are, of the true worship of the living God in spirit and in truth—are justified by the authority of the earliest ecclesiastical writers. Thus, Tertullian goes so far as to use the word "sacrament" in connexion with the purifications (or lustrations) undergone by the votaries of Mithras and the mysterious sign imprinted upon their foreheads. In this way the devil uses the same material elements which Christ has deigned to choose as the outward symbols of His inward grace. The same great African writer attributes to the direct intervention of the evil one the institution of such rites or observances as have in themselves an element of truth and beauty, but which we prefer to look upon as manifestations of the religious instinct, often sadly misled, of the human heart. But let us read Tertullian: "The devil, in the mysteries of idols, rivalleth even the very things of the mysteries of God (*ipsas res sacramentorum divinorum idolorum mysteriis aemulatur*). He too baptizes some, to wit, his own believing and faithful people; he promises a putting away of sin by washing, and, if I yet remember aright, Mithras there seals his soldiers on their foreheads. He celebrates also the oblation of bread.... If we turn over in our minds the superstitions of Numa Pompilius, if we consider his priestly offices, badges, and privileges, his sacrificial services, the instruments and vessels of the sacrifices themselves, and the curious niceties of the expiations and vows, has not the devil manifestly imitated the strictness which

---

8 *Georgics*, ii, 226: "He himself celebrates the festal days, and, stretched on the sward where the fire burns (on an altar) in the middle and his companions wreathe the bowl, invokes thee, Linaeus, with libations."

is in the Jewish Law?"⁹

In his treatise on Baptism, the fiery African writes in the same strain: "The nations [Gentiles] who are strangers to all understanding of spiritual powers, ascribe to their idols the imbuing of waters with the selfsame efficacy [as baptismal water]. So they do, but they cheat themselves with waters which are widowed [*i.e.*, lacking the presence and virtue of the Holy Ghost].... We recognize here also the zeal of the devil in rivalling the things of God, while we find him, too, practising baptism on his subjects. But what similarity is there? The unclean cleanses! the ruiner sets free! the damned absolves! He will, forsooth, destroy his own work by washing away the sins which he himself inspires! These things have been set down by way of testimony against such as reject the faith; if they put no trust in the things of God, they trust in the spurious imitations of them, made by God's rival."¹⁰

The rites which Tertullian here describes, were much used in the religion of Mithras. Like other ecclesiastical writers and in agreement with the Fathers, he attributes their institution to the devil, "the monkey of God," who is for ever travestying the ways and works of God. However, even though the devil may have had a share in the institution of expiatory and other rites (and no doubt it was a large share), we may safely affirm that many of these symbolic actions are based upon the instinct of human nature, and were often remnants of better and purer traditions. One great and fundamental principle we must deduce from the foregoing examples, namely, that the sacramental system and the symbolical ritual of the Church answer to the truest instincts of man, who can only see the spiritual and divine through sensible images. Hence we feel justified in concluding that, although He was eminently free in the choice of means by which to dispense His gifts, our Lord adapted Himself most admirably to our nature when He instituted the Sacraments—visible symbols of an invisible grace, and its instrumental, yet effective causes.

In like manner, the Liturgy of the Church is such as man requires, for it answers to the necessity of the dual element which constitutes his nature, giving him visible, tangible, material symbols and tokens

---

9 *De praescriptione haereticorum*, xl.   10 *De baptismo*, v.

by which he can give vent to the aspirations of his immortal spirit. In this way the Liturgy of the Church, which is no mere human conceit but the result of divine inspiration and guidance, is yet another example of that supreme law which rules all God's dealings with creation, namely, that even as He "reacheth from end to end mightily," He likewise "ordereth all things sweetly."[11]

Puritans, indeed, would have us worship in plain, whitewashed, barnlike buildings, practically without any of those outward observances which lend dignity to even ordinary human relationship and intercourse. It were mere sophistry to quote in support of so unnatural a theory the words of Christ to the woman of Samaria: "The hour cometh, and now is, when the true adorers shall adore the Father in spirit and in truth."[12] Here there is no anticipated condemnation of the glories of our ritual, but only a comparison between the material observances of the Old Law and the reality of the New Law, of which the former were the shadows. These things were "a parable of the time present: according to which gifts and sacrifices are offered, which can not, as to the conscience, make him perfect that serveth only in meats and drinks and divers washings...."[13]

Religion, being a supernatural thing, can never be unnatural or against the best instincts of nature, any more than there can ever be opposition between faith and true science. Both nature and religion are of God. We but obey the dictates of what is best in us, when we surround the public worship of the Author of nature with all the splendors that this earth can lend it.

It is scarcely necessary to point out that by the beauty of our Liturgy we do not seek to give to God anything that He stands in need of. His glory is supreme, for He fully knows, from before all ages, His infinite perfections in His Word and loves and enjoys them in the Holy Ghost. And, outside the divine circle, the Angels in their myriads stand around His throne and the echo of their undying *Sanctus* rolls for ever through the halls of eternity.

The external pomp of our worship is meant to impress the mind and imagination of man. The *external* glory of God consists in this, that

[11] Wisdom, viii. 1.
[12] John, iv. 23.
[13] Heb., ix. 9, 10.

He is known, loved and adored, not only by each human unit, but by the whole human family. Now, when many are gathered together, for whatever purpose it may be, each person is the more impressed with a sense of the importance of the object by the very reason that there are many brought together by the same motive or interest. Corporate and public worship is, in itself, an act of wonderful beauty and dignity. We all know the mysterious influence—so subtle, yet so irresistible—of the spirit of a crowd. He must be a strong man who is not swept off his feet by the passions of an excited crowd in which he happens to be lost. But, when many are gathered together in the Lord's name, there is at work much more than the mere spirit of the crowd, for even He Himself is then in our midst, according to the promise of the Gospel.

What could be more in accordance with right reason and sound instinct than that all the resources of the arts should be drawn upon to lend dignity and impressiveness to what is most sublime in itself? One of the primeval instincts of man is the wearing of a distinctive dress on certain solemn occasions. Again, those who held public offices, or discharged certain duties in the name and by appointment of the community, wore a special dress or peculiar ornaments, symbolical of their office. So it is not a matter for surprise that the Church, who always cherishes all that is true and good and beautiful, should have bestowed a special apparel upon her ministers, decking them with vestments and ornaments calculated to enhance the sacredness of the rites and ceremonies of the Liturgy: "All the beauty of the king's daughter is within, in golden borders, clothed round about with varieties."[14]

The ceremonial vestments of the Church are symbolical. We may be permitted to quote here a very true saying of the Philosopher of Chelsea: "All visible things," says Carlyle, "are Emblems; what thou seest is not there on its own account.... Matter exists only spiritually, and to *represent some idea and body it forth*. Hence, Clothes, as despicable as we think them, are so unspeakably significant. Clothes, from the king's mantle downwards, are emblematic, not of want only, but of a manifold cunning victory over Want. On the other hand, all emblematic things are properly Clothes, thought-woven or hand-woven:

---

14 Ps. xliv. 14, 15.

must not the Imagination weave Garments, visible Bodies, wherein the else invisible creations and inspirations of our Reason are, like Spirits, revealed, and first become all-powerful?"[15]

In speaking of ecclesiastical vestments, we shall confine ourselves to a study of those with which daily use has made all the faithful familiar—that is, the vestments worn in the celebration of the Mass. Here, the word *evolution* is the most appropriate, for only very gradually and by the slow process of time did certain garments come to be set apart as sacred, and to be used only by the ministers of the altar in the actual discharge of their liturgical functions.

---

15 *Sartor Resartus*, 1, xi.

CHAPTER II

LITURGICAL VESTMENTS

The Amice (*Amictus*)

THE Amice is the first among the sacred vestments put on by the priest as he vests for Mass; but, in order of time and origin, it was one of the last to come into general use, and cannot be traced back to a period earlier than the eighth or ninth century. Originally it appears to have been but a linen cloth with which the priest covered his neck, probably for the purely utilitarian purpose of protecting the more valuable upper garments from being soiled by perspiration. It may be, also, that it was introduced as a protection for the throat. What Amalarius and others say about the *custodia vocis* in connexion with the amice, may perhaps be taken to refer as much to the protection of the vocal organs as to the ethical "custody of the tongue."

Some would see in the amice a memory of the Jewish *ephod;* but the only possible point of resemblance can be found in that both ephod and amice are worn over the shoulders. In the Middle Ages the amice was not only worn over the shoulders, but also served to cover the head. Rupert of Deutz (1135) speaks of it as a head-covering. When the chasuble had been put on, the amice was thrown back over the shoulders. At an early date the amice came to be adorned with a *parura* (or "apparel"), that is, a band of more or less elaborately embroidered silk.

The amice is still used as a covering for the head in some of the older religious orders, at least in the *accessus ad altare* and again on the way back to the sacristy. Since the revival of the old forms of ecclesiastical vestments, amices with apparels have once more come into use.

In the ordination of a subdeacon, the bishop draws the amice over the head of the candidate, declaring that by it is signified *castigatio vocis* (that is, reserve in speech). But this spiritual signification by no means excludes the more utilitarian origin of the amice, which was introduced, as we have seen, to protect both the vestments and the throat. The heat of summer demanded that the vestments be preserved from perspiration, and the unheated churches of the Middle Ages made it necessary to protect the throat from the cold. The mystical meaning now attaching to the sacred vestments does not go back to a very high antiquity. About the tenth century, when it became customary to make of the amice (or humeral, as it was also called) a covering for the head as well as the throat, the symbolism now attaching to it was shown in all its appropriateness. The amice is a mystical helmet—an integral part of that spiritual panoply so graphically described by St Paul.[1] Hence, as he puts it on, the priest prays: "Place, O Lord, upon my head the helmet of salvation that I may overcome all the attacks of the devil."

Such is the evolution of the amice. At first, as far as we car see, it is but a kerchief or muffler to protect the throat and preserve the vestments. Gradually, it becomes an integral part of the liturgical vesture of the priest of the New Law, and, as such, is made symbolical of that protection which we expect from on high in our daily wrestling with enemies that are all the more dangerous in that they are unseen.

The Alb (*Alba*)

The Alb is one of the most remarkable among the vestments worn by priests and levites of today. It is a white garment, reaching to the ground, with close fitting sleeves, and is confined by a girdle or cincture. It is normally reserved to priests, deacons and subdeacons, and, as its name indicates, it must needs be white. But alb (*alba*) is only one of many names by which this vestment has been designated in the course of time. *Tunica, linea* or *talaris, poderis, camisia*, were names in common use at different epochs. The alb exists since the ninth century as a specific sacred vestment in its present shape. Since that time, and long before, it has been one of the many liturgical vestments used by the Church, but in the earliest times it would appear to have been

[1] Eph., vi. 13–18.

practically the only specific ritual vestment.

Originally the tunic was a garment commonly worn at Rome and Athens during the period of the Caesars. The tunic of the Greeks and that of the Romans was secured round the waist by a belt (except the *tunica laticlavia* of the Roman Senators). At first it was a sleeveless garment, or had only abbreviated sleeves; however, already in the days of St Augustine, it was considered unseemly to wear it without sleeves, or with only abbreviated ones.

This garment eventually became our alb. From the fourth century onwards, it is spoken of as a distinctly liturgical dress. In his "Dialogue against Pelagius," St Jerome asks: "What injury to God is it if ... the bishop, the priest, the deacon and the rest of the clergy go forth in white garments?" Canon 41 of the so-called Fourth Council of Carthage forbids the deacon to wear the alb, except when discharging his liturgical functions (*ut diaconus tempore oblationis tantum, vel lectionis, alba utatur*).

Most remarkable is the testimony of the Stowe Missal, in which we find the following prayer: *Rogo te, Deus Sabaoth, altissime Pater sancte, ut me tunica castitatis digneris accingere et meos lumbos baltheo tui amoris ambire* (I beseech Thee, God of hosts; holy and supreme Father, that Thou wouldst clothe me with the tunic of chastity, and gird my loins with the cincture of Thy love). Here we have a clear mention of both alb and girdle as early as the seventh century.[2]

Up to about the twelfth century the alb was worn by all clerics; since that time, a shorter alb (our surplice or rochet) has come into general use for minor clerics; and, except at Mass, is now commonly used by priests and bishops in most functions.

In the course of the twelfth century the alb begins to lose its plainness. Up till then only the lower edge had been adorned with a fringe or strip of costly material. "Apparels" now became general, as in the case of the amice. These are oblong pieces of embroidery or brocade, sewn on the lower part of the alb, both in front and behind, smaller ones being attached to the sleeves. The effect of these "apparels" (*parurae*, as they were called) is very striking. In the last three centuries

---

2 See Braun, *Die priesterlichen Gewänder des Abendlandes*, p. 27.

"apparels" have made room for lace decoration to the great loss of true liturgical art. However, since the revival of the old forms of vestments, apparelled albs are not infrequently seen, especially in England.

Durandus sums up the various mystical explanations of the alb.[3] Its color, white, symbolizes purity. It is made of linen, which is not naturally white, and only becomes so by a lengthy process of bleaching; in like manner purity cannot be preserved, unless we practise mortification. It is also a reminder of the white garment which Herod put on our Lord, when he and his whole court derided the Lord of glory and treated Him as a fool.

Holy Church looks on the alb as an emblem of priestly purity and freedom from sin; in that spirit she puts the following prayer on the lips of the priest as he vests himself in his snow-white alb: "Cleanse me, O Lord, and purify my heart, so that, having been washed in the Blood of the Lamb, I may enjoy everlasting bliss."

The Girdle or Cincture (*Cingulum*)

The Girdle is the third of the sacred or priestly ornaments. Its introduction, in one form or another, was rendered necessary by the alb. "The alb," says Durandus, "must be secured around the loins of the bishop or priest by means of the *zona*, or girdle, in order that he may not be hindered in walking by its loose and long folds, and in order that the priest may be admonished thereby not to allow his priestly purity, symbolized by this white garment, to be impaired by the fascination of the senses." The girdle serves, therefore, both a practical and a mystical purpose.

All liturgists of the latter part of the Middle Ages speak of the girdle. Its shape has varied in the course of the centuries; at present it is a plain cord, but a few surviving examples and some miniatures show it to have been an elaborately embroidered sash, though not as long as the modern cincture.

The mystical signification of the girdle is obvious; in fact, as Braun remarks,[4] there is far more agreement between the explanations of

---

3 *Rationale Divin. Off.* 4 *Op. cit.*, p. 50.

liturgists and the acceptance of these by the Church in respect to the girdle than there is with regard to any other liturgical vestment. There is an almost natural symbolism in the girdle, and the language of the Scriptures and the Fathers makes us all familiar with its meaning: "Let your loins be girt," says our Lord,[5] upon which St Gregory makes the comment with which we are so familiar: *Lumbos enim praecingimus, cum carnis luxuriam per continentiam coarctamus* (We gird our loins when we restrain the lusts of the flesh by continence).[6]

As we have seen above when treating of the alb, the Stowe Missal makes the priest pray for charity (*meas Jumbos baltheo tui amoris ambire*); the Roman Missal connects the girdle exclusively with the virtue of chastity. "Gird me, O Lord," we are made to pray, "with the cincture of purity and extinguish in my loins the ardor of lust, that there may abide in me the vigor (*virtus*) of continence and chastity."

The Maniple (*Manipulus*)

The Maniple has borne many names in the course of its evolution: *mappula, sudarium, manuale*. All these and other designations hint at its origin and purpose. The liturgical use of the maniple originated in Rome. Up to the ninth century and even beyond, it served a purely practical purpose, and was simply a napkin or handkerchief. Just as the amice was a plain linen cloth wrapped around the neck in order to protect the outer vestments from perspiration, so the *mappula* was a linen cloth, held in the hand or carried on the left arm, for the purpose of wiping either the face or the hands of both celebrant and ministers. It is obvious that, if a *mappa* or *sudarium* was necessary in private life, it was even more so in the public functions of the Church, especially when we consider the climatic conditions of the country of its origin.

Our maniple has undergone very much the same transformation as the so-called *mappa consularis*. At first the *mappa* of the consul was but an ordinary handkerchief, which he also used to give the signal for the beginning of the public games. In course of time it lost its obvious use and even its original form, and became an emblem of the consular

---

5 Luke, xii. 35.   6 *Lect. I. 2 Noct. Conf, n. Pontif.*

dignity. But it does not follow by any means that the liturgical *mappula* is derived from the consular one; only the origin of both is alike.

The appellation *manipulus* appears as early as 781 in a deed by which Aldegaster gives to the monastery of Obona (in Asturia, Spain) three *mantos*, six *stolas* and five *manipulos*.[7] It ranks among liturgical vestments at least since the ninth century, and in Spain, as we have just seen, even since the eighth.

According to the *Liber Pontificalis*, Pope Sylvester I (314–326) ordained that deacons should wear dalmatics in church, and that their left hands should be covered with a linen towel (*palliis linostimis levam eorum tegerent*). The *pallium linostimum* of the deacon was a linen cloth which he carried on his left forearm or in his left hand, and used, if the necessity arose, for the purpose of wiping the sacred vessels. We may gather this from a remark of Amalarius: "Afterwards the deacon places the chalice and his *sudarium* (napkin) upon the right-hand corner of the altar; it will be very handy to wipe up any trace of dirt that may befall, whilst the priest's own will thus remain quite clean." So both priest and deacon had each his own kerchief or maniple.

It is difficult to find any definite information as to the shape of the maniple prior to the ninth century. Amalarius declares expressly that in his time it was a linen cloth. We also know that at least from that time (that is, the ninth century) it was carried in the left hand (*manu sinistra portatur*, says Amalarius). The miniatures of that period show how it was folded and held between the thumb and forefinger, and allowed to fall down on both sides of the hand. About the twelfth century the custom of wearing the maniple over the left arm had become universal, and has not altered since. At the same period it underwent another and final alteration. From a simple piece of linen destined to serve a practical purpose, it became a mere ornament.

In the Museum of Durham there is preserved a most precious maniple of the tenth century. It was found in 1827 in the tomb of St Cuthbert in the Cathedral of Durham. This ornament had been made by command of Queen Elfled or Æthelflead, wife of Edward the Elder, for Bishop Frithestan of Winchester, who was consecrated

---

7 *Annal.* OSB, I, 25, quoted by Braun, *op. cit.*, p. 55.

in 905. It is "a strip of cloth of gold, most richly adorned with figures in needlework. It has a uniform width of two inches and a quarter, and is thirty-two inches long, thus hanging down for sixteen inches on either side of the wearer's wrist. The extremities terminate in a fringe of crimson purple an inch and three-quarters in length."[8]

When the maniple (the old-time *sudarium*) had become a mere ornament, the need of something more practically useful had not disappeared. So we find decrees of bishops and synods prescribing another *sudarium* in place of the ornamental maniple; this new *sudarium* was generally attached to the Missal. Thus, in 1200, Odo of Paris, commands as follows: *Districte praecipitur, ut quilibet sacerdos habeat in celebratione missae, propter munditiam vestimentorum servandam circa altare, unum manutergium pendens circa missale, ad tergendum os et nares, si fuerit necesse* (It is strictly enjoined that when he says Mass, and for the sake of the cleanliness which should adorn the altar, every priest should have a handkerchief attached to the Missal, for the purpose of wiping his mouth and nostrils, if the need were to arise).

In the same spirit, Bishop Grandison of Exeter (1327–1369) likewise prescribes a handkerchief or napkin, in addition to the maniple: "We enact that at Mass the priest, the deacon, and the subdeacon should constantly keep a little napkin (*parvum manutergium*) in their hands, that the vestments may not get soiled in front, and to wipe off the perspiration. So, too, when the wine and water are being poured into the chalice, or the water at the *Lavabo*, let a napkin be held underneath, and when they sit down, let some linen cloth, reserved specially for this purpose, be laid over their lap."[9]

Incidentally, it may be remarked here that the purificator, which we now place over the chalice, cannot be anything else but that same *sudariolum* or *parvum manutergium* so often mentioned by liturgists, bishops and synods of the latter centuries of the Middle Ages, when the maniple no longer served a practical purpose.

The conferring of the maniple on the subdeacon at his ordination does not go back further than the twelfth century.

The mystical interpretations of the maniple to be found in the

---

8 Cfr. Thurston in *The Month*, October, 1898, p. 405.
9 Thurston, *loc. cit.*, p. 402.

writings of liturgists are many and varied. The original purpose of this vestment is clearly pointed out in the prayer of the Ambrosian Missal: "Put, O Lord, the maniple in my hands for the removing of all bodily uncleanliness, that I may be worthy to serve Thee without stain." The word *manipulus* has led most commentators to base their interpretations upon Psalm cxxv. 6, 7: *Euntes ibant et flebant, mittentes semina sua: venientes autem venient eum exultatione, portantes manipulos suos* (Going they went and wept, casting their seeds. But coming they shall come with joyfulness, carrying their *sheaves*). *Manipulus* means "a handful," and at first our present-day vestment was but a folded linen carried in the hand. A *manipulus* is also a sheaf, or handful of stalks of wheat or any other cereal. So we pray, as we put on the maniple: "May I be worthy, O Lord, to carry the maniple of weeping and sorrow, that thus I may receive with exultation the reward of toil." The "maniple of tears" is an allusion to the pristine practical purpose of our sacred ornament; the prayer itself is of great antiquity and is already found in a Sacramentary of Troyes of the middle of the eleventh century.

The Stole (*Stola*)

The word *stola* (στολή) occurs in the Scriptures, where it has the meaning of *dress* (perhaps ceremonial dress), as for instance in the parable of the prodigal son: "Bring forth quickly the first robe" (*stolam primam*).[10] Again, St John describes the saints as standing before the throne "in white robes" (*amicti stolis albis*).[11] Originally, the word was used to designate the long flowing robe worn by Roman matrons. Liturgically, it is a long narrow strip of silk, most frequently richly embroidered, which is worn by bishops, priests and deacons, though differently by each of these three orders of the hierarchy.

As a distinctive dress or vestment, , the stole (also called *orarium*) does not appear to be of Roman origin. At Rome, says Msgr Duchesne,[12] *insignia* (viz., distinctive robes) were not looked upon with much favor. The *orarium*, both of priest and deacon, as a distinct *insigne*, remained unknown there until the tenth century, though it had been adopted

---

10 Luke, xv. 22.
11 Apoc., vii. 9.
12 *Origines du Culte*, p. 276.

everywhere else. The *Ordines* indeed make mention of the *orarium*, but we see it worn even by subdeacons and acolytes. It was not a distinctive badge, so to speak, but merely a *sudarium* (muffler or kerchief) which had come to be an integral part of the dress of the upper classes, and so came to be used by the clergy, who at first had no distinctive dress, but merely wore that generally used by the better classes. The word *orarium*, etymologically considered, bears out this interpretation. It comes from *os* (face), not from *orare* (to pray), as medieval liturgists would have it. The *orarium* was a cloth with which the face would be wiped, or which could be used to cover the face or even the head. The word *stola*, to designate the vestment at first called *orarium*, came into general use about the ninth or tenth century. In the Life of Bl. Leo IX, there is mention of *"orarium, quod vulgo stola dicitur."*[13]

The earliest mention of the *orarium* as a vestment exclusively reserved to the higher orders of clerics, occurs in the Acts of the Council of Laodicea (in Phrygia), which forbids subdeacons, lectors, and other clerics of the lower degrees to wear this garment.

In the decrees of synods held in the fifth, sixth and seventh centuries at Braga and Toledo, we meet with several ordinances concerning the stole. Thus, the fourth canon of the Fourth Council of Braga says: "When the priest prepares for Mass that he may offer the sacrifice ... he shall not do it unless he has put the *orarium* on both shoulders, as he received it at his ordination, and in such a manner that, placing one and the same *orarium* round his neck and shoulders, he may have the sign of the cross upon his breast." The First Council of Braga (561) had already prescribed that deacons should wear their *oraria*, not *under* their tonic, but *over* it, and hanging over their shoulder, "else," says the Council, "they would not appear to differ from the subdeacon."

In the canon quoted above, the Council adds that, if the Fathers order the priest to wear his *orarium* in the manner described, they do so because "it is an ancient prescription of the Church that, at his ordination, the *orarium* should be placed over both shoulders of the candidate. How then should he not wear, at the time of the Sacrifice, that which he has received in the sacrament [of Orders]?" From these

---

13 *Acta* ss., Apr. II,

words we are able to draw the very important conclusion that in the seventh century, at least in Spain, it was already an ancient law or practice of the Church for the priest to receive the stole at his ordination, and to wear it at Mass, crossed over his breast, just as priests do today. Moreover, it seems obvious that the stole or *orarium* of those days had very much the same shape as our own stole, and was looked upon as an emblem or *insigne* of a spiritual power and hierarchical standing.

The Council of Toledo (633) prescribes that the deacon's stole be worn on the left shoulder, falling down both in front and behind. The custom of wearing it like a scarf across the chest and back (*en bandoulière*) seems to go back to the ninth century, and was based upon a practice of the Roman Church.

In some countries, during the Middle Ages, the custom was introduced of wearing the stole at all times, even apart from any liturgical function. Thus the Council of Mayence (813) commands priests always to wear the *orarium, propter differentiam sacerdotii dignitatis* (that is, to render them always recognizable as priests). We must bear in mind that for several centuries the ordinary dress of priests and laymen of some standing was not distinguishable. We see this from the letter of Pope Celestine (422–432) to the Bishops of Provence. The Council of Tribur (895) renews the above-mentioned Decree of Mayence, and adds that the robbery or murder of a priest who, when on a journey, was vested in his stole, should be punished with a penalty three times as heavy as if he had been without it, since in the latter case he could not be so easily known to be a priest. Of St Thomas of Canterbury his historian relates that from the time he was ordained priest he always wore his stole: *Quodam sacro ordinis insigni, quod stola seu orarium dicitur, mox ut sacerdos, utrumque, quod sacerdotum est, humerum ambiebat, et hoc quotidie, et in omnium visu gestabat* (As soon as he was made a priest, he covered his shoulders, as is the practice of priests, with a certain sacred emblem of order, which is called stole, or *orarium*; this he wore daily and in sight of all).[14]

The mystical signification of the stole of both deacon and priest may be gathered from the words spoken by the bishop as he places

---

14 Migne, *Patr. Lat.*, CXC, 1095.

this sacred vestment upon the shoulders of the candidate at the moment of ordination. The deacon's stole signifies the power given him to minister at the altar and to distribute the Holy Eucharist. In this office of the deacon we may perhaps see the origin of the orarium, which, as we have said, was at first but a strip of linen, with which he covered or wiped his face and perhaps the mouth (*os, orarium*) of the communicant, after he had drunk from the sacred chalice. During the ordination of deacons, the bishop lays the stole on the candidate's left shoulder, saying: *Accipe stolam candidam de manu Dei; adimple ministerium tuum; potens est enim Deus, ut augeat tibi gratiam suam* (Receive this white stole or garment from the hand of God; fulfill thy office, for God is able to augment His grace to meet all thy needs). The ministry or office and the power to discharge it worthily, are from God, and the stole is the symbol of both.

The priest's stole is a symbol of the holy servitude undertaken by the minister of the altar. "The yoke of the Lord," is the burden of all the prayers of most of the early and medieval sacramentaries when there is mention of the priestly stole. But the stole is also a garment of joy and an emblem of the righteousness which should adorn the soul of the priest: *Accipe jugum Domini: jugum enim ejus suave est, et onus ejus leve* (Accept the yoke of the Lord, for His yoke is sweet and His burden light). Thus the *Pontificate Romanum*. This symbolism is more fully explained in the prayer which we say in the act of putting on the stole: "Restore unto me, O Lord, the stole of immortality (*sto lam immortalitatis*) which I have lost through the prevarication of our first parent: and though I be unworthy to draw nigh unto Thy mystery (*sacramentum*), may I yet merit everlasting joy."

The Chasuble (*Casula*)

The chasuble is the priestly garment *par excellence*. It is essentially *the Mass vestment,* and so is reserved exclusively to the priest. But it was not always so. Thus, at any rate in the Roman Church, the vestment we now call chasuble was commonly worn by deacons, subdeacons, and even by clerics in minor orders. The only survival of this practice in our present-day Liturgy is the custom by which the deacon and subdeacon wear folded chasubles in Lent and Advent. There can be little doubt that our chasuble was originally an article of ordinary and everyday wear. "At Rome in the fifth century," says Duchesne, "the outdoor dress of persons in position or office consisted of an undergarment—that is, a tunic, with or without sleeves—and a *paenula*—viz., a very ample cloak, without opening in front, and without sleeves. In the middle of this garment there was an opening through which the head was passed, and it was folded up on both sides, over the arms, when it was necessary to use the hands."[15] The color of this garment was generally purple or dark, whereas the tunic was bright colored. The *paenula* (also called *colobus,* and later on *planeta, casula, amphibalus*) seems to be identical with our chasuble. The *Codex Theodosianus,* at the end of the fourth century, forbids senators to wear the military cloak (*chlamys*), and prescribes for them a garment called *paenula* or *colobus.* This decree, however, did not abrogate the *toga* as the official dress of senators.

    Anyone who is at all familiar with the pictures or mosaics of the early Christian centuries must see an obvious identity between, I do not say the modern chasuble, but at least between what we call "Gothic" chasubles and the upper garment worn by priests and bishops in these mosaics and miniatures. A visit to any of our museums would change this impression into certainty, for we are fortunate enough to possess a great many specimens of chasubles of high antiquity. The color of this sacred vestment was not fixed by any law of the Church. In the Middle Ages only two vestments were required by Canon Law for the vestry of the ordinary parish church. So it would appear obvious enough that one and the same vestment did duty on days on which varying colors are now of obligation. The tunic of the deacon, as we have seen, was of a bright color, whereas the hues of the chasuble or *paenula* were generally dull or purple. Hence the custom arose for the deacon and subdeacon not to wear the tunic and dalmatic in Lent and on other penitential occasions, these garments being symbols of joy and gladness. So they would wear the chasuble, which was plain and of a subdued color. During that part of the Mass when he would

---

15 *Origines du Culte,* p. 365.

be most busy ministering at the altar (that is, from the Gospel to the Communion), the deacon, retaining his stole, would fold his chasuble like a scarf, and wear it like the stole on his left shoulder, pinning it under his right arm. This custom is very ancient and certainly goes back as far as the ninth century. In our own days the deacon wears a chasuble folded and pinned up in front, but lays it aside altogether at the Gospel, and in its place wears the *stolone* (or broad stole), which is simply the folded chasuble of old.

The practice of vesting the candidate for the priesthood with the chasuble at the time of his ordination is of very long standing, and we find traces of it from the seventh century onwards. In a *Pontificale* of Séez of the year 1045, the Bishop thus addresses the newly ordained: *Recipe planetam, ut possis legaliter celebrare Missam.*[16]

The spiritual and mystical signification of the chasuble may be gathered from the prayer uttered by the Bishop, when he puts the chasuble on the new priest. "Receive the priestly robe," he says, "by which is signified charity"; and when, at the end of the Mass, the chasuble is fully unfolded, he says: *Stola innocentiae induat te Dominus.*

The symbolism is easily perceived, and is pointed out by medieval liturgists and commentators with surprising unanimity. Just as the bell- or tent-shaped chasuble (*casula*, small tent) envelops the whole body and covers all the other garments, so is charity the perfection of man, giving the other virtues their final beauty and worth. In fact, all the other virtues have their root in charity, and by charity alone is man made righteous and acceptable before God. "Without charity I am nothing," says St Paul. This the Bishop points out to the young priest, when, having given him the chasuble and having explained that by it *charitas intelligitur,* he goes on to say: *potens est enim Deus, ut augeat tibi charitatem et opus perfectum* (for God has power to increase thy charity and to perfect thy works). The chasuble is also a symbol of the yoke of the Lord. So Holy Church makes us pray, as we put on the sacred "Mass vestment": "O Lord who didst say 'My yoke is sweet and my burden light,' grant that I may so wear this [vestment] that I may obtain Thy grace."

---

16 See Braun, *Die priesterlichen Gewänder des Abendlandes,* p. 150, note 1.

In the eyes of the Church, therefore, the chasuble, the most important vestment of the sacrificing priest, is a symbol both of charity, the queen of virtues, and of the yoke of Christ. Hence it is not a matter for surprise that, once it was decided to depart from pristine simplicity or even plainness, an embroidered cross, or the figure of the Crucified, became the chief ornament of the chasuble. We read in the "Imitation": *Habet (sacerdos) ante se et retro dominicae crucis signum, ad memorandam jugiter Christi passionem. Ante se crucem in casula portat, ut Christi vestigia diligenter inspiciat.... Post se cruce signatus est ut adversa quaelibet ... clementer pro Deo tolerat* (The priest hath before and behind him the sign of the cross of our Lord, that he may ever remember the Passion of Christ. Before him he beareth the cross on the chasuble, that he may diligently behold the footsteps of Christ.... Behind him he is marked with the cross that he may ... suffer for God's sake whatsoever adversities befall him).[17]

---

17 *Imitation*, IV, V, 3.

CHAPTER III

INTROIBO AD ALTARE DEI

The Priest's Mystical Identity with Christ

THOUGH most of the liturgical vestments were taken over from the ordinary uses of daily life, they soon became modified in shape and form as they began to be used exclusively at the altar in the service of the Church, and were regarded as appropriate symbols of divers virtues and spiritual powers. "Every high-priest taken from among men is ordained for men in the things that appertain to God."[1] For this reason it is right that his outward appearance also should single him out from among those in whose behalf he is to be a mediator between God and man, between heaven and earth. The adorable Sacrifice of the Mass, the offering whereof is the chief priestly function, is identical with the sacrifice which Jesus Christ offered once for all upon the altar of Calvary. Our Mass does not supersede or supplement the sacrifice of the cross; it continues it until the end of time, when the eternal designs of God shall have reached their fulfillment.

The Victim of Calvary was likewise the priest of that tremendous immolation. And, whereas Christ is a "priest for ever according to the order of Melchisedech,"[2] there is set up a wondrous identity between the priesthood of the Catholic Church and the priesthood of our Lord. Since we offer the same sacrifice that Christ offered, though the manner of oblation be different, there must needs be identity of power in Him and in us. Christ's priestly character and office are shared by the Catholic priest. The priest, whilst fully retaining his human personality, his human gifts, and alas! his defects and limitations, is taken up

---

[1] Heb., v. 1.   [2] Ps. cix. 4; Heb., *passim*.

by Christ. In the discharge of his sacerdotal function, the priest, so to speak, sinks his personality in that of our Lord: Christ speaks and acts through him, and the priest speaks and acts as if he and the divine High-priest were but one person. And so they are in very deed, the nature of the sacrifice itself demanding this mystical oneness. For who could have power over Christ's body, over His very life, but Christ Himself? "No man taketh it away [My life] from Me, but I lay it down of Myself, and I have power to lay it down: and I have power to take it up again."[3] The mystic immolation upon the altar of the Lamb of God is therefore accomplished, inasmuch as the priest and Jesus Christ are one.

What could be more becoming than that the oneness of the priesthood should be made sensible to all by the mysterious, highly symbolical garb worn by the priest in the sacrificial act? The priest is then taken from among, and raised above, his fellows. He is caught up by the mighty power of Christ's own priesthood. He enters into the cloud that shrouds the sanctuary wherein God dwells. As his office is wholly divine, let there remain in him and about him nothing that is of this earth, but let his very vesture, by its varied splendors, show forth the glory of his "kingly priesthood,"[4] which makes him the minister and the associate of the one High-priest who, "offering one sacrifice for sins, for ever sitteth on the right hand of God."[5]

Here it may not be amiss to make the remark that, even when the priest leaves the sacristy for the celebration of his own private Mass, his approach to the altar, though he be preceded by but one solitary altar boy, is yet in the nature of a ceremonial progress, and should be distinguished by unaffected dignity. The rubrics prescribe that he should have his head covered, the chalice being held in the left hand, the right hand resting upon and supporting the burse. It is scarcely necessary to say that *nothing* should be carried except the chalice, and nothing placed on the burse. Too many priests think the burse a suitable vehicle for their pince-nez. The present writer has known a venerable old canon, long since gone to his eternal rest, who invariably placed on the burse of his chalice both his pince-nez and a green bottle of smelling salts. Such practices obviously take away a great deal from

3 John, x. 18.   4 1 Pet., ii. 9.
5 Heb., x. 12.

the solemnity of our *Introitus ad altare.*

The priest, then, is now vested with the mystic splendors of the liturgical garments. His body is wrapped in the folds of a snow-white alb, the emblem of purity and innocence. On his head is "the helmet of salvation"; his loins are girt with the cincture of continence; from his elbow is suspended the maniple of sorrow which shall one day be changed into joy; the stole rests on his neck like the sweet yoke of Christ, and over all is spread the all-enfolding, all-covering priestly robe signifying charity, that queen of virtues which gives to the others their luster and consummate perfection. With such dispositions of his soul outwardly signified by the sacred vestments, the priest proceeds to the foot of the altar, whereon the undying Victim is about to be immolated.

His first act is to bend the knee, or at least (if the Blessed Sacrament be not present) to bow profoundly before the altar. Then, making upon himself the sign of the cross, he confesses his faith in the mystery of the Trinity, and at the same time proclaims that the sublime mysteries are to be accomplished by the power and to the glory of the Three Divine Persons. "In the Mass," says a holy soul of our own days, "the world, by the voice of the priest, calls down Jesus Christ. The adorable Trinity gives Him; the world and the priest receive Him, and again offer and give Him to the Holy Trinity that has bestowed Him on us."

Holy Church never begins any of her ceremonies or prayers unless it be "in the name of the Father, and of the Son, and of the Holy Ghost." The mystery of the Triune God is the basis of our religion. What should we be unless our spirit always enjoyed "the grace of our Lord Jesus Christ, and the charity of God, and the communication of the Holy Ghost"?[6] Moreover, all glory and honor belong to the ever-blessed Trinity, from whom all good things proceed. The Mass is earth's highest act of worship and homage to God: *Quando sacerdos celebrat, Deum honorat, angelos laetificat, Ecclesiam aedificat, vivos adjuvat, defunctis requiem praestat* (When the priest celebrates, he honors God, gladdens the Angels, edifies the Church, helps the living, procures rest for the dead).[7]

---

6 II Cor., xiii. 13.   7 *Imitation,* IV, v, *ult.*

Such great and glorious things can be realized only in the name and power of the Holy Trinity, whom the priest invokes as he takes his stand at the foot of the altar. Relying not on his own worth or righteousness, but solely upon Him from whom all blessings flow, the priest declares that he is even about to draw nigh unto God's altar: *Introibo ad altare Dei*. It is no small matter to approach the altar of God. In the Old Law death was the penalty inflicted upon any one who should dare to touch the Ark of the Covenant. When the Philistines restored the Ark of the Lord which had been in their land seven months, "the Bethsamites were reaping wheat in the valley: and lifting up their eyes they saw the Ark, and rejoiced to see it ... and He slew of the people seventy men and fifty thousand of the common people.... And the people lamented and said: 'Who shall be able to stand before the Lord, this holy God?'"[8]

But the altar of the Lord is no mere object of terror, precisely because it is the altar of the Lord: "How lovely are Thy tabernacles ... Thy altars, O Lord of Hosts!"[9] The altar upon which the priest sacrifices day by day is like the tree of life which God had planted from the beginning in the midst of the garden of delights. After the fall of Adam, God expelled him from the garden, and set a guard of cherubim with flaming swords "to keep the way of the tree of life, lest perhaps man put forth his hand and take also of the tree of life, and eat, and live for ever."[10] The tree of life produced fruits to which the Author of life had imparted a virtue which was beyond their nature—*viz.*, that of constantly renewing the physical life and energy of man. The wear and tear which is inseparable from existence itself should have been made good by the marvelous virtue of this mysterious tree, and mankind should have spent its allotted span of life upon this earth in the freshness and vigor of eternal youth, until the day when each of the sons of Adam should have entered, without tasting the bitterness of death, upon that vaster life which awaits him beyond this present period of probation.

There is now no tree of life for the body, but the altar of God is an unfailing source of spiritual and supernatural life. *Introibo ad altare*

8 I Kings, vi. 13, 19, 20.   9 Ps., lx.xxiii. 2, 4.
10 Gen., iii. 24, 22.

Dei: ad Deum qui laetificat juventutem meam. These words sound strange indeed when we ponder them with the attention of which lifelong familiarity is apt to rob us. God is life itself. As St John says: *In ipso vita erat, et vita erat lux hominum.* To come in contact with Him is to come in contact with life—hence to renew one's own vitality. God communicates of His own; He gives what He Himself is, in the measure in which we are able to receive. He is eternal and unchanging. What He was yesterday, He is today and shall be for ever more. He is "the High and the Eminent that inhabiteth eternity."[11] The changes and vicissitudes of this transitory universe do not touch Him, for He is raised above all changeableness, inasmuch as He possesses the fulness of life. So even though He is called the "Ancient of Days," age has written no wrinkles on His brow, and St Augustine rightly calls Him *Pulchritudo semper antiqua, semper nova* (Beauty ever old, ever new).

"Who gladdens my youth," says the priest. This sounds almost paradoxical. His very name (priest, *presbyter*, senior) implies old age, whereas he speaks of his youth. But the paradox is only apparent. Whatever may be the number of his years as a citizen of this world, in his priestly rôle he knows no change but remains ever the same, for he has a share in the changeless, eternal priesthood of Jesus Christ. Christ's priesthood and sacrifice are independent of the cyclic changes of the sun and moon. Though He was slain upon the cross on a certain date of our human calendar, the virtue of His sacrifice extends to all periods of time, both before and after; He is "the Lamb which was slain from the beginning of the world."[12]

In like manner our priestly office is above and independent of the chronology of our years. We share in Christ's own eternal youth and vigor, the more so since the altar to which we approach is Christ Himself, according to the words with which the bishop addresses the subdeacon on the day of his ordination: *Altare quidem sanctae Ecclesiae ipse est Christus, teste Joanne, qui, in Apocalypsi sua, altare aureum se vidisse perhibet, stans ante thronum, in quo et per quem oblationes fidelium Deo Patri consecrantur* (The altar of Holy Church is Christ Himself, on the authority of St John, who relates in his Apocalypse how he saw a

---

11 Ps. xlvii. 15. 12 Apoc., xiii. 8.

golden altar before the throne, upon which and by which the offerings of the faithful are consecrated to God the Father).

The Altar

Sacrifice, priesthood and *altar* are correlative terms. Where there is sacrifice, there is also a place set apart for its oblation, and the spot thus selected is invested with a special holiness. The word altar (*altare*) signifies *alta ara*, the word *ara* itself being derived from αἴρειν, which implies a lifting up or elevation. Among the pagan nations, as well as among the Jews, the altar was a lofty structure, so that the sacrifice could easily be witnessed by those who stood around. A natural instinct seems to have prompted men of every race to sacrifice on the tops of hills and mountains, rather than in the monotonous plain; and, where there were no natural heights, art and labor would often supplement nature. In the Old Testament we read that Abraham erected the altar, on which he was ready to sacrifice his son Isaac, upon the summit of a mountain which the Lord Himself showed him, and which the Father of all believers called: *The Lord seeth*.[13] Later on the altar of sacrifice was erected upon the holy hill of Sion. Our Lord Himself chose to offer His sacrifice upon Mount Calvary, and the Last Supper also, which was the first Mass ever said, took place, according to tradition, upon the slopes of holy Sion. St Paul calls the Christian altar θυσιαστήριον[14] and τράπεζα.[15] Both terms are properly applicable, not to the altar of the cross or Calvary, but to the altar upon which the Eucharistic Sacrifice is offered.

If we wish to rise to a fuller realization of the sacredness of the altar of the New Law, we need but read attentively the wonderful prayers and ponder the gorgeous ceremonial with which Holy Church dedicates her altars and imparts to them an abiding consecration. The consecration of an altar, like that of a church, is a very different thing from our common "openings".

By its consecration the altar is permanently removed from the ordinary uses of human life: *Deus, qui in omni loco dominationis tuae clemens*

13 Gen., xxii. 14.
15 1 Cor., x. 21.
14 Heb., xiii, 10.

ac benignus dedicator assistis, exaudi nos ... ut inviolabilis permaneat hujus loci consecratio (O God who by Thy merciful and salutary presence sanctifiest every place subject to Thy dominion, hear us and grant that the consecration of this spot may remain inviolable for ever more). The altar is a source of graces: *In hac mensa sint libamina tibi accepta, sint grata, sint pinguia, et sancti Spiritus tui semper rore perfusa; ut omni tempore hoc in loco supplicantis tibi familiae tuae anxietates releves, aegritudines cures, preces exaudias, vota suscipias, desiderata confirmes, postulata concedas* (May the offerings that are put upon this table always be acceptable to Thee; may they be pleasing, ripe and always watered with the dew of Thy Holy Spirit; mayest Thou at all times on this spot relieve the anxieties of Thy children who supplicate to Thee, heal their ills, hear their prayers, receive their vows, approve their desires and grant their petitions).

In a noble Preface, the Pontiff sings the ancient glory of our altar, foreshadowed by that altar which, at the dawn of history, Abel consecrated with his own blood. Later on, the altar of Melchisedech and that of Abraham (*seminarium fidei nostrae*) point clearly to the life-giving mystery of our Lord's Passion. The bishop prays that God would look upon this altar as upon that which Isaac erected, when he struck a well of limpid water; or as He looked down upon the stone upon which Jacob rested his head, and on the altar made of twelve stones, by which Moses foreshadowed the choice of twelve Apostles.

In the Preface sung at the consecration of a portable altar, the bishop beseeches God in words of wonderful beauty, which one despairs of rendering in English: *Inhaereas hic placido aeternae majestatis obtutu.... Adsit misericordia tuae ineffabilis pietas: ut, te largiente, referat praemium quisquis intulerit votum* (Do Thou fix upon this spot the serene gaze of Thy eternal Majesty.... May the ineffable kindness of Thy mercy be present: so that, through Thy bounty, every one who offers at this altar may receive his reward).

Our altar is no mere block of stone or wooden table; it is the living Christ, and the faithful are the mystic covering of the altar: *Altare sanctae Ecclesiae est Christus ... cujus altaris pallae et corporalia sunt membra Christi, scilicet fideles Dei quibus Dominus, quasi vestimentis pretiosis, circumdatur* (The altar of Holy Church is Christ ... of which altar the coverings or cloths are Christ's members, to wit, those who believe in God who form as it were a precious garment for the Lord).[16]

Moreover, our altar is identical with the altar which the Apocalyptic seer beheld in heaven, and to which there is an obvious allusion in the prayer which follows the Consecration of the Mass, when we pray that the Lord would command His angel to take up the Victim that lies slain upon our earthly altar, and place It upon that lofty altar which is ever before His presence in heaven. From the identity of the Victim, we rightly infer the identity of altars.

The proper material of an altar is stone. Should the altar be of wood, there must be placed in its center a stone "sepulchre," containing the relics of some Martyr and of perhaps some other canonized servant of God. The origin of this practice, which is now law, is traceable to the days of the Catacombs. The bodies of the more celebrated martyrs and confessors (bishops or priests) were often buried, not in the shelf-like tombs of the great dormitory of God's children (*coemeterium*), but in a sarcophagus abutting on the wall, and surmounted by a throne-like structure (*arcosolium*); upon the flat top of the sepulchre Mass was offered, and so we have the beginning of that universal practice of never celebrating the Holy Sacrifice except upon the bodies of the Saints. St John, in the Apocalypse, saw "under the altar the souls of them that were slain for the word of God, and for the testimony which they held."[17] These words must have inspired our predecessors in the faith. In the Martyrs our Lord continues His bloody sacrifice until the end of time. He is the origin and inspirer of martyrdom. *Sacrificium illud offerimus de quo martyrium sumpsit omne principium*,[18] says Holy Church in the Secret of the Thursday of the third week in Lent. Christ the *Head* is on the altar; the Saints, His *members*, are beneath it. Christus hostia ... super altari, qui pro omnibus passus est; illi sub altari, qui illius redempti sunt passione (Christ the victim ... is upon the altar, for He suffered for all; they are beneath the altar, who have been redeemed by His Passion).[19]

---

16 *In Ordinat. Subdiac.*   17 Apoc., vi. 9.
18 "We offer up that sacrifice from which every martyrdom has had its inception."
19 St Ambrose, *Ep. ad Marcell.*

CHAPTER IV

JUDICA ME AND THE CONFITEOR

IT is necessary that the priest should constantly react, by a lively faith, against the dulling effects of custom and familiarity. If he realizes daily that the altar at which he celebrates is the holiest spot in the universe, he will never be bereft of the joy that is God's daily gift to him, and his experience will not belie the triumphant assertion of his lips: *Introibo ad altare Dei, ad Deum qui laetificat juventutem meam.*[1]

Immediately after these words, which form its antiphon, the priest recites the forty-second Psalm. In this Psalm, David prays to be delivered from the wicked, from an unholy people. Left to his own resources, man walks alone and in sadness. Yet his soul need not despond, nor despair. God is his hope; He will send forth His light and His truth—that is, dissipate our present gloom by the light of faith, and at the same time fill our hearts with a joy which is for ever renewed in the sure hope that is ours that the God of truth will realize in our persons the promises He has made. These sentiments of the royal singer are also those of the priest, as he stands at the altar. His heart is swayed by contrary emotions; seeing his own weakness and proneness to evil, the priest might well feel despondent. But such sentiments are quickly overcome by the knowledge that God is with us, that His light and truth are ours, and thus fear is cast out by trust and love—trust in God, who is the source of joy.

The Psalm *Judica me* ends on a note of quiet, yet firm confidence in God, the God who is *the salvation of my countenance*—that is, the Saviour to whom I look up as unto my God. *My God*—that is, all the power and riches of God are mine, since He is *my* God and I am His.

---

[1] The full text of the Ordinary of the Mass will be found on pp. 217 sqq.

The greater our trust in God, the less we rely on self, the more so as our personal sins have only too often brought home to us the consciousness of our misery. Humility is the most suitable disposition of one who is about to enter into the Holy of Holies. The first act of a truly humble man is to acknowledge his sins, and such acknowledgment is the surest means of obtaining forgiveness. In the spiritual order our best excuse is self-accusation, because God will not despise a contrite and humble heart.

The *Confiteor* is an acknowledgment of whatever transgressions we may have committed, be it in thought, word or deed. We confess our guilt, not only before God Almighty, but also before the sinless Virgin, the great Princes of the Apostles, St John the Baptist, and the whole blessed company of heaven. We pray that these courtiers of the King of heaven would plead with Him on our behalf. "I saw," says Bl. Angela of Foligno, "in that I had offended my Creator, I had offended all creatures that had been made for me.... And I asked of all creatures—all of which I saw I had offended in that I had offended their Creator—not to accuse me before God. And it seemed unto me that all creatures had pity upon me, and all the Saints in like manner."[2]

His humble confession and the prayers of the Saints have obtained for the priest an all-embracing, all-including forgiveness: *Indulgentiam, absolutionem et remissionem peccatorum*. Strengthened from on high, he at last ascends the steps of the sacred altar, the while he once more pleads for mercy and forgiveness: *Aufer a nobis*... (Take away from us, we beseech Thee, O Lord, our iniquities, that we may be made worthy to enter with pure minds into Thy Holy of Holies).

He then kisses the altar, at the place where the relics of the Saints repose, and through their intercession renews his plea for pardon and forgiveness.

---

2 *Visions, etc., of Bl. Angela of Foligno*, vi.

CHAPTER V

THE INTROIT

THE prayers which are recited at the foot of the altar by the priest and his ministers were in reality the last addition to the Liturgy of the Mass. It is certain that originally the Mass began with the reading of the Epistle and Gospel. According to the *Liber pontificalis*, the custom of singing a psalm or psalms at the beginning of the Eucharistic Sacrifice was first introduced into the Roman Liturgy by Pope Celestine I (422–432): *Hic constituit ut psalmi David 150 ante sacrificium psallerentur antiphonatim ab omnibus, quod antea non fiebat, sed tantum epistolae Pauli recitabantur et sanctum Evangelium* (This Pope ordained that one, or some, of the 150 psalms of David should be sung antiphonally by all before the Sacrifice. This custom had not been previously observed, but only the Epistles of Paul and the holy Gospel were read). *Antiphonatim* describes the custom of singing psalms alternately, two choirs answering each other and, as it were, vying with each other. This custom originated in the East and was first introduced in the West by St Ambrose at the time when he and his people were besieged in his church by the troops of the Arian Empress Justina. In order to keep up the spirit of his people during the long hours of that night of alarms and terrors, the holy Bishop made them sing hymns and psalms, the multitude being divided into two choirs, each choir singing alternate verses. We learn this from *The Confessions of St Augustine*, Book VII, Chapter ix: *Tunc hymnis et psalmis ut canerentur secundum morem Orientalium partium, ne populus moeroris taedio contabesceret, institutum est, et ex illo in hodiernum retentum, multis jam ac pene omnibus gregibus tuis et per caeteras orbis partes imitantibus* (Then was it first introduced that hymns, and psalms should be sung, according to the custom of the Eastern Churches, lest the people should faint through the tediousness of grief;

and this custom, which is retained even to this day, is imitated by many, yea, by almost all thy congregations throughout the rest of the world).

The custom of singing the psalms and hymns in such wise that one choir alternated with and responded to the other, began early in what St Augustine calls the *Orientales partes*. It is not unreasonable to interpret in that sense what Pliny wrote to Trajan in his famous letter from Bithynia. Among other things, he tells his imperial master that the Christians were wont to meet in the early morning, when they would *carmen Christo quasi Deo dicere secum invicem* (that is, sing the praises of Christ in alternating chants). This would make our present-day psalmody almost as old as Christianity itself.

However, *antiphonal* singing implies more than *alternating* singing. The antiphon is a psalm verse which today is said, or sung, only at the beginning and the end of a psalm. But in the early centuries it used to be repeated between each verse of the psalm, as we still do in the Invitatory of Matins. This is the meaning of that great liturgist of the early centuries, St Benedict, when he prescribes that certain parts of the Office are to be sung "with an antiphon". The antiphon gave the key both to the meaning of the psalm and to the manner of its singing.

Our Introit of today is a survival of the psalm which was at first sung in its entirety, together with an antiphon, whilst the priest and his ministers proceeded from the *secretarium* (our modern sacristy) to the foot of the altar. The entrance of the clergy into the sanctuary must necessarily be stately and dignified. What could be more natural, then, than for the assistants to sing during that time some appropriate psalm—the psalms being practically the only hymns known to the faithful, at any rate before the days of St Ambrose, who introduced them and made them popular? In his *Rule*, St Benedict calls the hymn simply *Ambrosianus*, though St Hilary of Poitiers had also composed metric hymns some time before St Ambrose.

But the psalm was not for long sung in its entirety. Soon the antiphon alone was sung, together with the first verse of the psalm and the *Gloria Patri*, after which the antiphon was once more repeated. The *Gloria Patri*, as the normal conclusion of all psalms, was introduced in the Western Church by Pope Damasus—at the request of St Jerome, if we may admit as authentic the letter of Jerome to the Pontiff, in which he says: *Istud carmen laudis* (i.e., the doxology) *omni psalmo conjungi praecipias* (Command that this song of praise be added to every psalm).

The Introit is not found in the old Sacramentaries, but only in the Antiphonaries and *Ordines*, because neither antiphon nor psalm was read by the celebrant, but only sung by the choir and people.

Whilst the choir sang the introductory psalm, it was an obvious thing for the celebrant to prepare his own soul for the performance of his sacred functions. This he did in those preliminary prayers which he now says at the foot of the altar; "but for a long time," says a well-known authority, "no special prayers were appointed, they were not written in any official book. The fixed form we have now is the latest part of the Mass. No such prayers are mentioned at all before the eleventh century."[1]

Originally, as we have seen, the Introit and its psalm were sung by the choir or the people, but not read by the priest, but since the fourteenth century it has been customary for the celebrant to read both. This is now strictly enjoined by the rubrics. As soon as he begins to read the first words of the antiphon of the Introit, the priest makes upon himself the sign of the cross. Without a doubt this practice goes back to the time when the Introit marked the beginning of the Mass and when the preliminary prayers, now said at the foot of the altar, were still indeterminate and left to the private devotion and choice of the celebrant. At a Requiem Mass, the priest does not cross himself, but traces a cross over the book: *Manu dextera extensa, facit signum Crucis super librum, quasi aliquem benedicens*[2] (With his right hand extended, he makes the sign of the cross over the book, as if he were giving a blessing). We may see here the mind of Holy Church, which by this ceremony shows that the Mass about to be said is for the relief of the faithful departed, rather than for the help and wellbeing of the living, though this latter purpose is not and cannot be excluded from the Mass, even when specifically offered up for the dead.

Since the Mass during many centuries began directly with the antiphon of the Introit, its first words were used to designate the Mass of the day, or even the day or the feast itself. Thus even today we still call

---

1 Fortescue, *The Mass*, p. 225.   2 *Ritus Cel. Miss.*, XIII, 1.

a Mass for the dead a *Requiem;* the First Sunday of Advent is called *Ad te levavi;* the Second, *Populus Sion,* etc. But these denominations are not now so universal as they were in the Middle Ages, though even today we still speak of *Gaudete* Sunday or *Laetare* Sunday to designate the Sundays which occur in the middle of Advent and Lent, respectively.

The text of the Introit, as well as that of the Gradual and other varying parts of the Mass, is not taken from the Vulgate, but from the *Vetus Itala,* the oldest Latin translation of the Bible, based upon the Septuagint as regards the Books of the Old Testament. Hence the antiphons or psalm versicles do not always tally with the text of our breviaries, which give us the psalter of the Vulgate. The rubrics ordain that the Introit should be read *junctis manibus,* and at the *Gloria Patri* the celebrant *tenens junctas manus, caput inclinat versus crucem.*[3] The folding of hands is prescribed probably because of the *Gloria,* which, being an act of homage and adoration, demands this external manifestation of reverence.

The Introit is frequently of striking beauty and of singular appropriateness, to the day, or is specially applicable to the Saint whose feast is kept. Very often, also, the note struck in the Introit is heard again in the other variable parts of a Mass. The Introit, no less than the other parts of the Mass, can supply the priest with much matter for private prayer, or even for the pulpit. It marks the beginning of what was called the Mass of the Catechumens—that is, those readings and prayers which precede the oblation of the gifts of the faithful (the bread and wine that were to be changed into the Body and Blood of Christ, to be partaken of by them at the Communion). At the Offertory, the Catechumens had to withdraw from the assembly of the faithful. The readings from the inspired Books and the chants were thus chosen for the purpose not only of worship, but also of instruction and edification.

It will be helpful to give the text of the variable parts of a Mass in order to illustrate the remarks we shall have to make as we proceed. The Mass of Easter Sunday is eminently suited to our purpose. Let us first notice the rubric: *Statio ad Sanctam Mariam Majorem.* On certain solemn days the faithful of Rome, headed by their clergy, would

---

3 *Ritus Cel. Miss.,* IV, 2.

meet for the celebration of the holy mysteries in one of the many sanctuaries of the Eternal City. The Roman Pontiff himself celebrated Mass, assisted by the clergy of the whole city. The faithful were given a rendezvous in some church, and that first meeting was called *collecta*. From this meeting-place they went in procession to the church designated for the *Statio*, singing psalms and litanies, as we still do on the Rogation Days. At the *Statio* the Pope celebrated Mass and preached to the people. It was on these occasions that St Gregory delivered the forty homilies on the Gospels which we still possess. St Gregory fixed the churches where there were to be *Stationes*, but not all the *Stationes* indicated in the Missal are of his appointing. The word itself is a Roman military term corresponding to our own word "post" ("to post" troops to guard a place or building).

The antiphon of the Introit of Easter-day is made up of verses 18, 5 and 6 of Psalm cxxxviii, in the order here given and with slight variations from the text of the Vulgate: *Resurrexi, et adhuc tecum sum, alleluia: posuisti super me manum tuam, alleluia: mirabilis facta est scientia tua, alleluia, alleluia* (I have arisen, and am still with Thee, alleluia; Thou hast laid Thy hand upon Me, alleluia; Thy knowledge hath become wonderful, alleluia, alleluia) The psalm verse is verse 1 of Psalm cxxxviii, and is identical with the Vulgate text. David is the author of our psalm. He sings the all-embracing knowledge of God from whose vision nothing can be hidden. Holy Church puts some of his words on the lips of the risen Saviour: "I rose up and am still with Thee," Jesus Christ says to His heavenly Father, or, *in sensu accomodatitio*, to each faithful soul and to the whole Church. *Posuisti super me manum tuam;* for it is written: "Thou wilt not suffer Thy Holy One to see corruption."[4] The wisdom of God, as well as His infinite power, is marvelously shown forth in the Resurrection of our Lord; for in that great mystery He is revealed as the true Son of God: "Who was predestinated the Son of God in power... by the resurrection of our Lord Jesus Christ from the dead."[5]

Thus, our Introit is a very real introduction into the meaning of Easter-day. It sounds a ringing note of joy and triumph for Christ and for the Church. "*I am risen*, to die no more, and always shall I be with

---

4 Ps. xv. 10; Acts, ii, 27.   5 Rom., i. 4.

My Church, until the end of time." And for ever is the thought of His triumph over death a reminder of our own personal victory over the grave. *Tu cognovisti sessionem meam et resurrectionem meam:* God knows all things, even before they come to pass; hence, even as He knows the day of our *"sitting down"* (our death), so He beholds the day of our final *"rising up."*

CHAPTER VI

KYRIE ELEISON

IN the earliest centuries of the Church the Mass began, not with the Introit, as it does today, but with a lengthy Litany, of which the only remaining trace is the *Kyrie eleison*.

At Low Mass (which is the one we are studying), the priest, standing in the middle of the altar, alternately with his ministers or servers, invokes three times each of the three divine Persons. The *Kyrie eleison* (together with the *Agios o Theos*, etc., of Good Friday) bears witness to the fact that up to the third century, and possibly beyond, the whole of our Mass was in Greek. The invocation itself occurs many times in our Holy Books, both in those of the Old and the New Testaments, especially in the Psalms; for instance, in Psalm vi. 3: "Have mercy on me, O Lord, for I am weak"; in Matt. ix. 27: "Have mercy on us, o Son of David"; or in Luke, xvii. 13: "Jesus, master, have mercy on us."

Its liturgical use began in the East, and thence it passed into the West, about the sixth century. St Benedict, when describing the order to be followed in the divine psalmody, speaks repeatedly of the *Kyrie eleison*. His testimony is of great value, since he wrote in the early part of the sixth century: *sequatur ... supplicatio Litaniae, id est, 'Kyrie eleison.'*[1] We recite this invocation in the original Greek in order to emphasize the unity of the Christian people: *ut unum ejus populum esse ostendamus, unumque Deum utrumque populum credere*[2] (that we may show God's people to be one, and that each people believes in one and the same God).

Originally, the Litany consisted of a number of detailed prayers and petitions, called out or sung by a deacon, to each of which the people, especially the children, answered: *Kyrie eleison*. Such is the custom of

---

[1] *Reg. St Ben.*, ix.   [2] Alcuin, *De div. off.*, xl.

the Greek Church to this day. From the *Peregrinatio Silviae* we learn that a choir of boys sang the responses to the prayers of the deacon, *quorum voces sunt infinitae;* that is, the invocation, *Kyrie eleison,* was repeated by them an indefinite number of times.

When Rome and the Western churches definitely adopted the *Kyrie,* the preliminary or explanatory invocations were left out. Also, whereas the Greeks merely repeat *Kyrie eleison* without distinction, the Latin Church addresses its invocations to each divine Person separately. St Gregory the Great (590–604) comments on this difference between Rome and Constantinople: "We neither say nor have said *Kyrie eleison,* as it is said by the Greeks. For, whereas amongst the Greeks it is said together by all, with us it is said by the clerics and answered by the people; and *Christe eleison* is said as many times, which is by no means the case among the Greeks. But in the daily Masses we leave out some things which are generally said: we only say *Kyrie eleison* and *Christe eleison,* so that we may dwell rather longer on these words of prayer."[3]

The meaning of the holy Pontiff is that at Rome only the *Kyrie* is retained on ordinary days. On certain special occasions, however, as for instance the Rogation Days, the full Litany was retained.

The Litany, as has been said, marked the beginning of the Mass. We still see it in its ancient form in the Liturgy of Holy Saturday and the Saturday before Whit Sunday. There is no Introit; the *Kyrie* with which the Mass begins is but the conclusion of the Litany of the Saints, which thus marks the real beginning of the Mass.

According to Duchesne, the Litany of the Saints, as we now find it in our Roman Missal, preserves the ancient form of alternating prayers as used in the primitive Roman Church. It has undergone many alterations, especially in its opening section, which contains the invocations of the Saints. But the concluding section, when we respond *Te rogamus audi nos,* has a distinct flavor of antiquity, and bears a very close resemblance to some of the litany-like prayers of the Greek Church. Though we have no earlier text than one dating from the eighth century, it is probable that the Litany is of much greater antiquity.[4]

We may, then, attribute the introduction of the Kyrie, as we now

---

3 *Ep. ix ad Ioan. Episc. Syrac.;* see Fortescue, *The Mass,* p. 234.
4 Duchesne, *Origines du Culte chrétien,* p. 157.

say it at Mass, to St Gregory, as does his biographer, John the Deacon. It is easy to see how natural it was that, with the introduction of daily Mass, the long Litany with its acclamations, or responses by the people, should come to be omitted in its entirety. Rome has always avoided extremes, and we know by experience that mere length of prayer is not by any means synonymous with devotion.

St Benedict is no mean authority on liturgical questions. He makes mention of the "supplication of the Litany; that is, *Kyrie eleison*," as of something that was not in any way new or unusual in his time. There are reasons for believing that already in the fourth century the *Kyrie* was sung or said both at Mass and at the other sacred offices. In 529 the Synod of Vaison, in its third canon, ordains the frequent repetition of the *Kyrie*. The Council bases its prescription on the universal custom of the time: "Whereas both in the Apostolic See and in all the churches of the East, and throughout the provinces of Italy, a sweet and most salutary custom has grown up that *Kyrie eleison* be said very frequently with much devotion and compunction, it has pleased us that in all our churches this most holy practice be introduced at Matins [the Night Office and Lauds], at Mass and at Vespers."

The Council ordains that *Kyrie eleison* should be said or sung *frequentius* (that is, often, even very often). The number is not specified, neither did St Gregory determine the number of times each invocation was to be repeated; all he did was to ordain that the invocation should be said alternately by the priest (or deacon) and the people, and that mention should be made of the second Person of the Trinity.

The limitation to nine invocations is first met with in the eleventh century. Amalarius (ninth century) speaks indeed of the invocation of the three divine Persons, but not of the number of the invocations. "Let the cantors say: *Kyrie eleison*, Lord, the Father, have mercy; *Christe eleison*, have mercy, Thou who hast redeemed us by Thy Blood; *Kyrie eleison*, Lord, the Holy Ghost, have mercy."[5]

In the later Middle Ages, whenever it was sung, the *Kyrie* came to be "farced"—that is, interspersed with *tropes*. Tropes are words added to the text, by which its meaning is explained or amplified. The *Kyrie* is

5 *De eccl. off.*, III, c. 6.

generally sung to an elaborate melody, the voice, as it were, lingering on one syllable or vowel. So they fitted-in tropes between the *Kyrie* and the concluding *eleison* in such wise that a syllable of the trope was made to correspond to each note of the "neums" (melodies). These tropes were all abolished when the Missal was reformed by Pius v, though we find traces of them in the titles of some of the *Kyries* in the official Vatican chant books. Thus, for instance, the *Kyrie* No. 1, for Paschal time, bears the sub-title *Lux et Origo*, which words are simply the beginning of the tropes sung to this *Kyrie*. Or again, the *Kyrie* called *Fons Bonitatis*, refers to one which began thus: *Kyrie fons bonitatis, a quo bona cuncta procedunt, eleison*.

A supplication of such venerable antiquity should be said with reverence and deliberation. The priest should, therefore, avoid all unseemly haste, nor should he permit the servers to indulge in what often looks like speed-rivalry between celebrant and acolyte. Each petition must be said separately, not simultaneously by priest and acolyte.

"The *Kyrie* is said *junctis manibus*. To fold the hands, or to extend them crosswise, has always been preeminently the Christian attitude of prayer. This external attitude of supplication to the Triune God should be but the outward manifestation of the feelings of our hearts, as we repeat nine times a prayer of which it has been well said that, by itself, it signifies, or typifies, all other prayers (*omnes universales Ecclesiae preces significat*)."[6]

---

6 Rupert of Deutz, *De div. off.*, tit, 29,

CHAPTER VII

GLORIA IN EXCELSIS DEO

THE hymn *Gloria in excelsis Deo* is said on all Sundays except Septuagesima and during Lent and Advent, on Saints' days, on all *ferias* during Paschal time, but not on the *ferias* during the other parts of the year. It is also said at *solemn* votive Masses, unless the color of the Mass is purple, but not at private votive Masses, except at the Mass of Our Lady *in Sabbato,* because Saturday has long been regarded as a minor feast of Our Blessed Lady. It is also recited at the votive Mass of the Angels. The reason is obvious, for the *Gloria* is properly the *Hymnus Angelicus.* The Angels intoned it first in the blessed midnight hour of Christ's Nativity, then Holy Church took it up, added to it, and made it that perfect song of praise which, morning after morning, thrills and gladdens our hearts.

Yet for a long time the *Gloria* was not recited by the ordinary priest. It was the exclusive privilege of bishops to say the *Gloria* on Sundays and Saints' days, and the ordinary priest was only allowed to say it on Easter Sunday. About the middle of the eleventh century, Berno of Reichenau complains of this restriction, and asks that priests, as well as bishops, should say the *Gloria* on all Sundays and Saints' days, *ad augmentum laudis divinae.* The restriction was withdrawn before the end of the century, for we learn from his *Micrologus* that, outside Advent, the feast of the Holy Innocents and Septuagesima, priests and bishops alike recited the *Gloria* on all Sundays and feast-days.

It is certain that the *Gloria* comes to us from the East. It is a very old Greek chant, written in loose rhythm. The oldest documents in which our hymn is found are the *Constitutiones Apostolicae,* VII, and a work entitled *De Virginitate,* attributed with good reason to St Athanasius. In these documents our hymn is described as a morning prayer.

Its authorship is unknown, but some would attribute its composition to St Hilary of Poitiers. However, it seems scarcely credible that this great witness to the divinity of the Word should have used some of the expressions which occur in the original Greek text. What is more probable is, that he heard the hymn during the years of his exile in Asia Minor, and translated it into Latin. The following is the text of the Apostolic Constitutions:

> *Gloria in excelsis Deo et in terra pax, in hominibus bona voluntas. Laudamus te, hymnis celebramus te, benedicimus te, glorificamus te, adoramus te per magnum pontificem, te verum Deum, ingenitum unum, solum inaccessum, propter magnam gloriam tuam, Domine rex coelestis, Deus Pater omnipotens. Domine Deus, Pater Christi, Agni immaculati, qui tollit peccatum mundi: suscipe deprecationem nostram, qui sedes super Cherubim; quoniam tu solus Dominus Jesu Christi, Dei universae naturae creatae, regis nostri, per quem tibi gloria, honor et adoratio.*

In this text the entire hymn is addressed to God the Father. The concluding clauses savor strongly of what is called "subordinationism," that is, an apparently attenuated, yet real form of Arianism. The entire hymn was revised and corrected when it was definitely adopted by both the Greek and Latin Churches. According to the *Liber Pontificalis*, Pope St Telesphorus (138) ordered Masses to be said on the night of the Nativity of our Lord. He also ordered that the hymn *Gloria in excelsis* should then be sung, as it is in St Luke's Gospel. This means, probably, that only the opening sentences of the hymn were sung. So, if St Hilary is really the author, he only added the clauses beginning with *Laudamus te*, though, as we have observed above, it is far more likely that the holy Bishop of Poitiers only translated into Latin a hymn already popular in the East.

The *Gloria*, as we now say it at Mass, is divided into three parts, in which we successively render honor and glory and thanksgiving to the Father, the Son, and the Holy Ghost. Thus, our hymn is a perfect doxology, and is called the *great doxology,* in contradistinction to the *Gloria Patri, et Filio, et Spiritui Sancto,* which is called the *minor doxology*. Abbot Cabrol justly remarks that most of the titles and invocations of the *Gloria* occur almost word for word in the most ancient liturgical prayers, when liturgical language was at its very birth and in process of formation. To judge by the text, this hymn may date from the earliest ages of the Church. None of its formulas is out of harmony with the style of the most ancient authors, and it contains no expression which might not have been written in the first or second century.[1]

Some think that Pliny alludes to the hymn *Gloria in excelsis* in his famous letter to Trajan, in which he informs his imperial master that the Christians were wont to assemble early in the morning "to sing a hymn to Christ as to their God."

In the Middle Ages the *Gloria*, like the *Kyrie*, was frequently "farced" (that is, interspersed with tropes). This was especially the case in Masses on feasts of Our Lady. It would appear that these tropes on the feasts of Our Lady were particularly popular and not readily given up. This must be borne in mind if we want to understand the rubric of bur Missal, which run thus: *Sic dicitur Gloria in excelsis,* **etiam in Missis Beatae Mariae.** Here is the conclusion of the "farced" *Gloria* of Our Lady's Mass: *Quoniam tu solus sanctus;* **Mariam Sanctificans,** *tu solus Dominus,* **Mariam Gubernans,** *tu solus Altissimus,* **Mariam Coronans.**

One can only feel grateful that better taste should have restored to us the hymn of the Angels in all its old-world simplicity and grandeur. It would be a most excellent practice, were we to make of the Gloria the habitual expression of our praise and adoration of the Blessed Trinity. *Homo creatus est ut laudet,* and it would be difficult to find a nobler expression of praise and worship than this sublime canticle, which contains the substance of our inspired Books and is redolent of the wonderful spirit of prayer that was the peculiar gift of the early Church.

---

1 *Liturgical Prayer,* p. 101.

CHAPTER VIII

THE COLLECT AND ITS CONCLUSION

The Collect

WHEN the priest has completed the recitation of the *Gloria*, he kisses the altar, and, turning around, he greets the assistants with the words, *Dominus vobiscum*. If the celebrant is a bishop and the Mass has a *Gloria*, he says *Pax vobis*, instead of *Dominus vobiscum*. To kiss the altar is a sign of reverence and love. The heart is considered by all men as the symbol and organ of love. Of this love of the heart the lips give external evidence, both by words and by physical contact with the object loved. True love necessarily implies reverence for the thing beloved. *Adoration* literally signifies kissing—the thing worshiped is approached to the lips (*ad os, adorare*).

The Christian altar is no mere insensible block of stone or wooden table. It stands for Christ Himself, who is for us priest, victim and altar (*Altare sanctae Ecclesiae ipse est Christus*). The altar must be of stone, because this enduring material is an apt image of the abiding presence of Christ in His Church, daily immolating Himself in the mystic sacrifice of the Mass. He is indeed the living cornerstone, upon whom rests the universal Church. "Jesus Christ Himself being the chief corner-stone," says St. Paul;[1] and St Peter: "A living stone, rejected indeed by men, but chosen and made honorable by God."[2] When the priest kisses the altar, he pays homage to the spot whereon the august Sacrifice is about to be offered, but over and above he is mindful of our divine High-priest in heaven, of whom our consecrated stone is a sacred and venerable image.

[1] Eph., ii. 20.   [2] 1 Pet., ii. 4.

This sacred, liturgical kiss is an act of homage addressed, in the first instance, to our Lord Himself; but it includes likewise the Saints whose relics rest in the altar tomb. The Saints are the members of Christ's mystical body; they cannot be separated from Him. Hence the strict law of the Church that the holy Sacrifice should always be offered upon the bodies of the Saints.

Facing the congregation, the priest now extends and again immediately folds his hands, saying: *Dominus vobiscum*. This greeting, as well as the now exclusively episcopal *Pax vobis*, is of the highest antiquity. For the Eastern Liturgies the formula is Εἰρήνη πᾶσιν (Peace to all), and precedes every exhortation to prayer. In the Greek Liturgy both priest and bishop use this one formula of salutation. We find the formula in the books of both the Old and the New Testaments; thus, for instance, when Boaz came out of Bethlehem into his fields, he said to the reapers: "The Lord be with you; and they answered him: The Lord bless thee."[3] In Galatians, vi. 18, St Paul prays thus: "The grace of our Lord Jesus Christ be with your spirit, brethren, Amen." The same wish ends the Epistle to the Philippians, and to Timothy he writes: "The Lord Jesus Christ be with thy spirit. Grace be with you. Amen."[4] The Epistles also begin with a like salutation: *Gratia vobis et pax*.

The grace and peace of Christ are sanctifying grace, by which we are made the children and friends of God. When the priest, or bishop, prays that the Lord be with us, or that peace be unto us, he does far more than express a pious wish. When he stands at the altar, the priest is the mediator between God and man, the authentic dispenser of the mysteries and graces of God, and hence also of His peace—that peace of God which surpasseth all understanding, which the world can neither give nor take away from us, if we are fortunate enough to possess it. "Into whatsoever house you enter, first say: Peace be to this house. And if the son of peace be there, your peace shall rest upon him...."[5] The greeting *Dominus vobiscum* is, therefore, a sacramental, an infallible sign and means of grace, if those to whom it is addressed are properly disposed. The peace of the Lord will be given

3 Ruth, ii. 4,   4 II Tim., iv. 22.
5 Luke, x. 5, 6.

them in the measure in which they are "sons of peace".

Here we may perhaps be pardoned if we insist on how important it is for the priest to realize what his lips utter. If it is necessary that the faithful should pay attention to the liturgical greeting, it is not less requisite that the celebrant should put his whole heart into it. We turn towards the people, not to take stock of the congregation, but to dispense God's grace and peace to them. The whole movement should be slow and dignified. There is nothing more unedifying, and withal grotesque, than to see a priest swing around on his heels in a whirlwind, as if he were carrying out a military movement on the parade ground of some barracks at the bidding of a drill sergeant.

St John Chrysostom speaks thus of our liturgical salutation, and complains of the listlessness of many: "Is it I who give you peace? No, but Christ deigns to speak by my mouth. Were we altogether void of grace, yet are we not then, for your sakes. If the grace of God could act upon a soothsayer and his ass... for the sake of the people of Israel, He will assuredly not fail to act upon us also, for your sakes."[6]

The answer to the priest's greeting is *Et cum spiritu tuo*, which signifies simply: "And with thee." The faithful pray for the priest, that the grace and peace of which he is the dispenser may also sustain his spirit.

Before reading the Collect the priest exhorts the faithful to pray: *Oremus*. In the Greek Liturgy the deacon warns the people with the words: "Let us stand well; in peace let us pray to the Lord"; or simply: "Let us pray to the Lord."

Our present-day *Oremus* is the survival of a much longer and more detailed exhortation to prayer, such as we still have in the intercessory prayers of Good Friday. The invitation to prayer, and the detailed exposition of its object, would be followed by a more or less prolonged private prayer of the faithful, after which the priest would once more raise his voice in supplication, and, as it were, sum up, collect, or gather in one the prayers of the multitude. That may well be the origin of our "Collect" (*collecta*, from *colligere*, to gather up, gather together, or sum up).

---

6 *Hom. in Ep. ad Colos.* iii, c. 4-

According to Dom Cabrol, "this prayer was at first improvised, its subject-matter only being given out. By degrees such prayers as were distinguished by their genuine piety, their eloquence, or theological importance, were committed to writing, and thus from very early times, probably not later than the fourth century, collections of prayers were formed, a good number of which have been preserved in our liturgical books. In this respect the Roman Liturgy is exceedingly rich."[7]

It is, however, more likely that the Collect owes its name to the fact that it was a prayer which was recited when the faithful had all assembled in the place or church, from which they walked in procession to the church where the *Statio* was to take place. As soon as the faithful were gathered together, an antiphon with a psalm would be sung—or more likely, whilst the people were flocking together, a psalm would be sung with an antiphon interpolated after every verse. When all were assembled, a short prayer was said (*oratio super collectam*). We see traces of this practice to this very day; on Candlemas Day, for instance, an antiphon taken from Psalm xliii, with the first verse of this same psalm, is sung with the *Gloria,* and followed by a Collect. The word *Collect* has now almost wholly disappeared from the Missal, and we invariably speak of the "prayer" (*oratio*) of the day or feast.

The great mass of our Collects are addressed to God the Father; a few are addressed to God the Son (especially those of more recently instituted feasts), and none at all to the Holy Ghost, though there are prayers to the Holy Ghost in other Liturgies than the Roman and in the rituals of some Orders (for instance, in that of the Benedictine Order).

The composition of the Collects is subject to some very definite, but simple rules. The *oratio* begins with an address to God: *Omnipotens sempiterne Deus*. This constant appeal to the omnipotence and eternity of God is very striking. What could be more natural than this call to One who can do all things, and who is ever the self-same, whereas "all flesh is as grass, and the years of our life are but few and evil."

---

7 *Liturgical Prayer,* p. 38.

The appeal to God's omnipotence is often followed by a brief exposition of the motive of our prayer, or by some allusion to the day or the event commemorated. The petition itself is always expressed with great directness and terseness. Especially is this so in the oldest Collects—those of the Gelasian and Gregorian Sacramentaries, of which many are read on the Sundays after Pentecost. The conclusion invariably mentions the three divine Persons. The simplicity, terseness, unction, and theological accuracy of these venerable prayers are unequalled. It is impossible to tell who is the author of these masterpieces. Some attribute them to the great Pope of the fourth century, St Damasus. What is certain is, that there was in those early days a peculiar gift both of conception and expression, a peculiar outpouring of that *spiritus gratiae et precum* spoken of by the prophet. Nothing is more striking than the brevity of the old, and, if one may say so, the verbosity of the more modern Collects. It would be easy to compile a list of particularly impressive Collects; in fact, it is difficult to say that one is more beautiful than another, where there is such superabundance of wealth of thought and phrase. The Collect of Easter-day is an excellent illustration of what we have said. It opens with a direct address to God: *"Deus."* This is followed by a brief reference to the event commemorated that day: "Who through Thine only-begotten Son didst today overcome death and open unto us the gates of everlasting life." No translation can adequately render the petition thus nobly expressed: *Vota nostra, quae praeveniendo aspiras, etiam adjuvando prosequere* (To our good resolutions which Thou didst anticipate with Thy holy inspirations, grant furtherance also by Thy gracious aid).

The Collect of the Mass is now the concluding prayer of all the offices of the day, and sometimes it is repeated for an entire octave (for instance, the Collect of the Epiphany and that of the Ascension). It expresses the spirit of the day, and is a terse summary of the thoughts called forth by the feast. As such, it is an eminently appropriate subject for our personal meditation and prayer, and a rich source of inspiration for the pulpit. It would be an immense gain to both priest and people, if the preacher would seek inspiration, not only in the Epistle and Gospel, but likewise in the Collects. Thus, to speak only of the above-mentioned Collects of the Epiphany and the Ascension, the star which led the Magi to the feet of the Emmanuel is obviously a symbol of the light of faith by which we too have known God. What could be a more natural and logical inference than to pray that, having known the only-begotten Son of God by faith here below, we may be led to behold the splendor of His countenance hereafter (*usque ad contemplandam speciem tuae celsitudinis perducamur*). And, on the day on which our Lord's victory ended in a sublime triumph, it is meet to pray that we might at least in thought dwell with Him in heaven (*ipsi quoque mente in caelestibus habitemus*).

Nothing could surpass in dignity the noble phrasing of the conclusion: *Per Dominum nostrum Jesum Christum.* "Who first wrote this no one knows. Whoever he was, he has immortalized himself by words that for centuries have closed our prayers with the splendid rhythm of their accent and the roll of their vowels."[8]

During many centuries only one Collect was said at Mass. About the twelfth century the custom of saying more than one Collect or prayer was universal throughout the Western Church. Sicardus of Cremona, who wrote at the end of the twelfth century and the beginning of the thirteenth, lays down the rule that only one prayer be said. However he adds that "by the institutions of the Fathers, three or five or seven are sometimes said" (*ex patrum institutionibus quandoque dicuntur tres, vel quinque, vel septem*). Medieval writers find, of course, the most wonderful reasons for these various numbers. The above-mentioned Sicardus goes so far as to quote Virgil as an authority in favor of the uneven number of Collects, for, according to the poet, *numero gaudet impare deus.*[9]

On the greater solemnities of the year we still observe the primitive custom of saying but one Collect. If the Blessed Sacrament is exposed during Mass, the Collect of the Mass of Corpus Christi is said as well, but *sub unica conclusione.* The same is done at the Mass of Ordination, when the prayer for the ordinands is said under the same conclusion as the prayer of the day.

If, in a prayer addressed to God the Father, mention has been made

---

8 Fortescue, *The Mass,* p. 250.
9 "Uneven numbers delight the god."—*Eclog.,* viii, 75.

of the Son, the conclusion is: *per eumdem Dominum nostrum*. If the Holy Ghost has been mentioned we conclude thus: *in unitate ejusdem Spiritus Sancti*. According to the rubric of the new Missal, the Holy Ghost is to be understood as expressly mentioned in the Postcommunion of Easter-day (*Spiritum nobis, Domine, tuae caritatis infunde*), so that the conclusion must be: *in unitate ejusdem Spiritus Sancti*.

Amen

The prayers of Holy Church, as well as her hymns, psalms and canticles, end with one of the most venerable words in human language, *Amen*. It is a Hebrew word and has remained untranslated in the Liturgy, though in some modern languages it has been translated for extra-liturgical use. Thus the French conclude their prayers with *"Ainsi soit-il!"* and the Italians with *"Cosi sia!"* It is a matter for real satisfaction that we have not attempted to say "So it be!" but have retained the Hebrew *Amen*.

The word *Amen* may be taken as an adjective, and as such signifies firm, true, loyal; as a substantive, it signifies fidelity, God's fidelity in realizing His promises. Thus we read in Isaias: "He that is blessed upon the earth shall be blessed in God, *Amen*; and he that sweareth in the earth shall swear by God, *Amen*."[10] So also in the Apocalypse: "These things saith the *Amen*, the faithful and true witness, who is the beginning of the creation of God."[11] As an adverb, it signifies an emphatic affirmation, the adhesion or assent of the mind to some statement, or a wish that what is said or promised may be accomplished. Thus, for instance, in Rom., xv. 33: "The God of peace be with you all. *Amen!*" Then we have the repeated words of our Lord Himself: "*Amen, Amen,* I say unto you," which in His mouth signify a solemn declaration and affirmation.

When the people respond *Amen* at the end of the Collect, that short word is in itself yet another prayer, as well as the outward declaration that they are at one with the priest who, has given public expression to what is in the minds and hearts of all. *Amen nostra subscriptio est, consensio est, adstipulatio est*, says St Augustine. We should

---

10 Is., lxv. 16.   11 Apoc., iii. 14.

pronounce this sacred word with due reverence and attention. The word is still frequently used by the Jews. The Talmud says that, if a man says a hurried *Amen*, his days shall be curtailed, but, if he lingers over it, his days shall be lengthened. St Augustine tells us that *Amen* remained in its original Hebrew in order that it might not become trivial, like some ordinary, familiar interjection: *Non est interpretatum, ut honorem haberet velamento secreti, non ut esset negatum, sed ne vilesceret nudatum. Amen* has not been interpreted, in order that secrecy might procure it more honor; not because its meaning was to be withheld, but lest it should be considered common if fully explained;[12] and this was done by the authority of the Saints who have gone before us (*propter sanctiorem auctoritatem*).[13]

Very touching and most appropriate are the words of the great Benedictine mystic, St Gertrude, at the end of the first of her "Exercises." The Saint declares that God is Himself the true *Amen*, inasmuch as He is truth itself. It is worthwhile quoting the entire passage, for it is calculated to rouse our interest and suggest a train of thought which will prevent us from a mere perfunctory utterance of a word which is so frequently upon our lips. "May the faithful God, the true *Amen* which knoweth neither pause nor interruption, condescend to excite within me a thirst for that beloved *Amen* of which He is the source; may He render sweet to my taste that sweetest *Amen* wherewith He doth ever nourish His friends; may He make me perfect in the blessedness of that *Amen* wherewith He completeth and endeth all things; may He grant me to enjoy for ever more the delights of the ravishing and eternal *Amen*, who will show me after this exile, according to my sure hope, the true *Amen*, Jesus, the Son of God, who alone sufficeth to him that loves; who, with the Father and the Holy Ghost, is the source of all good things, and who despiseth nothing that He has made: *Amen, Amen, Amen*."[14]

---

12 *In Ioan. Tract.*, xli., 3.   13 *De doctrina christ.*, xi.
14 *Exercises of St Gertrude*, 1 (London), p. 17.

CHAPTER IX

THE EPISTLE AND DEO GRATIAS

The Epistle or Lesson

FROM the very beginning of the Church the reading of the Holy Books has been an integral and most important part of the Liturgy. In his famous "Apology" addressed to the Emperor Antoninus, St Justin Martyr, who died about 167, gives us a fairly complete account of the religious ceremonial of those early days, which, according to him, began with the reading of selected passages of the Bible. It is more than likely that the Christian Church followed more or less closely the practice of the Synagogue, for reading was part of the worship of the Jews. The Acts bear witness to the liturgical reading of the Law and the Prophets: "For Moses of old time hath in every city them that preach him in the synagogues, where he is read every sabbath."[1] When Saul and Barnabas came to Antioch in Pisidia, they entered the local synagogue upon the Sabbath day. "And after the reading of the law and the prophets," they were invited to address the assembly. In the course of his address, St Paul blames them "that inhabited Jerusalem, and the rulers thereof," inasmuch as they, "not knowing Him (Jesus) nor the voices of the prophets which are read every sabbath, judging Him, have fulfilled them."[2]

At first the various readings were from the volume of the Bible itself. The president of the assembly designated the parts that were to be read, and gave the signal to stop the reading when he judged it expedient, or when the allotted time was over. Moreover, the reading of the sacred volume was continuous—that is, the various books of

---

[1] Acts, xv. 21. [2] Acts, xiii. 27.

the Bible were read integrally and without regard to the character of the time or feast. However, already in the fourth century, the choice of the book was more or less in keeping with the character of the season of the year. Thus, we gather from St Augustine that the Acts of the Apostles were read during Paschal time, as well as the Gospel of St John.[3] In course of time the full text was no longer read, but only selections, and these were gathered into one volume. According to medieval liturgists, St Jerome was the first to draw up such a list of readings, called *comes* (that is, a companion for the lectors of the Church, or catalogue of lessons). Originally the number of lessons was not determined. Since the sixth century, in the Roman Church at any rate, there have been only two lessons except on special occasions, such as the Ember Days or the eves of Easter and Pentecost.

In Old Testament days the Scriptures were divided into two sections: the Law and the Prophets. In like manner, the New Testament was broadly divided into two classes of writings, those of St Paul and those of the Evangelists. Thus, it came about that the two readings were simply called "the Apostle" and "the Gospel". In the Missal or Sacramentary of St Gregory, the expression, *sequitur Apostolus,* is frequent. St Benedict, who wrote in the sixth century, speaks repeatedly of "the Apostle" (*lectio Apostoli sequatur*).[4]

It is very difficult to account for the choice of one section of the writings of St Paul or of the Gospels rather than of another, though of course the selection is most appropriate on certain days. As St Augustine already remarked, there are some lessons from the Gospels so intimately connected with certain days or times of the year that they must be read. Thus, the connection between the Epistle and Gospel of Christmas, the Epiphany; or the Ascension, is apparent to everyone. But it is not the case as regards the Epistles and Gospels of (say) the Sundays after Pentecost. On the feasts of the Saints, the Epistle is frequently most appropriate, though sometimes it must be taken *in sensu accomodatitio.*

The Epistle is invariably announced as *Lectio* (Reading)—from the Epistle of St Paul to the Romans, for instance. If the reading is taken

---

3 *Tract. in Ioan,* vi, 18.   4 *Regula,* ix.

from Proverbs, or Ecclesiastes, Ecclesiasticus, the Canticle of Canticles, or Wisdom, it is always announced as *Lectio libri Sapientiae*. Medieval liturgists have indulged in some curious speculation as to the reason why the name of Moses or Solomon is not mentioned when the lesson is from their books. De Ruberis tells us that the name of Moses is not mentioned because he provoked the Lord to anger, and that of Solomon because, *deceptus a mulieribus, in idololatriam lapsus est!*[5]

At first the Lesson or Epistle was sung by a reader. When the singing of the Gospel became the exclusive privilege of the deacon, the subdeacon also secured the honor of being alone permitted to sing the Epistle. However, even in our own days the Bishop may allow a cleric in minor orders to sing the Epistle at Mass and to discharge some of the other duties of the subdeacon. But he may not wear the maniple or purify the chalice.

The reading of the Epistle serves a distinctly catechetical purpose. It constitutes the first part of the Mass of the Catechumens, from which none were excluded, because it was intended for the instruction of the people: *Episcopus nullum prohibeat ingredi ecclesiam et audire verbum Dei, sive gentilem, sive haereticum, sive Judaeum, usque ad Missam Catechumenorum* ("Let the bishop forbid none to enter the church to hear the word of God, be he a pagan or a heretic or a Jew—up to the Mass of the Catechumens"—inclusively, we must suppose).[6]

The Epistle is read before the Gospel, because it is symbolic of St John the Baptist, who went before the Lord, whereas the Gospel is the preaching of Christ Himself. It also typifies the disciples whom our Lord sent two by two "before His face into every city and place whither He Himself was to come."[7]

The injunction which the bishop addresses to the newly ordained lector may well be pondered sometimes by the priest. We should read the Epistle *distincte et aperte, ad intelligentiam et aedificationem fidelium*. The faithful, especially the more instructed and intelligent among them, love to follow the Mass and to hear the noble phrases of the sacred tongue. Let us see to it that we do not deprive them of

5 *Rationale div. off.*, II, 28.   6 *Concil. Carthag.* IV, Can, 24 (AD 398).
7 Luke, X. I.

this satisfaction by a careless, slurring, or too hurried reading.

It has been said above that the Epistle is frequently, if not always, chosen because of its appropriateness to the day or the time. This is eminently so in regard to the Epistle of Easter Sunday, the Mass of which we have taken to illustrate these Notes. It begins with the address, *Fratres,* with which Holy Church prefaces all the readings she has culled from the writings of St Paul.

"Brethren: Purge out the old leaven, that you may be a new paste, as you are unleavened. For Christ our pasch is sacrificed. Therefore let us feast, not with the old leaven of malice and wickedness, but with the unleavened bread of sincerity and truth."[8]

The Sunday sermon is commonly based on the Gospel, but what a rich vein of lofty thought meditation on the Epistle will open to us! Let us seek inspiration there, as well as in the Collect, and our weekly homily will gain much in freshness and persuasiveness.

Deo Gratias

When the Lesson or Epistle is ended, the people, now almost exclusively represented by the server or acolyte, answer: *Deo gratias!* The words are found in St Paul. Writing to the Corinthians, the Apostle says, towards the end of his letter: *Deo autem gratias, qui dedit nobis victoriam per Dominum nostrum Jesum Christum.*[9] And again: *Deo autem gratias, qui semper triumphat nos in Christo Jesu.*[10] *Deo gratias* has become one of the most frequent of the exclamations, or acclamations, which Holy Church uses in her Liturgy. It is said not only at the end of the Epistle, or Lesson, but likewise after the *capitulum,* and it is the response of the people to the invitation of the priest when, at the end of the Hours of the Divine Office, he bids them bless God: *Benedicamus Domino.* ℟. *Deo gratias!*

The exclamation, *Deo gratias,* is of hoary antiquity. We might say that it is one of those ejaculatory prayers which were frequently on the lips of the early Christians. In the words of Cardinal Pitra (quoted by Dom Cabrol), "in these primitive chants was reflected all that was

---

8 I Cor., v. 7, 8. 9 I Cor., xv. 57.
10 II Cor., ii. 14.

most simple, most expressive, most familiar.... These acclamations of the people, these cries of the Christian soul, have come down to us through the ages from the early Christians, and still form a link between the Churches of the East and West. Even to this day the sun never rises without hearing the same words uttered in the midst of the same mysteries."[11]

In his forty-first Epistle; St Augustine writes to Bishop Aurelius, thanking him for allowing simple priests to preach in his presence. As is well known, in those early days the preaching of the Word of God was reserved exclusively to bishops. When St Augustine, as yet a simple priest, began to preach instead of his bishop, no small sensation was caused. "What better thing," says the holy Doctor, "can we bear in mind, utter with the mouth, or write with the pen, than 'Deo gratias'? It is not possible to say aught shorter, to hear aught sweeter, to understand aught grander, to do aught that could be more profitable" (*Quid melius et animo geramus, et ore promamus, et calamo exprimamus quam Deo gratias? Hoc nec dici brevius, nec audiri laetius, nec intelligi grandius, nec agi fructuosius potest*).[12]

In his Commentary on Psalm cxxii, the same Doctor tells us that the monks of those days greeted each other with the words *Deo gratias*; whereas the Circumcellions used to say *Deo laudes* instead: "He who says: *Deo gratias!* gives thanks to God. See whether a brother ought not to return thanks to God when he sees his brother. Is it not matter for congratulation when they meet who abide in Christ? Yet you scoff at our *Deo gratias!* but men weep because of your *Deo laudes!*" (*Qui dicit 'Deo gratias,' gratias agit Deo. Vide si non debeat frater Deo gratias agere, quando videt fratrem suum. Num enim non est locus gratulationis quando se invicem vident qui habitant. in Christo? Et tamen vos 'Deo gratias' nostrum ridetis: 'Deo laudes' vestrum plorant homines*).[13] The greeting, *Deo gratias*, distinguished the orthodox Christian from the heretic.

In the sixth century St Benedict ordained that the door-keeper of the monastery should exclaim *Deo gratias*, as soon as he had heard the "knock of a caller, or the cry of a poor man."[14]

11 *Liturgical Prayer*, p. 52.
12 *Loc. cit.*
13 *Enarrat. in Ps. cxxrii*, 6.
14 *Regula*, LXVI.

So popular was our ejaculation that a holy bishop of Carthage took it as his Christian name. Thus, year after year on the twenty-first day of March, we read in the Roman Martyrology the announcement for the following day of the feast of St Deogratias, who brought back into the true fold many Arian Vandals.

CHAPTER X

THE GRADUAL, TRACT AND SEQUENCE

The Gradual

THE Gradual follows immediately upon the Epistle. The Gradual, as we now find it in our Missal, is composed of only two psalm verses, but originally a whole psalm was sung between the reading of the Epistle and the Gospel. The interspersing of singing with reading is a very early innovation, and was introduced for the purpose of renewing and sustaining the interest of the faithful during the long hours of divine worship.

There is no doubt that the Gradual was sung as a *psalmus responsorius;* that is to say, a deacon (or cantor) sang each verse, and the people repeated the first verse (or some other acclamation) after every verse sung. We see this already practised by the Synagogue, the classical instance being Psalm cxxxv:

> *Confitemini Domino quoniam bonus:*
> *Quoniam in aeternum misericordia ejus,*
> *Confitemini Deo deorum:*
> *Quoniam in aeternum misericordia ejus:*[1]

and so on throughout its twenty-six verses, when the whole of the first verse is once more repeated. St Augustine speaks very definitely of the singing of a Gradual consisting of an entire psalm: *Primum lectionem audivimus Apostoli ... deinde cantavimus psalmum, exhortantes nos invicem una voce, uno corde dicentes: 'Venite adoremus.'...Post haec evangelica lectio decem leprosos mundatos nobis ostendit* (First we heard the lesson of the

---

[1] Praise the Lord, for He is good: for His mercy endureth for ever.
Praise ye the God of Gods: for His mercy endureth for ever.

Apostle ... then we sang a psalm, exhorting one another by saying with one voice and one heart: 'Come, let us adore.' After that the lesson from the Gospel showed us ten lepers made clean).[2]

From about the time of St Gregory the Great, the Gradual became reduced to only two psalm verses. There are even a few Graduals of which the text is not from the book of psalms, or even from the Bible.

It is called *Gradual,* because it was customary to sing it on the *ambo* (*gradus*), where the lessons also were read. Like the Epistle, it was sung by only one cantor, the people only taking up the last neums of the melody, as we do to this day. Until the time of St Gregory, the rule was that the deacon alone had the right to sing the Gradual. Duchesne cites some epitaphs in which deacons allude to this privilege of theirs. One good bishop assures us that his people raised him to episcopal honors in acknowledgment of his beautiful singing:

> *Psallere et in populis volui, moderante propheta.*
> *Sic merui plebem Christi retinere sacerdos.*

The great liturgist of the sixth century, witnessing the abuses to which this custom not unfrequently led, abolished the exclusive privilege of deacons in this matter. It did not seem right that a man should be raised to the diaconate solely or mainly because he had a good voice, or could sing.

The singing of the Gradual is a very ancient practice of the Church; in fact, it is as old as the reading of the lessons. Duchesne warns us not to put the Gradual on the same footing as the other chants of the Mass, such as the Introit and others, which were only introduced in order to occupy the attention of the people during long ceremonies. The Gradual is sung or said for its own sake. During that time both celebrant and people have nothing to do but listen, though of course, in our days, the celebrant must read the Gradual, even though it is sung by the cantors.

The Gradual is generally inspired by the feast or the character of the liturgical season. This is emphatically true of the Gradual of Easter-day: *Haec dies quam fecit Dominus: exultemus et laetemur in ea.* This

---

[2] *Sermo clxxvi,* 1.

verse, which we might describe as the chorus or refrain, is followed by the first verse of Psalm cxvii: *Confitemini Domino quoniam bonus: quoniam in saeculum misericordia ejus.* Then *Haec dies* may be repeated, according to the rubrics of the Vatican *Graduale* (xv, 4), in order to make it once more a *psalmus responsorialis (juxta ritum responsialem, quando magis id videtur opportunum, post versum a solis cantoribus. aut a cantore expletum, cuncti repetunt primam partem responsorii usque ad versum).*

The words, *Haec dies,* are the refrain of every Gradual in Easter week, the verse being always from the same Psalm cxvii. Easter-day is indeed a day on which it behoves us all to rejoice. "Let none withhold himself from the universal joy because of the consciousness of sin: for on this day the sinner must not despair of pardon... if a thief merited paradise, shall not a Christian merit forgiveness?"[3]

The Alleluia

Alleluia, like *Amen,* is now an acclamation or exclamation, a kind of ejaculatory prayer of the Old Law, which has remained untranslated, in order that its very strangeness may impress the mind all the more forcibly. *Alleluia* (Praise ye Jehovah), originally two words, occurs most frequently in the Psalms. Very soon it became, as it were, one word, signifying joyful praise of God. It is a cry of joy. Thus, for instance, in Tobias, when the inspired writer describes the glory of the Jerusalem above, of which the splendor of the earthly city is but the faint image, he asserts: "All its streets shall be paved with white and clean stones: and Alleluia shall be sung in its streets."[4]

Psalms cxii–cxvii were called by the Jews the great Hallel, and the singing of them was one of the features of the ceremonial supper of the Pasch. In the Apocalypse, St John hears the heavenly choirs, and the burden of their song is Alleluia. "I heard, as it were, the voice of much people in heaven, saying: Alleluia, Salvation, and glory, and power is to our God.... And again they said: Alleluia.... And the four and twenty ancients, and the four living creatures fell down and

[3] St Ambrose, *Hom. ii in Pasch.*   [4] Tob., xiii. 22.

adored God...saying: Amen; Alleluia."[5]

In the Latin Church, Alleluia was at first sung only at Easter and during the Paschal time. When it came to be said during other parts of the year, it nevertheless ceased at the beginning of the penitential season. St Augustine has left us some eloquent homilies on the Alleluia. From them we learn how the Christian people looked forward to the Alleluia of Easter. "Alleluia," he says, "is the consolation of our journey through this life. Now Alleluia cheers us on the way.... We journey over a rough road towards our peaceful country, where, all other endeavors being set aside, our one occupation shall be to sing Alleluia" (*Tendimus autem per viam laboriosam ad quietam patriam, ubi, retractis omnibus actionibus nostris, non remanebit nisi Alleluia*).[6] And again: *O felix illic Alleluia! O secura! O sine adversario! ubi nemo erit inimicus, nemo perit amicus! Ibi laudes Deo, et hie laudes Deo: sed hic a solicitis, ibi a securis; hic a morituris, ibi a semper viventibus; hic in spe, ibi in re; hic in via, illic in patria* (O the blissful Alleluia of heaven! how secure! without adversary! Where there shall be no enemy; and where we shall miss no friend! There we give praise to God, and here also we give praise to God: but here it is given by anxious ones, there by secure ones; here it is given by them that shall some day die, there by them that shall live for evermore; here we praise God in hope, there in actual possession; here we praise Him on our pilgrimage, there in our home).[7]

St Benedict, when ordering the daily task of praise and prayer, prescribes a frequent repetition of Alleluia, and in Paschal time he commands that it should be said continually (*sine intermissione*).[8]

St Gregory the Great, on hearing of the conversion of the Angles, was transported with joy. In one of his homilies of that period, he expresses his delight at the thought that a people, who hitherto had only emitted barbarous sounds, had now learned to say the Hebrew Alleluia: *Ecce lingua Brittaniae, quae nil aliud noverat quam barbarum frendere, jam dudum in divinis laudibus hebraeum coepit Alleluia resonare.*[9]

So popular was the sacred word, Alleluia, that it was with keen

---

5 Apoc., xix. 1, 3, 4.   6 *Sermo, cclv,* 1.
7 *Sermo cclvi,* 3,   8 *Regula,* xv.
9 *Moral.,* xxvii, 8.

regret that the faithful saw themselves deprived of it at the beginning of the penitential season. Many churches bade an elaborate farewell to this heavenly chant. The church of Autun had a complete Office in which the word Alleluia recurred again and again. The Collect of this Office is as follows: "O God, who permittest us to celebrate the solemnity of the suspension of the Alleluia, grant that we may sing Alleluia for ever more in bliss, together with Thy Saints, who sing Alleluia in eternal happiness."

The Alleluia is repeated twice. This repetition, according to Durandus, symbolizes the twofold glorification to which we look forward—that of our soul and body. At the end of the versicle yet a third Alleluia is said. The verse itself is generally a psalm verse, and its choice is frequently inspired by the character of the feast or the time of year. Some Alleluia versicles are taken from other sources than the Bible, like that of Pentecost, for instance, or that of the Mass of Sts John and Paul, which last is sung at the Mass of Martyrs who are also brothers: *Haec est vera fraternitas*. The Alleluia verse of Easter Sunday is St Paul's triumphant cry that "Christ our Pasch is sacrificed."

Alleluia is a cry that should naturally and frequently rise from the heart of the priest. To praise God is his principal duty. This duty is sadly neglected in this modern world. Men do not, perhaps, blaspheme God; they just forget Him, and are wholly indifferent where He is concerned. Let the priest's voice rise frequently to the throne of God in acknowledgment of His wonderful deeds. *Alleluia* will faithfully express our loving gratitude, our praise and admiration of Him whom "angels and archangels praise together with cherubim and seraphim" in the splendors of the heavenly city.

The Tract

On certain occasions of a penitential nature, the Alleluia is omitted, and its place is taken by a Tract, or second psalm (*psalmus tractatus*). Such days are the Ember Days out of Paschal time, Requiem Masses, and all days from Septuagesima until Holy Saturday. On the latter day, however, the Tract follows upon the Alleluia, which has been only just restored to us after the long silence of Lent. The name is derived from some peculiarity in its musical execution—that is, it used to be sung rather slowly (*trahendo*), with a certain dignity and slowness of movement.

The Sequence

The Sequence follows close upon the Alleluia. It owes its origin to the long series of notes, to which the last syllable of that word is sung- the *jubilus*, as it is called. The *jubilus* is, according to St Augustine, *vox quaedam exultationis sine verbis, ita ut appareat ... ipsa voce gaudere ... quasi repletum nimio gaudio non posse explicare verbis quod gaudet* (a joyful sound, without articulate words, so that the very voice shows forth joy—the joy of one who cannot utter in words the delight of his soul).[10]

"When we sing, *Alleluia,* we rejoice rather than sing," says Rupert of Deutz, "and we hold one short syllable of this venerable word the while the voice sings several neums, that so the mind of the listener may be filled with wonder, and raised to where the Saints shall rejoice in glory and shall be joyful in their beds."[11]

St Bonaventure assigns the same reason to the prolonged melody of the last syllable of Alleluia: "We are wont to sing many notes on the latter a which terminates Alleluia, because the joy of the Saints in heaven is interminable and ineffable."[12]

Great joy, like great sorrow, is inarticulate. Do we not likewise daily hear children sing by the hour without articulating a word? The apparently inarticulate *jubilus* of the Alleluia is but the manifestation of the joy of God's children rejoicing *in spe,* while waiting and longing for the day when they shall rejoice *in re:* "That joyful sound (*jubilatio*), which singers call sequence, brings to our mind that state when there will be no need of words for speech; but mind will commune with mind by a direct manifestation of its innermost thoughts."[13]

The long-sustained singing of one syllable demanded a great effort and much *breath* (*pneuma* in Greek); whence the transition to *neum* was easy. We must also bear in mind that the introduction of lines, or staves, is of comparatively recent date. The only musical notation

10 *In Ps. xcix.*
11 *De div. off.,* I, 35.
12 *Expos. Miss.,* 11.
13 Amalar., *De eccl, off.,* III, 16.

known for many centuries consisted solely in certain signs, or accents, written above the text that was to be sung. When these accents were in great number, without any text, and only serving as an indication of how one syllable was to be drawn out or trilled, they proved a great strain on the singer's memory, and differences in execution arose easily enough when the chant was performed by many. So already in the ninth century certain words came to be written under the notes, or neums, of the Alleluia *jubilus*. In other words, the *jubilus* came to be "farced." At first these additions were only prose compositions (hence their name, *prosa*). From the twelfth century these "proses" became more elaborate; in fact, they vied with the more stately hymns of the Church, though always retaining their native simplicity and a naïve homeliness both in conception and expression.

The earliest composer of sequences (so called because they *follow* upon the Alleluia) appears to be Notker Balbulus, a monk of the celebrated Abbey of St Gall, who died in 912. He took the idea from a monk who had come to St Gall from Jumièges in Normandy. This monk had with him an office book in which words had been written under each of the notes, or at least under each neum, of the Alleluia *jubilus*, probably merely to assist the memory of the cantors. This was enough to inspire Notker with the idea of a number of lengthy compositions, all of which were but a development, sequence, and expression of those feelings of holy joy which had been excited by the singing of the *Alleluia*.

Sequences became exceedingly popular in the Middle Ages, at least in England, France and Germany. Rome was very slow in admitting them, and Spain never did so at all. The composition of sequences became at one time the fashion. They were composed not only for use at Mass, but for other occasions as well.

The best and most popular author of sequences is undoubtedly Adam of St Victor (twelfth century). His sequences strike at times a very solemn note; he maintains a high level both of thought and expression, and rarely, if ever, falls into the platitudes and trivialities which disfigure many such compositions of that period. Guéranger calls him the greatest poet of the Middle Ages. "The exquisite art and variety with which his verse is managed and his rhymes disposed, their rich melody...most of all, the evident nearness of the things which he celebrates to his own heart of hearts—all these and other excellencies render him, as far as my judgment goes, the foremost among the sacred Latin poets of the Middle Ages. He may have no single poem to vie with the austere beauty of the *Dies irae,* nor yet with the tearful passion of the *Stabat Mater*...but then it must not be forgotten that these stand well nigh alone in the name of their respective authors."[14] The best edition of Adam's work is Gautier's, who published 106 sequences, which he proves to be from the pen of the Victorine. In 1881 the Rev. Digby Wrangham, MA, a Yorkshire clergyman, published these sequences, together with a very fine translation in which the meter and rhymes of the original are preserved as far as this is possible. Whatever we may think of medieval poetry, assuredly the work of Adam of St Victor deserves to be better known than it is. To mention it only in passing, our popular hymn books would be very much rejuvenated and rendered more interesting were we to draw upon this rich storehouse of melodious verse for the entire cycle of the Church's calendar.

In the Roman Missal of today only five sequences survive out of the immense number of such compositions which have come down to us from the Middle Ages. The Council of Trent (1545–1563) decided on a reform or revision of the Missal of the Latin Church, with a view to a return to pristine simplicity and, if possible, uniformity throughout the Latin Rite. A commission was appointed, but it terminated its labors only during the pontificate of Pius V. On July 14, 1570, the holy Pontiff published the Bull which we still read at the beginning of our Missals. It commands that "Mass shall be sung or said according to the rite, manner and standard which is given in this Missal, nor in celebrating shall anyone dare to add or recite other ceremonies or prayers than those that are contained herein." The ideal that the commission steadily kept before its eyes was a return to sober and stately antiquity. So the ornate accretions of the later centuries of the Middle Ages went by the board, and with them the innumerable proses and sequences which had ended by unduly lengthening the

---

14 Archbishop Trench, *Sacred Latin Poetry.*

Mass without any compensating addition to its beauty or impressiveness; all were rejected but five, but these are undoubtedly the best, and worthy to be retained. They were retained solely on their intrinsic merits, not at all with a view to lending an added solemnity to the days on which they are recited. The five are: the sequences of Easter (*Victimae paschali*), Pentecost (*Veni Sancte Spiritus*), and Corpus Christi (*Lauda Sion*), the *Stabat Mater* and the *Dies irae*. The *Victimae paschali* is the work of Wipo, chaplain to the Emperors Conrad II and Henry III, and thus dates back to the eleventh century.

The *Veni Sancte Spiritus* has been attributed to various authors, but it is now almost beyond doubt that it was composed by the great Pope Innocent III.

St Thomas is, of course, the author of the *Lauda Sion*.

The ever-popular *Stabat Mater* is the work of Jacopone da Todi. After the death of his wife, Jacopone, who had been a lawyer, became a member of the Franciscan Order, and as such led a most austere and holy life. In his contempt of all things worldly he castigated rather too freely the manners of monks and priests and even Popes. At one time he was excommunicated by Boniface VIII, whose opponent he had been. He died a most holy death in the year 1306, in the midnight hour of Christ's Nativity, as the priest at the altar was intoning the *Gloria in excelsis Deo*. By the end of the same century the *Stabat Mater* was exceedingly popular, though it found a place in the Roman Missal only in 1727, when Benedict XIII extended to the universal Church the Feast of the Seven Dolors of Our Lady.

The *Dies irae* is rightly attributed to Thomas of Celano, the friend and first biographer of St Francis. Originally an extra-liturgical poem describing the terrors of the last day of the world, it became the sequence of Requiem Masses as early as the thirteenth century. The last verses, beginning with *Lacrymosa dies illa*, were added to the original poem in order to render it more suitable to its new use.

Our Easter sequence, as we have seen, is the composition of the chaplain of Conrad II and Henry III. Apparently, he is the author not only of the text, but likewise of the noble melody to which it is sung. In respect of the latter, we may make our own the words of Dr Fortescue: "The clanging melody (like the blare of trumpets) is one of the very finest pieces of plainsong that we have. It seems the perfect musical expression of Easter, and its immemorial connection with the words makes it almost incredible that anyone should ever want to replace it by a modern composition."[15]

During the Middle Ages, our Sequence was used in many places for a dramatic presentment of the mystery of the Resurrection. Choir boys, representing the Angels, Mary Magdalen and the other holy women, went to the Easter sepulchre at the end of Matins, singing a dialogue referring to the various episodes of the early hours of the first Easter Sunday. Into this dialogue were woven the verses of the *Victimae paschali*, the whole being followed by the singing of the *Te Deum* and the solemn office of Lauds.

The first strophes of our Sequence call upon Christians to praise the paschal Victim, that guileless Lamb who has brought about a reconciliation between us sinners and our outraged Father. We have here an allusion to Apoc., v. 6 : "And I saw ... a lamb standing, as it were slain...." And again to Apoc., v. 9 : "Thou art worthy, O Lord, to take the book and to open the seals thereof: because Thou wast slain and hast redeemed us to God in Thy Blood...."

> *Mors et vita duello conflixere mirando,*
> *Dux vitae mortuus regnat vivus.*[16]

The tremendous single combat of Christ, the "author of salvation (in Greek ἀρχηγός, *dux*, prince), ended apparently in the discomfiture of the Lord of life. But His very defeat was for Him the hour of victory, and, in the moment when death seemed to triumph, death was swallowed up in victory (*absorpta est mors in victoria*). "I am the First and the Last, and alive and was dead, and behold I am living for ever and ever, and have the keys of death and hell."[17] *Dux vitae mortuus regnat vivus!*

Turning abruptly to Mary Magdalen, the poet bids her relate what

---

15 *The Mass*, p. 276, note.
16 In this great triumph death and life
   Together met in wondrous strife,
   The Prince of Life, once dead, doth reign.
17 Apoc., i. 17, 18.

befell her on the way and what she saw at the sepulchre. The "apostle of the Apostles" replies by narrating how she found the tomb empty, how angels proclaimed His Resurrection, above all that she has seen the glory of the risen Saviour (*et gloriam vidi resurgentis*). Finally, she breaks forth into a sublime confession of faith at a moment when the Apostles were still wavering (*Surrexit Christus spes mea*), at the same time reminding the Eleven of the words of the Master: "After I shall be risen again, I will go before you into Galilee."[18]

Finally, speaking in the name of the Church, the poet also proclaims his faith in the fundamental mystery of our religion:

Scimus Christum surrexisse a mortuis vere.[19]

The revisers having definitely dropped the lines with which our Sequence concluded during many centuries,

Credendum est magis soli Mariae veraci
Quam Judaeorum turbae fallaci,[20]

we now end on a note of humble supplication to our glorious King:

Tu nobis, victor, Rex, miserere.[21]

"If," says St Ambrose, "Christ is merciful to the thief in the hour of His crucifixion, He will be even more inclined to mercy towards the Christian in the hour of His Resurrection. If in the hour of His humiliation He conferred so great a boon upon him who confessed His Divinity, what will not the glory of the Resurrection procure for us?" *Largior enim ad praestandum solet esse, sicut ipsi scitis, laeta victoria, quam addicta captivitas.*[22]

---

18 Mark, xiv. 28.
19 "We know that Christ is risen indeed."
20 "We should credit the simple testimony of truthful Mary rather than the deceitful crowd of Jews."
21 "Thou, Victor King, have mercy on us."
22 *Hom. lii in Pasch.*, 2.

CHAPTER XI

THE GOSPEL AND HOMILY OR SERMON

The Gospel

THE reading of the Gospel constitutes the climax of the first part of the Mass—the Mass of the Catechumens, which is made up of prayers and carefully selected passages (*pericopes*) of our holy Books of both the Old and the New Testaments. Our English word *gospel*, from the Anglo-Saxon *god* (good) and *spell* (tell, speak), has the same meaning as the Greek εὐαγγέλιον, and signifies glad tidings, good news. Our Lord Himself took the word in that sense. On His first public appearance in the synagogue of Nazareth at the beginning of His public ministry, "He rose up to read," and, the Book of Isaias the Prophet having been handed to Him, He unfolded the volume and read the passage appointed for the day, which was as follows: "The spirit of the Lord is upon Me, wherefore He hath anointed Me to preach the gospel to the poor (εὐαγγελίσασθαι)."[1]

The Gospel is primarily the spoken word—the preaching of the kingdom of God which has come. "Go ye into the whole world," the Master said, "and preach the gospel to every creature."[2] The preaching of the Apostles is "the gospel of salvation."[3] St Paul is "called to be an apostle, separated unto the gospel of God, which he had promised before, by His prophets, in the holy scriptures."[4] Hence he declares to the Galatians that "the gospel which was preached by me is not according to man."[5]

However, the spoken word was very soon to be supplemented

1 Luke, iv. 16–18.   2 Mark, xvi. 15.
3 Eph., i. 13.   4 Rom., i. 1, 2.
5 Rom., i. 11.

by the written word. Though the Apostles were primarily bidden to go forth into the world, not to write, but to preach the Gospel, it was found expedient—and the Holy Ghost prompted some of those who "from the beginning were eyewitnesses and ministers of the word"—to write down what they had seen or heard, or to dictate it to others, such as St Mark and St Luke. Thus, the *ipsissima verba* (very words) of the Word of life have been handed down to us, "upon whom the ends of the world have come." "From none other have we learned the scheme of our salvation, than from those through whom the Gospel has come down to us; this they first delivered orally, but afterwards, by the will of God, handed down to us in writing."[6] Just as there is but one Lord, one Faith, one Baptism, so there is but one Gospel. St Irenaeus speaks of εὐαγγελίον τετράμορφον—one Gospel under four different aspects, or presentments. "*In quatuor evangeliis, vel potius quatuor libris unius Evangelii*" (In four Gospels, or rather four books of one Gospel), says St Augustine.

The custom of reading the sacred text of the Gospel during the liturgical services of the Church is of very ancient date. In fact, we must trace it back to apostolic days. It is clear that St Luke's Gospel was read throughout the Church, St Paul himself being a witness to it: "We have sent also with him [Titus] the brother, whose praise is in the gospel through all the churches."[7] This brother is not St Barnabas, as the Greeks hold, but St Luke. This is proved by a text of St Ignatius of Antioch, also by St Jerome. Eusebius tells us in his "Ecclesiastical History"[8] that St Mark composed his Gospel at the request of the Romans, who asked to have a written record of the preaching and teaching of St Peter, whose disciple Mark was St Peter, delighted with the eagerness of his converts, is said to have given his approval to the volume, which was to be read consecutively in the churches (*ut deinceps in ecclesiis legeretur*). To this fact witness is borne by Clement in his "Institutions," and by Papias of Hierapolis.

It was natural to read the Gospel after the Prophets of the Old Law, or even the apostolic writers. They were but the heralds who prepared us for a worthy hearing of the voice of the Master Himself:

6 St Irenaeus, *Adv. Haeres.*, III. II.   7 II Cor., viii. 18.
8 Book II, chapter 13.

"God, who at sundry times and in divers manners, spoke in times past to the Fathers, by the prophets, last of all in these days hath spoken to us by His Son."[9]

At first the Gospel was read, not merely in sections as in our days (so that certain parts are never read at all and others constantly repeated), but was the object of *lectio continua;* that is, one of the Gospels was read right through, irrespective of the day or time of the year. When enough had been read for the day, the bishop (or presiding priest) gave the signal to the reader to stop, the reading being resumed where it had been left off at the next assembly. After peace had been granted to the Church, Pope Damasus was the first to organize the liturgical year, and to make a selection from the Sacred Books of passages which were mote especially appropriate, either to the mystery celebrated or to the spirit of the season. Thus arose our present-day *pericopes.* These various texts were at first written in separate volumes. There were the *Psalterium* (containing only the Psalms), the *Epistolarium* (containing only the Epistles), the *Sacramentarium* (containing the rites and prayers of the Mass), and the *Evangelarium* (containing the sections of the Gospel appointed to be read on certain days). The Book of the Gospels, since it contained the words of Christ, was treated with the utmost reverence. It was generally beautifully written and sumptuously bound; in fact, reverence was rendered to it as to the person of Christ Himself.

Originally, simple lectors read the Gospel, just as they read the other books of the Bible. From the fourth century onwards, however, the deacon has been the sole reader of the Gospel. At his ordination the bishop tells him that "a deacon should preach" (*diaconum oportet...praedicare*), by which we are to understand not only the office of instructing (or that of explaining the text of the Gospel), but also the solemn and ceremonial singing of the Sacred Text. Hence the Book of the Gospels is handed to him by the bishop, with power to sing the Gospel at Mass, whether said for the living or the dead.

At the Office of Matins on Christmas night, it was the privilege of the Emperor of the Holy Roman Empire to sing the Gospel which

---

9 Heb., i. 1, 2.

begins with the words: *Exiit edictum a Caesare Augusto* (There went out a decree from Caesar Augustus). The Emperor, vested in a dalmatic, sang this Gospel, and before singing it he drew his sword and brandished it three times, thus signifying his readiness to fight in defence of the word of God.

The Gospel is sung by the deacon (or read by the priest), facing North. There is a deep mystical signification in this. According to Biblical symbolism, the cold darkness of the North is an image of spiritual darkness and desolation: "Howl, O gate; cry, O city...for a smoke shall come from the North, and there is none that shall escape his troop."[10] "Strengthen yourselves, stay not: for I bring evil from the North, and great destruction."[11]

Before the reading or singing of the Gospel, we recite a most beautiful and appropriate prayer, by which we prepare ourselves for the high office of acting as the mouthpiece of Jesus Christ. *Sancta sancte!* seeing that we are about to utter, not our own words, or those of some great writer or poet, but the words of the Son of God. The prayer *Munda cor meum* is of comparatively recent origin, though not the blessing which follows it. The prayer alludes to one of the most striking scenes in the book of the visions of Isaias. "In the year that King Ozias died," the Prophet "saw the Lord sitting upon a throne high and elevated," and His glory "filled the temple." And he heard the Seraphim crying to one another: "Holy, holy, holy, the Lord God of hosts, all the earth is full of His glory." Then the awestruck Prophet, who had kept silence (for he durst not join in the song of the angels), exclaimed: "Woe is me, because I have held my peace; because I am a man of unclean lips.... And one of the Seraphims flew to me, and in his hand was a live coal, which he had taken with the tongs off the altar. And he touched my mouth, and said: Behold this hath touched thy lips, and thy iniquities shall he taken away, and thy sin shall be cleansed."[12]

When he reads or preaches the Gospel, the priest does not merely proclaim the judgments of God, or foretell impending punishments. His is a much higher office: he may even make his own the words

---

10 Is., xiv. 31.   11 Jer., iv. 6.
12 Is., vi. 1–8.

first spoken of the mediator between God and man—the man Christ Jesus: "The spirit of the Lord is upon me; wherefore, He hath sent me to announce glad tidings...." But how dare he take into his mouth the word of God, unless his lips shall first have been purified, even as the Prophet's lips were cleansed by the messenger of God? So the rubric of the Missal (that is, the commandment of the Church) bids him stand in the middle of the altar, raise his eyes for a moment to heaven, and then at once bend low before the majesty of an all-holy God, while he recites the prayer that cleanses and purifies and makes him in a manner worthy to utter in his turn the words first spoken by the Word of life.

When the Gospel is sung by a deacon, he kneels before the celebrant and asks his blessing, saying: *Jube domne benedicere* (Deign, sir, to grant thy blessing). *Domnus* is an abridgment of *dominus* (lord), and is only applied to man. When the priest himself asks the blessing, as he does at Low Mass, he says *Jube Domine benedicere* (Deign, O Lord, etc.), addressing God directly and asking Him for a blessing. Incidentally, we may remark on the appropriateness of the words of the blessing as an immediate preparation for the sermon, when the priest acts as a herald of glad tidings: "May the Lord be upon my lips and in my heart, that I may proclaim His Gospel [the divine message of glad tidings] worthily and suitably in the name of the Father, and of the Son, and of the Holy Ghost."

The reading of the Gospel is always preceded by the apostolic salutation, *Dominus vobiscum,* and the announcement of the Evangelist from whom the *pericope* is taken. During the Gospel everybody stands, with head uncovered and turned either towards the altar or the place where the deacon sings the divine message. At the conclusion the server, in the name of all, answers *Laus tibi Christe.* Formerly custom varied very much with regard to this final acclamation to Christ, who, through the Gospel, has spoken to His people. From the Rule of St Benedict we learn that in his day (that is, during the fifth and the beginning of the sixth centuries) it was customary to answer "*Amen,*" thus expressing assent to what was read. The words of the great legislator of monks, whose Rule is so important a source of liturgical information, may well be quoted here as being applicable to all, both priest and people. St Benedict speaks of the Gospel which, in the Monastic Breviary, is read at the end of Matins: *Legat Abbas lectionem de Evangelio, cum honore et tremore stantibus omnibus, qua perlecta, respondeant omnes: "Amen"* (Let the Abbot read the lesson from the Gospel, while all stand in awe and reverence. When it has been read, let all answer: Amen).

When the priest has read the Gospel, he reverently kisses the sacred text, except in Masses for the dead. The liturgical kiss is an expression of reverence and love for Christ, who is represented by the sacred text. Hence arose the custom in the Middle Ages of carrying the text of the Gospel in the procession of Psalm Sunday. *Sanctum Evangelium, quod intelligitur Christus, statuitur in ecclesia ante aram* (The Holy Gospel, by which is understood Christ, is placed in the Church before the altar), says the twelfth *Ordo Romanus*.

The Homily or Sermon

Immediately after the reading of the Gospel follows the sermon. This is one of the oldest Christian customs, so that the *Caeremoniale Episcoporum* ordains that *Sermo regulariter infra Missam esse debet, de Evangelio currenti* (The sermon, as a rule, should be preached during the Mass, and about the current Gospel—*viz.* the Gospel of the day). In the early centuries the bishop himself invariably addressed the assembly in a familiar discourse (ὁμιλία), based on the passage of the Gospel just read. The great bulk of the discourses and addresses left to us by the Fathers is formed of these simple explanations of the Scriptures. We learn from the Acts of the Apostles[13] that already in apostolic days the sermon was part of the Liturgy: "On the first day of the week, when we assembled to break bread [that is, for the celebration of the Holy Eucharist], Paul discoursed with them [the Church of Troas], and he continued his speech until midnight. "When the reader pauses," says St Justin Martyr, "the president addresses the people, exhorting them to imitate the beautiful things they have heard."[14]

We may conclude from this remark of Justin that not only the

---

13 Acts, xx. 7.   14 *Apol.*, II.

Gospel, but the Epistle also, may legitimately form the subject-matter of our discourses. It would certainly not be right habitually to set aside both Epistle and Gospel in our Sunday morning discourses in favor of, let us say, "topics of the day." The sacred text has a virtue all its own, and our people love to hear it. The more a priest is like Apollo *potens in scripturis* (powerful in the Scriptures), the greater the efficacy of his words. The Gospel is capable of many interpretations. The Fathers loved allegorical explanations and adaptations, often more ingenious than convincing. The Homilies of St Augustine and St Gregory the Great are conspicuous examples of this latter mode of treatment. In our own days we prefer sober reality to elaborate symbolism. If we wish to be truly eloquent, let our doctrinal statements be in the words of the Gospel or the apostolic writings, and let our moral exhortations invariably be based on the text of the sacred volume.

Since, by way of illustration, we have been studying the text of the Mass of Easter Sunday, let us also look at its Gospel. It may be treated either allegorically or historically. The Homily of St Gregory the Great, which is read at Matins, is an example of the former mode of exposition. Our people will be more interested if we point out to them that our Gospel is obviously a narrative of an historical event, every detail of which is calculated to emphasize the reality of the fundamental fact of the Christian religion. *Jesum quaeritis Nazarenum, crucifixum: surrexit, non est hic, ecce locus ubi posuerunt eum* (You seek Jesus of Nazareth, who was crucified: He is risen, He is not here; behold the place where they laid Him). What force there is in that marvellous antithesis: *"The crucified: He is risen*—He is no longer here, you only see the place where they laid His dead body, but go, tell Peter and the others that soon they shall behold Him in Galilee, according as He told them."

CHAPTER XII

THE CREDO

THE *Credo* forms, as it were, a bridge between two clearly marked-off parts of the Mass; namely, the Mass of the Catechumens and the Mass of the Faithful. The recitation of the *Credo* during the Holy Sacrifice is of comparatively recent institution. It certainly was not part of the early Liturgies in either East or West. The Mass of the Catechumens always ended with the sermon or homily, which followed the public reading of the Gospel. Up to that moment Catechumens and baptized Christians prayed together. But no sooner was the homily or exhortation of the bishop ended, than the aspirants to Baptism were bidden to leave the sacred edifice, and not only they but all penitents and such as were not permitted to take part in the Eucharistic Sacrifice.

We see a curious illustration of this in a story related by St Gregory the Great in his life of St Benedict. The Pontiff tells us how St Benedict had warned two nuns of noble birth that, unless they bridled their tongues by which they sorely tried the patience of the *religiosus vir* (religious man) who looked after them, he would feel compelled to excommunicate them. But they took no heed of the Saint's warning. Now, when both died within the space of a few days, they were buried within the sacred edifice. But it came to pass that, whenever the Holy Sacrifice happened to be offered in that church, at the moment when the deacon cried out that those who did not communicate (that is, were not in full communion with the Church) should leave, the nurse of these two women, who was wont to offer the oblation for them (*quae pro eis oblationem offerre consueverat*), saw them come out of their graves and leave the church. When this was related to St Benedict, he had an offering made in their behalf with wonderful effects: *Quae dum oblatio pro eis fuisset immolata, et a diacono juxta morem clamatum est, ut non communicantes ab ecclesia exirent, illae exire ab ecclesia ulterius visae non sunt* (When the offering was made at the altar and the deacon cried out, according to custom, that those who were not in communion with the Church should leave the building, these two were no longer seen to depart from the sacred edifice).

This story is of great interest, inasmuch as it clearly supposes an elaborate, well-established Liturgy divided into two separate sections—one in which all might take part, and another to which only full membership with the Church could give admittance. The Mass of the Catechumens was, therefore, immediately followed by that of the faithful, and began with the oblation of the elements that were to be changed into the Flesh and Blood of the Lamb of God and restored to the faithful, as such, at the Communion of the Mass.

The public and solemn profession of faith, in the words of the Creed, comes very appropriately at the conclusion of the prayers and readings which form the preliminaries of the Sacrifice. When the faithful have listened to the word of God as contained in the pages of the Old and New Testament, it comes almost as a spontaneous act to proclaim aloud the faith that is within us. The mysteries, also, in which we are about to take part, are, above all others, a matter of faith (*mysterium fidei*). Hence, it is but natural that, besides professing our belief in the reality of Christ's Body and Blood, we should likewise confess those other truths which form a golden chain in which the Eucharist is the most precious link.

From the earliest days of Christianity, the recitation of the Creed formed an integral part of the rite of Baptism. The possession and profession of the Symbol was to the soldier of Christ what the military *symbolum* (watchword, *consigne* in French) was to the soldier in Caesar's army. Just as soldiers recognize each other by the exchange of the watchword, so are we known to belong to the one flock or army of Jesus Christ by the external profession of the same faith. The *Symbolum* is our common bond of union.

The Creed is a complete, though not necessarily an explicit, statement of the truths of our religion. It aims necessarily at terseness and conciseness, since it is in the nature of a watchword. It must, therefore, be fairly easy to commit to memory. This is all the more so, as during long centuries there was no written Creed: it was handed down from generation to generation by an unbroken oral tradition. This was done in order to safeguard the faith of the Church from corruption, and was part of that policy of secrecy (the famous *disciplina arcani*), which the Church applied during several centuries: *In symbolo fidei et spei nostrae, quad ab Apostolis traditum, non scribitur in charta et atramento, sed in tabulis cordis carnalibus* (As regards the symbol of our faith and hope, which has been handed down from the time of the Apostles, it is written not with paper and ink, but is engraved upon the fleshly tablets of our hearts).[1]

One of the chief occupations of the clergy during the whole time of Lent was the instruction of the Catechumens. On several occasions during its course there were special meetings for them (plenary sessions, so to speak), of which the Lenten Liturgy retains traces to this very day. One of these special meetings was for the precise purpose of making known the text of the *Symbolum*—the ceremony being called *traditio symboli*.

The earliest and most venerable of the various Creeds that have been or still are in use in the Church, is that which is called the Apostles' Creed. Tradition has it that, ere they parted from one another in pursuance of the divine command that bade them go forth into all the world to make of all men their disciples, the twelve Apostles framed a succinct statement of the glorious faith they were about to preach, and eventually to seal with their blood.

Tertullian (about the end of the second century or the beginning of the third) gives us, not indeed a complete text, but a full summary of this apostolic "tablet of the faith" (*tessera fidei*): "The rule of faith is absolutely one, immutable, unalterable; it is this: We must believe in one only God, Creator of the world, and in His Son Jesus Christ, born of the Virgin Mary, crucified under Pontius Pilate, who rose from the dead on the third day, who ascended into heaven, and is now seated at the right hand of the Father, and will come to judge the living and the dead, at the resurrection of the body."[2]

We need attach no undue importance to the legendary accounts

---

[1] St Jerome, *Ep. ad Pammach.*   [2] *De virgin. veland.*, 1.

of the formulation of the Apostles' Creed, for the important fact is that the Church has always used some formula by which her children were able to recognize one another.

During more than three hundred years (that is, until the First General Council), the Apostles' Creed was the only one in use. The 318 Fathers who met at Nicaea formulated once more the faith of the Church in the words of what we now call the Nicene Creed. When the text of this Creed was read before the assembled bishops, they exclaimed as with one voice: "This is the Catholic faith, in this faith we have been baptized, in this faith we likewise ourselves baptize."

The Nicene Creed ends at the words: *Et in Spiritum Sanctum* (And in the Holy Ghost). What follows was added by the Second General Council (that of Constantinople) of 381. New heresies demanded the addition of fresh clauses, defining more explicitly the work and mission of the Holy Ghost. The famous *Filioque* (defining the relation of the Holy Ghost to God the Son) was not part of the Creed as formulated at Constantinople, but was added by the Churches of Spain in the fifth century, and was afterwards adopted by the Church of Gaul. Everybody knows to what controversies this apparently slight addition gave rise, and how in the end it became one of the motives (or rather one of the pretexts) that led up to the lamentable schism which has so long severed the Eastern from the Western Church.

The practice of reciting the Creed during the Eucharistic Sacrifice is not of very great antiquity in so far as the Roman Liturgy is concerned. The Greek Church began to recite the Creed of Constantinople about the end of the fifth century. The orthodox bishops chose this Creed in preference to that of Nicaea, because its greater explicitness did not lend itself to the subterfuges of the heretics who affected a special loyalty to that of Nicaea. In the Latin Church, as has just been said, the practice originated in Spain at about the same time as in the Greek Church. In 589 the Third Council of Toledo decreed that "in all the Churches of Spain and Galicia, after the manner of the Eastern Chutches, the *symbolum* of the Council of Constantinople, (that is, that of 150 bishops) be recited, and that it be sung in a loud voice (*clara voce*) by the people before the recitation of the Lord's Prayer, in order that faith may be openly professed and that the hearts of the people may be purified by faith."

After the condemnation of the Adoptionist heresy of Felix of Urgel and Elipandus at the Council of Frankfort in 754, the Creed with the clause *Filioque* began to be universally recited throughout Gaul and Germany. Leo III sanctioned the custom, but expressed a wish that the *Filioque* be omitted, lest an occasion for quibbling be given to the Greeks. However, no notice was taken of this wise request.

Finally, the Church of Rome herself took up the practice (even though with some reluctance) at the request of Emperor St Henry in the year 1014. Berno of Reichenau, who accompanied his imperial master to Rome on the occasion of the latter's coronation by Benedict VIII, relates how the pious emperor was astonished that in the holy city the Creed was not sung at Mass, as he was wont to hear it in Germany. He asked the Pope for the reason, and was told that, whereas in most Churches some one or other article of the Creed had been denied, the Roman Church had never fallen into heresy. However, the emperor would not be denied, and persisted in his request until the Pope granted it. Baronius, when relating the incident in his "History of the Church," comments thus upon it: "We are satisfied, but we should have been even more pleased, had less respect been paid to a novelty and more to a custom of a thousand years' antiquity."

According to the rubrics, the Creed is said (or sung) on all feasts of our Lord and on all Sundays of the year; likewise on the feasts of Our Lady and the Angels; also on the feasts of the Apostles, who were the heralds of the faith we profess. St Mary Magdalen has a *Credo*, because she became the apostle of the Apostles, inasmuch as she was bidden by the risen Christ Himself to go and tell His brethren: "Behold, I am risen and go before you into Galilee." The feasts of Saints of the first and second class have a *Credo*. But the feasts of Saints of the Old Testament have no *Credo*, unless they happen to be the patrons of a church or country. St Joseph has a *Credo*, because he is the patron of the Universal Church. On the other hand, St John the Baptist has no *Credo*, except in a church dedicated to him. An octave is but the continuation of a feast, so, if the day itself has a *Credo*, the days within the octave have one also, not however the days within a simplified octave, as we now have them, according to the new rubrics of the Missal. It is also recited on the feasts of Doctors of the Church and in a *solemn* votive Mass, even if it be celebrated in purple vestments. But there is no need of a complete list here, since the *Ordo* of each diocese invariably indicates the days on which the *Credo* is to be recited.

The rubrics of the Missal prescribe that the *Credo* should be intoned when the priest has returned to the middle of the altar—not whilst he returns there, as so frequently happens. He must extend and raise his hands whilst he says *Credo*. When he says *in unum Deum* (in one God), he folds his hands and bows the head towards the crucifix. The remainder is said *junctis ante pectus manibus,* except during the genuflexion. This genuflexion must begin at the words: *Et incarnatus est,* and only terminate when the words *et homo factus est* have been said. We bow the head to the cross at *Jesum Christum* and at the words *simul adoratur* (equally adored), and make the sign of the cross whilst saying *Et vitam venturi saeculi,* joining the hands at the *Amen.*

CHAPTER XIII

THE OFFERTORY

Historical Development of this Prayer

IN earlier centuries, when the Mass of the Catechumens was ended (that is, after the Gospel and homily), the faithful alone remained within the sacred edifice. The first part of the Mass of the faithful was a common act of prayer and intercession (the prayer of the faithful), of which nothing remains in our present Liturgy except a rather general invitation to pray. Turning towards the people the priest greets them with the salutation: *Dominus vobiscum*, to which they answer: *Et cum spiritu tuo*. Then the priest says: *Oremus*. However, no prayer follows. As Duchesne quaintly remarks: "It is odd that this invitation should be followed by no result, in the eighth no more than in the present century: nobody prays! The offerings of the people are gathered." It seems fairly obvious that here something has dropped out of the Liturgy; probably some such prayers as we still recite on Good Friday. Those prayers are not, in reality, peculiar to Good Friday; they are general intercessions for various needs and for different classes of people. They used to be offered, without any doubt, at this moment, before the gifts of the people were placed on the altar. Eventually, they came to be left out because of their essential identity with the prayers for the living and the dead, which are said in the Canon of the Mass. Their length may very well have had something to do with their omission. The general exhortation to pray is now all that remains, together with some form of popular "bidding prayer" which has survived in most churches and countries.

The Offertory, as we now read it in our Missal, is reduced to a mere antiphon, like the Postcommunion or even the Introit. Originally it was but the first of a number of psalm verses; in fact, a whole psalm was assuredly sung whilst the people walked up to the sanctuary with their offerings of bread and wine. It is quite clear that the Offertory chant, like the Introit, was introduced for the sole purpose of occupying the mind of the assistants whilst something was being done. The Offertory chant is very ancient: it was introduced at Carthage during the lifetime of St Augustine, who had to defend the practice against the criticism of a certain Hilarius. The pamphlet which was written by the great African Doctor upon this subject and which he alludes to in his *Retractationes,* is unfortunately lost, but it is of interest to note that he calls the Offertory chant a hymn from the Psalms. The Psalms are, in effect, the ordinary source of our Offertories, though some are from other books of the sacred volume, and a few are simply liturgical compositions (such as the Offertory of the Mass of the Dead, in which the antiphon still retains its verse).

The Preparation of the Matter of the Sacrifice

The singing or recitation of the antiphon of the Offertory brings us to the Mass of the faithful. The Offertory supplies the keynote to the interior dispositions of the faithful as they are about to offer to the heavenly Father those gifts of Christ's own choosing, which are so soon to be changed into His Flesh and Blood. Thus, the Offertory of Easter, with its note of triumph and victory, brings home to our minds that the Victim we are even now preparing to slay in a mystic Sacrifice, is the risen Lord of glory and the Judge of all: *Terra tremuit, et quievit, dum resurgeret in judicio Deus* (The earth trembled and was still, when God arose in judgment).

According to our present use and discipline, as soon as the priest with hands folded before his breast has read the Offertory antiphon, he uncovers the chalice and proceeds to say the prayer of oblation over the host. The bread and wine are no longer brought to the altar by the people, but are supplied by the priest or his minister. But it was not thus in the beginning and for long centuries afterwards. The faithful, men and women alike, deemed it a privilege and a duty to supply the *matter* of the Eucharistic feast, and did so in the very act of the Sacrifice. A procession would then be formed of those who took their offering into the sanctuary, or at least as far as the barrier (*cancelli*), which invariably separated the sanctuary from the nave. According to Amalarius (ninth century), the priest came to the sanctuary railings, and there received the offerings of the people. Then he returned to the altar to dispose, either personally or by the ministry of the deacon, the offerings which he intended to present to the Lord in the course of the Mass. Even the celebrant and his ministers made their offering, but at the altar itself. Already in the sixth century the Council of Mâcon, in France, ordained "that on all Sundays both men and women should make an offering at the altar of bread and wine, that by this oblation they may be freed from the burden of their sins and made partakers of the sacrifice of Abel and all the just." That these offerings were made in the hope of receiving a share in the fruits of the Mass is borne out by an incident in the life of St Benedict which we have already related. Two dead nuns were seen to leave their graves whenever the deacon cried out that the excommunicate should leave the church. Though dead, they were seen obeying this command by their former nurse, who was wont to make an offering in their behalf (*quae pro eis oblationem Domino offerre consueverat*). When St Benedict heard of the dreadful event he at once made an offering: *Qui manu sua protinus oblationem dedit, dicens: Ite, et hanc oblationem pro eis offeri Domino facite.... Quae dum oblatio pro eis fuisset immolata ... illae exire ab ecclesia ulterius visae non sunt* (With his own hand, he gave an offering, saying: Go, and have this offering made to God for them.... When the offering had been made, these two were no longer seen to leave the church."[1] From this story we gather that offerings were made by the faithful, not only for themselves, but for others also, even for the dead.

As late as the eleventh century a Roman Synod prescribed that "every Christian should offer something to God during the solemn celebration of Mass, and call to mind that which God spoke by the mouth of Moses: 'Thou shalt not appear empty-handed in My presence.' For it is made clear by all monuments of the holy Fathers that it is an an-

---

[1] St Gregory, *Dialog.* I, ii, 33.

cient custom which ordains that all Christians should offer something to God." This canon is inserted in the old *Corpus juris canonici*.

Bread and wine were not the only offerings made by the faithful; other gifts were also offered to serve either for the maintenance of the clergy or for distribution to the poor. So the transition to the offering of money alone was a natural and easy one. St Peter Damian (at the end of the eleventh century) and Honorius of Autun (in the twelfth) already make it clear that in their time people no longer offered bread and wine, but money. Our "collection" of money during the Offertory has, therefore, a venerable antiquity to commend it. There can be no doubt that, if priests would explain to their people that to contribute to the collection is an act of worship, based upon an age-long tradition, the faithful would be moved to greater generosity and would derive more fruit from the Holy Sacrifice, since, as has been shown above, the purpose of the oblation was to secure a share in the fruit of the Sacrifice.

Our present-day Mass stipend is another normal development of this ancient practice. The stipend is not *payment* for Mass; it is an offering, freely made, but when it has been accepted by the priest he is bound in justice to apply the Holy Sacrifice according to the mind and intention of the donor. The sum which the faithful are to offer for a Mass is determined by the bishop of the diocese or the bishops of a province or country. It should be made clear to the people that the word "stipend" (*stipendium*) was a Roman military term signifying, not the pay of a soldier, but his allowance for food and whatever else he required for his sustenance. So the offering or "stipend" for a Mass should be the equivalent of the sum required to "keep" a priest on the day on which the donor has secured that part of the fruit of the Mass of which the priest may dispose according to his own will.

The necessary matter of the Sacrifice of the New Law is bread and wine. We know it to be so from the record of the institution of the Eucharist by Jesus Christ, who, at the Last Supper and there only, officiated as priest according to the order of Melchisedech. Our Lord is a priest *secundum ordinem Melchisedech*, because of the external resemblance of the Sacrifice of the Mass to the oblation of the King of

Salem, who brought forth "bread and wine, for he was the priest of the most high God."[2]

There can be no doubt that our Lord instituted the Holy Eucharist with unleavened bread, even if it were proved, as some assert, that He anticipated the Paschal feast by a day. The Last Supper began with the eating of the Paschal Lamb, and we know that only unleavened bread was allowed to be on the table on that occasion. Notwithstanding, during several centuries, both the Eastern and the Western Churches were wont to use indifferently leavened and unleavened bread. Since about the eighth century the Western Church has used unleavened bread exclusively for the Holy Eucharist, whereas the Greeks used ordinary leavened bread long before the schism. The Council of Florence (1439) defined that "the body of Christ is truly consecrated in either leavened or unleavened bread, and that every priest must use either the one or the other, according to the practice of the Church to which he belongs."

So long as the faithful were in the habit of offering the bread which was to be consecrated, ordinary loaves were used. St Gregory relates the story of a woman who laughed during Mass, because, at the Communion, she was given the very loaf she had presented at the Offertory. At least since the twelfth century, the Eucharistic bread has a round shape, like a coin. According to Honorius of Autun, it has the shape of a coin, because Christ, who is the Bread of life, is also the coin which is given as the reward of those who have toiled in the vineyard of the Lord. The name *hostia* (host or victim) is given to the Eucharistic bread, not because it is itself the oblation—for we do not sacrifice bread—but by *anticipation,* inasmuch as the substance of the bread is to be changed into the Body of Him who is our true Victim (*O salutaris Hostia*).

The bread used at the altar must be wheaten bread—baked from dough made without admixture of anything whatsoever except pure natural water. The wine which is used in the Holy Sacrifice must be pure, unadulterated wine. The use of unfermented wine would be valid, but gravely illicit. It is immaterial whether white or red wine

---

[2] Gen., xiv. 18.

is used, but cleanliness demands that white wine should be used by preference, though our Lord most probably consecrated with red Palestinian wine. To the wine must be added a few drops of water. To avoid the danger of pouring in too much water, which would dilute the wine so as to make it doubtful matter of consecration, the priest may use a small spoon to draw the water from the cruet. The use of such spoons is many centuries old. In the early Middle Ages, when the faithful made their offerings in kind, the water was presented by the *schola cantorum* (the school of Chanters), at the foot of the altar or at the sanctuary rails.

The Holy Eucharist is both Sacrifice and Sacrament, a sacred repast in which is consumed that which has been offered in the Sacrifice. Our Sacrifice was prefigured by that of Melchisedech and predicted by the Prophet Malachy. God is described as weary of the offerings of the priests of the Old Law; He has no pleasure in them and will receive no gift at their hand. A new sacrifice, a pure oblation, presented to God from every point of the globe, is about to take the place of the blood of sheep and oxen, shed so long upon the one altar of Israel. Jerusalem is to be no longer the only place of sacrificial worship. Countless altars, yet substantially all one, are to be erected among the nations, for "from the rising of the sun to the going down, My name is great among the Gentiles: and in every place there is sacrifice and there is offered to My name a clean oblation."[3] The Eucharistic Sacrifice is the glorious fulfilment of this divine oracle.

The Victim immolated in our Sacrifice is eaten in Holy Communion, for our Victim is the source and cause of our true life: "My Flesh is meat indeed and My Blood is drink indeed...he that eateth this Bread shall live for ever; he that eateth My Flesh and drinketh My Blood, hath everlasting life."[4] Now bread and wine are simply food itself. Our Lord bids us pray for our "daily bread," by which is meant all that we need for food and drink. "Bringing forth grass for cattle, and herb for the service of man. That thou mayest bring bread out of the earth and that wine may cheer the heart of man. That he may make the face cheerful with oil: and that bread may strengthen man's heart."[5]

3 Mal., i. 11. 4 John, vi. 55.
5 Ps. ciii. 14, 15.

Bread and wine are also symbols of unity—unity, that is, with Christ and with one another. "For to this end (as also men of God who were before us have understood this matter) did our Lord Jesus Christ betoken unto us [leave unto us] His Body and Blood in things which are out of many units reduced to some one whole. For out of many grains are several made into one."[6] The Eucharistic repast does not merely symbolize our union with our Lord; it produces it. Oneness with Jesus Christ is the chief effect of Holy Communion. "The chalice of benediction which we bless, is it not the communion of the Blood of Christ? And the bread which we break, is it not the partaking of the Body of the Lord? For we, being many, are one bread, one body, all that partake of one bread."[7]

It is the peculiar property of this divine Bread that, unlike material bread, we do not assimilate it after eating it; rather are we transformed into its likeness, for this is a "living bread" which alters and transforms us into the likeness of the Son of God. In his *Confessions*, St Augustine has a fine passage which may pertinently be quoted here. Describing how the light of God unchangeable beat upon his eyes, he says: "Thou didst beat back the weakness of my sight, streaming forth Thy beams of light upon me most strongly, and I trembled with love and awe: and I perceived myself far off from Thee, in the region of unlikeness, as if I heard this Thy voice from on high: 'I am the food of grown men; grow, and thou shalt feed upon Me; nor shalt thou convert Me, like the food of thy flesh, into thee, but thou shalt be converted into Me.'"[8]

The bread of our Sacrifice is azym-bread (that is, unleavened). Leaven brings about fermentation, and hence a certain corruption, in the dough of which the bread is made. So it came to be looked upon as a symbol of sin by which the soul is corrupted. For this reason the law prescribed that all leavened bread should be burnt ere the Israelites partook of the azyms and the flesh of the Paschal lamb. We have already seen the symbolism of the azyms in the Epistle of the Mass of Easter: "Purge out the old leaven, that you may be a new paste, as you are unleavened. For Christ our Pasch is sacrificed. Therefore, let

---

6 St Augustine, *In Ioan.* xxvi; cfr. *Library of the Fathers,*, p. 412.
7 I Cor., X. 16, 17.   8 *Confess.*, VII, 16.

us feast, not with the old leaven of malice and wickedness, but with the unleavened bread of sincerity and truth."[9]

The water which we mix with the wine is symbolic both of the Incarnation, in which the Eternal Word united a human nature to Himself in the unity of one person, and of the union of the faithful with Christ our Head. This is the explanation given by the Council of Trent of a practice which goes back to the days of the Apostles (*Hoc ex apostolica traditione perpetuo sancta Ecclesia servavit*).[10] The Fathers of Trent quote a passage from a letter of St Cyprian, in which the holy Bishop says: "Inasmuch as Christ bore us and our sins [in the Incarnation], the water signifies the people and the wine the Blood of Christ. When the water is mixed with the wine of the chalice, it symbolizes the oneness of the people with Christ." That the water is a symbol of the people appears from Apoc., xvii. 15: "The waters which thou sawest... are peoples, and nations and tongues." The symbolism is the more expressive, since the few drops of water poured into the chalice lose their nature and become wine, according to the teaching of Innocent III, which St Thomas makes his own: *Si aqua omnino non apponeretur, totaliter excluderetur significatio; sed cum aqua in vinum convertitur significatur quod populus Christo incorporatur* (Were no water mixed with the wine, the symbolism would be destroyed; but when the water is turned into wine, it signifies that the faithful are incorporated in Christ).[11]

We are made one with Jesus Christ in order that we may receive "grace upon grace," and share in the glory which He had with the Father before the world was made; but so sublime an end can only be achieved if we identify ourselves likewise with the Sacrifice of our High Priest and our Victim. This is well expressed by a servant of God of our own days: "All religion is summed up in sacrifice: Jesus is a priest in order that He might immolate and offer a twofold victim, His natural and His mystical body. He came down into this world for the purpose of offering this sacrifice; hence, the heavenly Father can only acknowledge and receive us as His own, if we have put on Jesus Christ immolated, and are in such wise united to His sacrifice."

9 1 Cor., v. 7, 8.
10 *Catech. Concil. Trid.*, Part II, c. iv, 16.
11 *Summa Theol.*, III, Q. lxxiv, a. 8.

The Offertory Prayers

The oblation of the Victim to God is the essential part of the Sacrifice, even more than its actual slaying or destruction. So it comes about that the Offertory forms a preliminary to the Consecration, by which alone the Eucharistic Sacrifice is accomplished. The oblation which takes place in the Offertory is of comparatively recent origin—at least the prayers which accompany the presentation of the gifts, are of comparatively recent institution. In any case, the Offertory oblation is specifically different from the implied, or even explicit, oblation which is identical with the consecration of the elements of bread and wine. It would be truer to say that our Offertory is a fuller or more detailed reënactment of our Lord's own action at the Last Supper, when He Himself instituted and celebrated the unbloody Sacrifice of the New Law. Taking bread into His holy and venerable hands, He raised His eyes to heaven, towards His divine and omnipotent Father, and blessed it. By His blessing our Lord set aside and sanctified the bread He held in His hands, that it might be substantially changed into His Body by the words of omnipotence: "This is My Body."

In like manner, when the Eucharistic elements have been placed upon the altar, Holy Church, by her blessing and oblation, withdraws them from all profane and common uses. By offering them to God, she liberates these lowly elements from every subtle influence of the evil one. According to Innocent II, the bread, wine and water are blessed with the sign of the cross in order that "the power of the cross may drive away every effort of the ill-will of the devil, lest he should be able to do aught against either the priest or the sacrifice itself."

The Offertory is, therefore, a preliminary consecration of the elements, which receive their highest consecration when their substance is indeed, not lost, but changed into the substance of the Flesh and Blood of the Son of God. For many centuries the only prayer accompanying this oblation is that which we now call the *Secret*, but which the Gelasian Missal calls *Oratio super oblata* (Prayer over the Offerings). Our present Offertory prayers are only a development of what is more concisely expressed in the Secret. For that reason they are likewise recited secretly, except the prayer which accompanies the oblation of the chalice at the High Mass, when it is said by the celebrant and the deacon together, and for that reason must be said in such wise that priest and deacon may hear each other.

Having uncovered the chalice and placed it outside the corporal, the priest takes, with both hands, the paten on which the host lies, and holds it before him (*usque ad pectus,* says the rubric; that is, at the height of his chest). Then he raises his eyes to God for a moment, lowers them immediately and lets them rest upon the host, whilst reciting the prayer by which the bread is blessed and presented to God for His blessing. The prayer of oblation opens with an appeal to the holiness, power and eternity of God our Father. To Him, and to Him alone, may sacrifice be offered. *Suscipe* (Receive it), prays the priest, for He alone is the true and living God. Him we serve, but His service does not enslave; on the contrary, it invests us with a regal dignity: "You are a chosen generation, a kingly priesthood, a holy nation, a purchased people."[12] For this cause it is granted to us, inasmuch as we are "a holy priesthood, to offer up spiritual sacrifices, acceptable to God by Jesus Christ."[13] Soon we shall offer Him His only Son, in whom He is well pleased; now we only offer this spotless bread (*hanc immaculatam hostiam*).

What is offered to the Most High should be flawless, for, even when we give of earth's best, we give but little, and our offerings are always of His giving. In that very prophecy which so clearly foretells the perfect oblation of the New Law, we hear God's complaint that the priests of the Old Law dishonored Him: "To you, O priests, that despise My name, and have said: Wherein have we despised Thy name? You offer polluted bread upon My altar, and you say: Wherein have we polluted Thee? In that you say: The table of the Lord is contemptible. If you offer the blind for sacrifice, is it not evil? and if you offer the lame and the sick, is it not evil? offer it to thy prince, if he will be pleased with it, or if he will regard thy face, saith the Lord of hosts."[14]

However, the whole tenor of our prayer compels us to see in the "spotless host" not merely flawless, stainless bread. Holy Church looks

12 1 Pet., ii. 9. 13 *Ibid.*, ii. 5.
14 Mal., i. 7, 8.

ahead and anticipates upon what is to be accomplished in the Canon. In the *immaculata hostia* which now lies upon the paten, which her prayer and oblation withdraws from the common uses of human life, she already beholds the spotless Victim whose immolation alone can take away the stains of our innumerable transgressions: "Christ hath loved us, and hath delivered Himself for us, an oblation and a sacrifice to God for an odor of sweetness" (*Christus dilexit nos, et tradidit semetipsum pro nobis oblationem et hostiam Deo in odorem suavitatis*).[15] Hence it would be a deplorable whittling down of the rich significance of the *Suscipe*, were we to think of the bread only; in fact, it would be a grievous error, inasmuch as we expressly declare that the "spotless host" is offered "for my innumerable sins, offenses and negligences" (*pro innumerabilibus peccatis et offensionibus, et negligentiis meis*), an end for which the oblation of bread would avail but little.

All this is very forcibly stated by Cardinal Bona, who tells us of a great controversy between a certain Austin Friar named Hofmeister and some learned, unnamed personage. The latter expressed his amazement that bread and wine should be called a spotless sacrifice, when God is asked to accept it for the wellbeing of the living and the dead. "Not bread and wine do we call a spotless sacrifice," answered the friar, "but the Body and Blood of the Lord, into which they are changed. Hence they are deemed worthy of such appellation, not by reason of what they now are, but of what they are about to become. Such an appellation harmonizes with Scriptural language. Thus Judas is styled 'the traitor,' from the beginning of his vocation, because he became a traitor later on." In short, we speak of the material elements of our sacrifice in the same terms as we should speak of the divine realities that underlie them after the words of omnipotence have been pronounced over them. So we call the host lying on our paten *immaculatam hostiam*, and with perfect propriety because of the intimate and immediate relation between the bread that is now and the sacred Flesh of Christ that is presently to take its place.

We need waste no time in scrutinizing the exact shade of meaning of the three words, *peccatis, offensionibus, negligentiis;* they include

---

15 Eph., v. 2.

all our sins, great and small, both of omission and commission, by which our life has been at variance with the supreme rule of conduct, the all-holy will and essence of God. Moreover, in this very act of preliminary oblation and anticipatory consecration of the elements, the priest is reminded of the catholicity of his sacrifice. He offers it not for himself only, but also, and that in a peculiar manner, "for all here present" (*pro omnibus circumstantibus*). Those nearest to a big fire get most warmth out of it; hence, other things being equal, those who surround the altar at the moment of sacrifice receive more of its efficacy than those who take part in it only because they belong to the mystical body of Christ, and thus somehow share in whatever advantages accrue to the Church. Then, our sacrifice is made for the living and the dead, for our present wellbeing in the order of nature and grace, that so we may come to life everlasting (*ad salutem in vitam aeternam*).

After the prayer of oblation the priest makes the sign of the cross with the paten over the place where he is to put the spotless host which he has just presented to the gaze of the heavenly Father. Then he allows the host gently to slip from the paten. The paten itself is hidden under the corporal in such wise that only the edge of it is visible. We find traces of this custom as far back as the eleventh century. Medieval liturgists see various symbolic meanings in the act, of which no doubt the truest explanation is also the obvious one: namely, that the paten, being a sacred vessel but not required until the end of the *Pater noster*, it was found desirable to put it out of the celebrant's way, yet so as to hide it from the gaze of the people. Hence, at High Mass, it is taken off the altar altogether and held under a veil by the subdeacon.

After the offering of the bread, the priest pours wine into the chalice, then blesses the water by making the sign of the cross, and pours two or three drops into the chalice. The prayer which accompanies the blessing and pouring in of the water gives us the meaning of the ceremony. The prayer is very old, for it is found in both the Gelasian and Gregorian Missals as a Collect for Christmas Day, with only the omission of a reference to water and wine, which was inserted when the Collect was placed among the Offertory prayers. The addition of water to the Eucharistic wine (that is, the addition of a lowlier to a nobler substance) signifies the union of the human with the divine nature in Christ and our own consequent raising to a dignity far excelling the primeval and essential nobility inherent in our nature. God has wondrously created us, but has even more marvelously renewed us; and the purpose of Christ's assumption of our nature is but that we may be made one with Him, "by whom He [God] hath given us most great and precious promises: that by these we may be made partakers of the divine nature."[16]

"Let us hide ourselves in the sacred chalice," the saintly foundress of a religious institute said to her daughters, "like the drop of water which the priest mingles with the wine of the altar, in order that our lowly expiations and our sacrifice be mingled with the Sacrifice of the Redeemer, and that His oblation and ours may constitute but one offering." And we have the authority of Holy Church herself to bear out this interpretation. The *Secret,* as has been said already, is the real Offertory prayer, the only prayer *super oblata* used by the Church during many centuries. Thus, the Secret is the authentic expression of the mind of the Church in the Offertory act, which is seen in every Secret. It is, thus, seen in the Secret of Easter, but most vividly in that of the Fourth Sunday after Easter: *Deus qui nos per hujus sacrificii veneranda commercia, unius summae Divinitatis participes effecisti* (O God, who by the venerable communion in this sacrifice hast made us partakers of the one supreme Godhead).

The prayer which accompanies the oblation of the chalice is spoken in the plural. It is supposed to be said simultaneously by the priest and the deacon, the latter being in a peculiar manner (and, as it were, by right) the minister of the chalice, so much so that it was he who formerly offered it to the faithful at the Communion. St Lawrence said to St Sixtus, the Pope: *experire utrum idoneum ministrum elegeris, cui commisisti Dominici sanguinis dispensationem* (try whether thou didst choose a fit minister when thou didst commit to me the dispensation of the Blood of the Lord). The plural, moreover, emphasizes once more the universality of the sacrifice. Now there is but wine in

---

16 II Pet., i. 4.

the cup—we lift it up on high, and at the same time we keep our eyes raised to heaven—and as the heavenly Father blesses and accepts our offering, He already perceives the sweet odor of the cup of salvation (*in odorem suavitatis ascendat*).

After the oblation of the wine, the priest folds his hands, rests them on the edge of the altar and says a prayer reminiscent of Daniel's pitiful complaint to the Lord that in his day there was no longer either holocaust or sacrifice "that we might find mercy; nevertheless, in a contrite heart and humble spirit let us be accepted."[17]

Then, raising his eyes and hands to heaven and lowering them again, the priest blesses simultaneously both elements of the Sacrifice, and prays: "Come, O Sanctifier, almighty and eternal God, and bless this sacrifice prepared for Thy holy name" (*Veni, sanctificator omnipotens, aeterne Deus, et benedic hoc sacrificium tuo sancto nomini praeparatum*). Who is meant by *Sanctificator omnipotens*? It seems wellnigh impossible to call in question that the Holy Ghost is meant here. Other Liturgies than the Latin seem to make the point certain. But the question is: Have we here the famous *epiclesis*, in which the Eastern Church asks the Holy Ghost to work the ineffable change of bread and wine into the Body and Blood of Christ? We are at liberty to look upon our prayer in that light—there is as much—nay, more—reason to ask the Holy Ghost to act upon these elements *before* the Consecration than after it, as is done by the Greeks. The sole cause of the tremendous change which takes place at the Consecration is the efficacy of the words of Jesus Christ, first spoken by Himself at the Last Supper and repeated in His name by the priests of the Catholic Church. There can be no manner of doubt that the Holy Ghost coöperates in the mystery, inasmuch as the three divine Persons are inseparable and coöperate in all things. *Pater meus usque modo operatur, et ego operor* (My Father worketh until now, and I work), said Christ, and the same is true of the Holy Ghost. That these operations are undivided is theological truth, because operation follows nature and the divine nature, though subsisting in three Persons, is one.

---

17 Dan., iii. 38, 39.

The invocation of the Holy Ghost in the *Veni sanctificator* is immediately followed by a highly symbolic rite—namely, the washing of hands (or rather, of the fingers with which the priest is about to touch the sacred species). At a time when all the assistants offered their gifts in kind, and the priest received them at their hands, there was an obvious reason for the washing of his hands. The fourteenth *Ordo Romanus* prescribes that the thumbs and forefingers alone be washed, adding that, after washing them, the priest should not touch anything with them until after the Communion. Whilst washing and wiping his hands, the priest recites part of Psalm xxv, in which David protests his innocence when subjected to calumny and persecution. The washing of hands is an external sign of inward purity. In a like spirit Jesus washed the feet of His Apostles before He instituted the Eucharistic Sacrifice and the priesthood of the New Law: "He that is washed needeth not but to wash his feet, but is clean wholly."[18]

When he has returned to the middle of the altar with folded hands, the priest raises his eyes to heaven (*oculosque ad Deum elevans*), lowers them immediately, bends the head and shoulders, and, resting his folded hands upon the edge of the altar, recites a prayer addressed to the Blessed Trinity: *Suscipe, Sancta Trinitas*. This prayer, with the Secret, was at one time the only Offertory prayer. Its text has come down to us with many variations. As it now stands in our Missal, it is one of the very few liturgical prayers directly addressed to the Blessed Trinity. It is interesting for the theologian as one more official expression of the dogma of the Communion of Saints. In the very act of sacrifice, which may be made to God's majesty alone, we declare that we perform this supreme act of worship in remembrance of the mysteries of our Lord's life in time, and to the honor also of Christ's Mother and the Saints, some of whom are mentioned by name—namely, the Precursor and the princes of the apostolic college. After *et istorum* (and of these), we may suppose that the names of the Saints were mentioned, whose relics were on the altar or beneath it—the more so since many versions of the prayer expressly say: *et eorum quorum reliquiae hic sunt reconditae* (and of these Saints whose relics are here concealed).

---

18 John, xiii. 10

Our Sacrifice procures an increase of glory for the Saints; for us it obtains salvation; so, whilst we are mindful of them on earth, we crave their intercession in heaven. But both their glory and our salvation are due solely to our one common Lord Jesus Christ, whose Passion, Resurrection and Ascension are the hope and stay of our lives in this world, for He alone can open the gate of life for His followers (*Tu devicto mortis aculeo, aperuisti credentibus regna coelorum*).

Orate Fratres

When the celebrant has recited the prayer addressed to the Blessed Trinity (*Suscipe Sancta Trinitas*), he kisses the altar. This ceremonial kiss of the altar is never omitted whenever the priest has to turn round to salute the faithful or to ask their prayers, as in the present instance. Since the altar is a symbol of Christ, reverence paid to it is given to Christ. Extending his hands, and at once folding them again, the priest says: *Orate fratres*. This is the very last time that the celebrant turns towards the assistants before he wraps himself in the holy silence amid which the tremendous Sacrifice is offered to God's majesty.

There is a strange anomaly between the words of the invitation (which, apparently, is addressed to the whole assembly), and the manner in which it is made. The rubric prescribes that the words be uttered *voce paululum elevata* (that is, in a slightly raised tone of voice). Apparently the invitation is not intended to be heard throughout the sacred edifice, but only by those who are in the immediate neighborhood of the altar. Various interpretations of the seeming contradiction have been proposed. One is that the Offertory chant is supposed to be still going on; another, which is one probably nearest the truth, explains that the words were addressed only to the priests who celebrated simultaneously with the sacrificing priest (*concelebrantes*). The General Rubrics[19] prescribe that at a Low Mass the *Orate fratres* should be said in a loud voice (*clara voce*), which seems to be at variance with what is expressly stated in the rubrics of the *Ordo Missae* and in the *Ritus celebrandi* which is printed at the beginning of the Missal.

---

19 XVI, 1.

The call to prayer at this moment is certainly addressed, in the first instance, to the ministers of the altar. In the *Breviarium ecclesiastici ordinis*, published by Muratori,[20] it is prescribed that after the Offertory the officiating priest shall turn to his fellow-celebrants (*concelebrantes*) on either side of the altar (*Tunc sacerdos ... aliis sacerdotibus postulat pro se orare*).

The same thing might be said about the *Nobis quoque peccatoribus*, which is also said *parum elevata voce*, and designates the ministers of the altar (*famulis tuis*), as distinct from the rest of the faithful. This distinction between celebrant, ministers and assistants is very emphatically stated in the prayer which follows the consecration: "Wherefore, O Lord, we Thy servants, as also Thy holy people" (*Unde et memores, Domine, nos servi tui, sed et plebs tua sancta*).

The faithful, however, are not excluded from the invitation to prayer; in fact, the ministers at the altar are but the representatives of the people. They are called *fratres*. We are all brethren, inasmuch as we all have one common Father, whom we acknowledge whenever we say: "Our Father, who art in heaven." Or, as one of the earliest Christian writers has it: "Whence is it that you are all brethren? Because we have one Father, Christ, and one Mother, the Church."[21]

Neither the invitation of the priest nor the answer of the people has always been expressed as it is in the Mass of today. Durandus, in the thirteenth century, makes the priest say: *Orate pro me, fratres, et ego pro vobis*.

Our prayer is one more proof of the universality of our Sacrifice; it is offered by the priest: *ut meum ... sacrificium* (that my sacrifice); but it is likewise the people's oblation: *ac vestrum* (and yours). Very beautiful indeed is the answer of the people. The Mass is offered, primarily, "to the praise and glory of God," then for the peculiar benefit and advantage of those who take an immediate and personal part in it; finally, for the help and profit of the universal Church.

Since the holy Sacrifice is the Sacrifice of all and the highest act of worship that we can render to the majesty of God, we should unite with and include in this supreme and truly divine oblation all

---

20 *Liturg. Rom.*, II,   21 Arnobius, *In Psalm, cxxxiii*,

the prayers, efforts and sacrifices which make up our daily life. In the words of a contemporary servant of God, whom we have already quoted on several occasions (the foundress of the Daughters of the Sacred Heart): "Let us add to the sacrifice of the Mass whatever our misery can give: renouncements, sacrifices, sorrows, love without reserve. Jesus, who suffers now no longer, thirsts for *our* sufferings. He wishes to offer them, together with His own, to the glory of His Father and for the salvation of souls. Let us give them to Him generously and thus fill up, in ourselves, what is wanting to the sufferings of Christ, for the formation of His body, which is the Church."[22]

A practical remark in connexion with the *Orate fratres* may not be amiss, and the writer hopes it may not be considered offensive. The rubrics of the *Ritus celebrandi*[23] prescribe very explicitly that, when the priest has kissed the altar before turning towards the people, he should do so *demissis oculis ad terram* (with his eyes lowered), and, when he has said the first words of his invitation to prayer (*Orate fratres*), he should at once turn round towards the altar, completing a full circle, and meanwhile reciting secretly the remainder of the prayer. The whole movement should be slow and deliberate; but there must be no pause. The celebrant should remain facing the faithful no longer than it takes to say *Orate fratres*. This rubric is not unfrequently set aside or forgotten. Too often one sees priests taking advantage of the *Orate fratres* to make a deliberate halt in order to have a good look at the congregation. This practice is at variance with the spirit and letter of the rubric.

It is a matter of debate among rubricists whether the server or other ministers should wait until the priest has finished his part of the *Orate fratres* before beginning *Suscipiat*. The directions given in the Missal do not clinch the matter. It is customary for the server to wait for a few moments—that is, at least until the priest once more faces the altar. However, it would not be in the least inappropriate to begin *Suscipiat* at once, inasmuch as this is the audible answer to the only audible part of the priest's invitation to prayer. Possibly we have here an instance of what is so common in the Greek Liturgy;

---

22 *Lettres de Mère Marie de Jésus*, p. 289; cfr. Col., i. 24.
23 VII, 7.

namely, the simultaneous recitation by the priest and the deacon, or choir, of prayers which were at one time said after one another. Furthermore, we know that for a considerable period the priest only said *Orate fratres,* or *Orate pro me.* What follows this invitation was added as an afterthought; it is only a detailed statement of the object for which prayers are asked. When these clauses came to be added to the *Orate fratres,* they were said in silence. So there would seem to be no reason why the response, *Suscipiat,* should not at once follow the call to prayer. When the people's response, spoken in their behalf by the server, is ended, the priest says *Amen* in a low voice, and at once turns to the Missal to read the secret prayers.

The Secret Prayer (*Secreta*)

We have seen that our present Offertory prayers are of comparatively recent introduction. Originally there was but one prayer of oblation which was recited by the priest after the faithful had presented their gifts at the altar. In the Sacramentary (or Missal) of St Gregory, this Offertory prayer is called *Secreta;* another name for it is *Oratio super oblata.* The former name became the usual one during the Middle Ages. It was most appropriate, inasmuch as the prayer was and still is recited by the priest in a low, inaudible voice. It was thus recited even at a time when the Canon was still said in a clear, audible voice. This silent prayer is not without its own significance. "Such is the nature of man," says the Council of Trent, "that it cannot easily rise to the contemplation of the things of God without external help. Hence, like a kindly mother, Holy Church has adopted certain rites, and ordained that in the celebration of Mass certain things should be said in a low voice, others in a somewhat higher tone."[24]

The reformers, in order to emphasize their conception of the priesthood as a mere delegated function performed in the name of the people, ordered that the Liturgy (or what part of it they had retained) should be said aloud. For that reason the Council justifies the age-long tradition according to which certain parts of the Mass (espe-

---

24 Sess, XXII, cap. v, *De Sacrif. Miss.*

cially the more solemn ones and above all the Canon) were to be said in secret. The priest is no mere delegate or spokesman of the people; he is a true *mediator* between God and man, dealing with God on behalf of man and offering sacrifice to the Most High on behalf of the people. The Secret is said inaudibly, because sacrifice is the exercise of a function proper to the priesthood. The priest alone may offer victims: "For every high priest taken from among men, is ordained for men in the things that appertain to God, that he may offer up gifts and sacrifices for sins. Neither doth any man take the honor to himself, but he that is called by God, as Aaron was."[25] In like manner, it is part of the priestly office to select the matter of the Sacrifice, to give it its preliminary sanctification and present it for God's acceptance.

Thus, it comes to pass that the Secret is, in a peculiar manner, a priestly prayer, the prayer of a mediator. It is addressed to God, as a preliminary of the Sacrifice, and "in it the name *oblatio* is first used in connexion with our sacrifice."[26]

The Secret is not preceded by *Oremus*. The *Orate fratres* may be looked upon as sufficient exhortation to pray. Moreover, before the Offertory chant the priest has already greeted the people and asked them to pray. The *Oremus* which precedes the Offertory antiphon is to be held as immediately preceding the Secret. Originally the Offertory prayers which now follow *Oremus* and precede the Secret, did not exist. The Secret is the *original,* and was for a long time the *only* prayer over the offerings (*super oblata*). As it is essentially a personal supplication of the celebrant in his rôle as sacrificing priest, there is no reason to call upon the people to pray with him at that particular moment.

The structure of the Secret is identical with that of the Collect, the only difference being that, whereas the latter is a prayer suitable to any office of the day, the Secret invariably contains a direct reference to the objects offered upon the altar—sometimes also to the prayers, the devotion, and such like dispositions of the faithful. In not a few of these prayers the thought of Holy Church is already of the Body and Blood of Christ which are so soon to take the place of the earthly ele-

---

25 Heb., v. 1, 4.   26 Durandus, *De eccl. off.*, III, 20.

ments now lying upon the altar. Thus, for instance, we pray in the Secret of the Fourth Sunday after Easter: *Deus qui nos per hujus sacrificii veneranda commercia unius summae divinitatis participes effecisti*.... Here we have an obvious reference, not to the bread and wine that are now on the altar, but to the divine realities which are to be substituted by the act of consecration.

The names by which the priest frequently designates the gifts which he presents for God's acceptance are such as the following: *debitum servitutis nostrae* ("debt of our servitude," that is, a moral, not a physical offering); *oblationes;* even *sacrificium*, by anticipation of course, as, for instance, in the beautiful Secret of the Seventh Sunday after Pentecost: *Deus ... accipe sacrificium a devotis tibi famulis ... ut quod singuli obtulerunt ad majestatis tuae honorem, cunctis proficiat ad salutem* (O God... accept the sacrifice made to Thee by Thy devoted servants ... so that what each has offered to the honor of Thy majesty, may avail to the salvation of all).

Very frequently the Secret contains a reference to the feast of the day or the mystery commemorated by the oblation of the holy Sacrifice, as well as to the gifts offered by the faithful for consecration by the priest. Hence the Secret, like the Collect, frequently gives us the keynote of our feasts and solemnities, and makes us ask for the spirit or the graces peculiar to the day or the time. We find a perfect instance of this in the Secret of the Mass of Easter, which we have hitherto used so often to illustrate these notes and comments on the Liturgy of the Mass: *Suscipe, quaesumus Domine, preces populi tui cum oblationibus hostiarum: ut Paschalibus initiata mysteriis, ad aeternitatis nobis medelam, te operante, proficiant* (Receive, we beseech Thee, O Lord, the prayers of Thy people together with their offerings, so that the mysteries which have their origin in the Paschal festival, may, by Thy operation, become for us the means of everlasting life."

In this Secret we have allusions to the prayers of the people, as well as to their offerings in kind. The mystery of Easter (that is, its spiritual effect) is a birth to a new life, more precious than that of the body. The grace of this blessed day is so to instill the supernatural life into our soul that what is begun so graciously upon earth and in time, may endure unto all eternity in heaven.

At the conclusion of the Secret, which like the Collect is said with hands extended and uplifted, the priest folds his hands, saying: *Per (eumdum) Dominum nostrum Jesum Christum,* etc. Thus is the Trinitarian character of the Church's prayer preserved in the Secret also. Jesus Christ is our Sacrifice, His Flesh and Blood are offered to the sweet majesty of God the Father, the Holy Ghost likewise coöperating in the tremendous change wrought by the words of consecration. It is right, therefore, that in the act of oblation of the matter of the great Sacrifice express mention should be made of the Divine Three, for of them "is all our sufficiency."[27]

The conclusion, *Per omnia saecula saeculorum,* is always said aloud in order to warn the assistants that the secret prayer is at an end. This raising of the voice is called *ecphonesis* by the Greeks, in whose Liturgy it is of frequent occurrence. The words, *Per omnia saecula saeculorum,* do not mark the beginning of the Preface, as many people imagine. They are said aloud only in order to let the assistants know that the Preface is about to be said. Their *Amen* is their joint, solemn ratification of the prayer of the priest, the expression of their moral oneness with him.

---

[27] II Cor., iii. 5.

CHAPTER XIV

FROM THE PREFACE TO THE SANCTUS

The Preface

THE Preface, though its name and form may vary as rites differ, is common to all Liturgies. The name *praefatio*, properly speaking, is only used in the Roman Liturgy. In the Gallican Liturgy it is styled *contestatio*—that is, a simultaneous, public attestation of faith, or a solemn testimony of priest and people to the majesty of God. In the Mozarabic (or Spanish) Liturgy, it is called *illatio*, perhaps to describe the final offering or presentation in the sanctuary (*inferre, illatum*) of the gifts of the faithful. Cardinal Bona makes the suggestion that from the acclamations of the people the priest *infers* (*illatio*) that it is their wish to give praise and thanksgiving to God. It may be also that in the Preface our praise and prayer is carried into (*infertur*) the very sanctuary of heaven, since at its conclusion we expressly pray that our voices may be allowed to mingle with the chant of the court of heaven: *Cum quibus et nostras voces ut admitti jubeas, deprecamur.*

The Preface is sometimes described as the beginning of the Canon—that is, the fixed and most sacred part of the Mass. So it was considered, at any rate, for a considerable time. Thus, the Sacramentary (or Missa) of St Gelasius has this rubric placed before the Preface: *Incipit Canon Actionis*. We now look upon the Preface as a final and immediate preparation for the prayers of intercession and consecration recited in the Canon, and the words *Canon Missae* are placed before the prayer, *Te igitur*, in all our Missals.

The characteristic note of the Preface in all Liturgies is found to consist in an expression of praise and thanksgiving to God. So striking a uniformity is in itself a proof of high antiquity. Its origin must be sought as far back as apostolic days. We can readily imagine that whenever the Apostles carried out the command given them on the night in which the Lord was betrayed (Do this in memory of Me), they would not depart from what they had seen the Master do whilst they were at table with Him. Now we know that the singing of hymns of praise (the great Hallel), as well as certain blessings pronounced by the head of the household, were part of the Paschal supper. Our Lord officiated as priest according to the order of Melchisedech towards the close of the Last Supper, when at least part of the psalms which accompanied the Paschal repast would have been sung. "Taking bread, He gave thanks,"[1] and "in like manner, taking the chalice after He had supped" (*similiter et calicem postquam caenavit*).[2] Hence we may be sure that, as they were "continuing daily with one accord in the temple arid breaking bread from house to house,"[3] thanksgiving was an integral part of the liturgical act. Many authorities might be quoted to prove that it was so. Thus, for instance, the Preface in the Liturgy of St James is a lengthy and detailed thanksgiving for the benefits of God in the order both of nature and grace.

The Preface begins with a dialogue between the priest and the assistants. This also is of very great antiquity. Thus St Cyprian (third century) writes: "When we stand at prayer [*"orationem,"* *oratio* being Cyprian's name for the Eucharistic prayer or sacrifice], we should be watchful, and give all our attention to it. Let every carnal and worldly thought depart, and let the whole energy of the mind be concentrated upon the object of our prayer. Hence it is that the priest says a Preface before the prayer [the Eucharistic *oratio*], that thereby he might dispose the minds of the brethren, saying *Sursum corda,* in order that, when the people answer *Habemus ad Dominum,* they may be admonished to think of naught but the Lord."[4]

Here we meet with the very word *Preface,* used in the same sense as we use it today. *Gratias agamus Domino Dea nostro* is mentioned by St Augustine: "You know in what Sacrifice the words are used: *Gratias agamus Domino Deo nostro.*"[5] The same holy Doctor, in fact, quotes the

1 Luke, xxii. 19.
2 Luke, xxii. 20; 1 Cor., xi, 25.
3 Acts, ii. 46.
4 *De orat. domin.,* xxxi.
5 *Ep. ad Dardan.,* 57.

entire dialogue in different parts of his writings and bears witness to the universality of its use, as in the following interesting passage: "Daily, throughout the entire universe, the human race answers almost with one voice that they have their hearts on high with the Lord (*humanum genus una paene voce respondet, sursum corda se habere ad Dominum*)."[6] Equally interesting is the following piece: *Inter sacra mysteria cor habere sursum jubemur. Ipso adjuvante id valemus: et ideo sequitur ut de hoc tanto bono 'Domino Deo gratias agamus,' quia hoc dignum, hoc justum est recordari* (In the sacred mysteries we are bidden to lift our hearts on high. By His help we are able to do so; hence it follows that we should 'give thanks to God' for so great a good, for it is worthy, it is meet, that we should bear this in mind).[7]

The Greek Church uses our *Sursum corda*—in fact, our Latin exhortation is but a translation of an old Greek formula. Hence, the great African Doctor is fully justified when he asserts that practically the entire human family knows the exhortation which bids them raise their hearts on high, and that they are wont to reply that they do in effect keep them united to Him who dwelleth in the heights.

Prefaces, we have seen, are common to all Liturgies. The general disposition, or the main idea of their structure, is everywhere more or less identical: praise, worship, thanksgiving, supplication, are the keynote of all Prefaces. The oldest—also the most detailed—of all Prefaces is that found in the eighth book of the *Constitutiones Apostolicae*.

When the people's responses have, as it were, assured the priest that their attention is truly fixed upon the sacred rites, he, in their name and his own, addresses the majesty of God the Father: *Vere dignum et justum est, aequum et salutare* (It is truly meet and just, right and salutary, that we should at all times and in all places give thanks to Thee, holy Lord, almighty Father, eternal God). Commentators give all kinds of explanations of *dignum, justum, aequum, salutare*. The mind of the Church is to make her children realize that thanksgiving to God through Jesus Christ is a duty, a privilege and a source of grace (*salutare*). Gratitude for favors received is the surest means of

---

6 *De vera relig.*, III.
7 *De bono viduitatis*, XVI.

obtaining yet further benefits—it is a law of the natural as well as of the supernatural order.

The ordinary Preface does not specify the benefits of God for which thanks are rendered. These thanks are given *per Christum Dominum nostrum*. Through Him and with Him do all the heavenly hierarchies praise the majesty of God with a holy awe and joy. With lowliest supplication we too pray that even our voices may be allowed to mingle with the voices of those who stand for ever around the throne of God.

The Roman Liturgy knows only thirteen Prefaces. In the old Sacramentaries there are a great many more, of varying lengths and for all sorts of occasions. Thus, the Leonine Missal contains one for almost every day of the year. The Gregorian Sacramentary contains only ten, but an eleventh (that of Our Lady) was added by Urban II. Tradition has it that this Pope himself composed it, and sang it for the first time at the Synod of Gaustalla (1094). Two more have been added within the last few years—one in honor of St Joseph and another for Requiem Masses. The last-mentioned Preface had long been in use in many dioceses before it was extended to the Universal Church. The substance of its text is already found in the Sacramentary of St Gregory; older Missals have the Preface with some slight variants, but, of course, the text as published by the Vatican Press is definitive.

Like the Collects, the proper Prefaces invariably contain a special allusion either to the feast that is being kept or to the character of the time or the Mass itself, as in the instance of the Mass for the Dead. These allusions are always brief, but full of significance, and describe in terse and arresting phrase the spirit of the feast.

The Preface of Easter will serve to illustrate our remarks. The Paschal Preface, like that of the Apostles, lacks a lengthy introduction: "It is truly meet and just, right and salutary to praise God at all times. Yet does it behove us to do this with even greater enthusiasm [we may be permitted so to translate *gloriosius*] at this time when Christ our Pasch is immolated." Christ is declared to be "the true Paschal Lamb who took away the sins of the world, who by Himself dying destroyed our death, gave us a remedy against death, and by rising from the grave restored life to us." In these words is described the mystical purport of our annual commemoration of Christ's Resurrection. The mystery of Easter is a mystery of life. We were dead by sin; the Lamb of God took away our guilt; by His bodily death He caused us to pass from spiritual death to a divine life. This divine life becomes a principle of everlasting and blissful existence even for our mortal body, which otherwise would of necessity share, in its own way, the death of the soul. For, as the body is dead when it can no longer retain the soul and respond to its quickening influence, so is the soul in a manner dead when, owing to its perversion, it can no longer respond to the sweet influence of God's goodness.

The conclusion of the Preface always contains a more or less complete enumeration of the Angelic choirs with whom we pray to be allowed to sing in unison: *Et ideo cum Angelis et Archangelis, cum Thronis et Dominationibus, cumque omni militia coelestis exercitus, hymnum gloriae tuae canimus....* In the ordinary Preface the conclusion is somewhat different: It is meet and just that we—on earth—should always return thanks to our heavenly Father through Christ our Lord (*per Christum Dominum nostrum*), for He is our only Mediator and Advocate: "We have an advocate with the Father, Jesus Christ the just;"[8] "There is one God and one Mediator of God and men, the man Christ Jesus."[9] In like manner do the heavenly choirs praise the majesty of God and exult in its presence with awe and trembling; through the same Christ, who is their Head as well as ours, "for in Him were all things created in heaven and on earth, visible and invisible, whether thrones, or dominations, or principalities, or powers.... And He is the Head of the body, the Church, who is the beginning... that in all things He may hold the primacy."[10]

Angels and men owe their grace and glory, though diversely, to the one universal Mediator. The right order, therefore, demands that thanksgiving should be sent up to God through the same channel through which grace comes to every creature (that is, *per Dominum nostrum Jesum Christum*).[11]

The Preface of the Apostles presents special points of interest. Its peculiarity consists in this, that it is directly addressed, not to God

8 1 John, ii. 1.
10 Col., i. 16, 18.
9 1 Tim., ii. 5.
11 St Thom., *Comment. in Ep. ad Rom.*, 1.

the Father, but to Jesus Christ, the true, supreme and immortal Shepherd of His flock. The Apostles keep ward and watch over Christ's flock, but their pastoral office is a vicarious one (*quos operis tui vicarios ... contulisti praeesse pastores*); in their person, by their ministry, Jesus Christ, the *Pastor aeternus,* is for ever with His flock. "Behold I am with you all days, even to the consummation of the world."[12]

The *Sanctus* or *Trisagion*

In the concluding sentence of the Preface the priest prays that all the faithful may be permitted to mingle their voices with those of the Angels on high (*Cum quibus et nostras voces ut admitti jubeas deprecamur,* or, *hymnum gloriae tuae canimus, sine fine dicentes* ...) The threefold *Sanctus* is found in all Liturgies, and is indeed one of the oldest features of the Eucharistic prayer. It is a song which earth has learned from heaven. Isaias first heard the chant of the "blessed Seraphim": "In the year that King Ozias died, I saw the Lord sitting upon a throne high and elevated, and His train filled the temple. Upon it stood the seraphims ... and they cried one to another, and said: Holy, Holy, Holy, the Lord God of hosts, all the earth is full of His glory."[13]

In the Apocalypse, St John likewise saw four living creatures round about the throne, "and they rested not day and night, crying: Holy, Holy, Holy, Lord God Almighty, who was, and who is, and who is to come."[14]

The thrice repeated exclamation *Sanctus* is a public profession of our faith in the mystery of mysteries. Three times the Seraphs cry out "Holy," to honor each of the three divine Persons, but the Three are but One Lord and God.

It is not possible to ascertain when the *Trisagion* was introduced in the Liturgy. Tertullian (end of second century) mentions its liturgical use when exhorting to perseverance in prayer: "It is right at all times and in all places to bless God ... whom those surrounding choirs of angels address without ceasing: 'Holy, Holy, Holy'" (*cui ilia Angelo-*

---

12 Matt., ult,, ult. 13 Is., vi. 1–4.
14 Apoc., iv. 6, 8.

rum circumstantia non cessat dicere: Sanctus, Sanctus, Sanctus).[15] Clement I also speaks of its use. The *Liber Pontificalis* does not say, as some would have it, that Sixtus I (119-128) introduced it. What it affirms is, that this Pope ordained that priest and people should sing it together. The obvious inference is that the priest recited it even before that time, but alone.

The Council of Vaison in Gaul (A D 529) commanded that the *Sanctus* be not omitted at any Mass, not even in Lent or at Masses said for the departed. It goes on to give a reason for this prescription: namely that "so sweet and delectable a word, even were it possible to say it day and night, cannot cause weariness" (*quia tam dulcis et desiderabilis vox, etiamsi diu noctuque possit dici, fastidium non potest generare*).[16] In the Middle Ages the *Sanctus* (like the *Kyrie*) was not unfrequently "farced" or interpolated—an abuse which has happily disappeared without leaving any trace in our present Liturgy.

The *Sanctus* of the Roman Mass is the common property of the Latin as well as of the Greek Church. It may not be uninteresting to remark here that there are two *Trisagions*—the one we have just spoken of, and that which the Latin Church sings on Good Friday only, but which is part of the daily Liturgy of Constantinople, namely *Agios o Theos* (*Sanctus Deus*, etc.). The fact that the hymn is so popular in the Greek Liturgy, and was used by the Fathers of the Council of Chalcedon (451), is indicative of great antiquity. It is certainly older than the date assigned to it by the legend according to which a boy, having been raised into the sky for the space of about an hour while the emperor and people of Constantinople were praying for preservation from an earthquake, heard the Angels sing: "*Agios o Theos*, etc." When the boy came down to earth once more, he told the people to repeat these acclamations, for thus would they be preserved from all harm. When he had delivered his message, the boy suddenly expired.

Some liturgists distinguish three heavenly hymns, to wit: the *angelic*, the *cherubic* and the *seraphic*. The *angelic* hymn is, of course, the *Gloria in excelsis Deo*. The *cherubic* hymn is one of the most beautiful liturgical pieces of the Greek Church, and derives its name from the

15 *De orat.*, III.   16 Cfr. Bona, *Res. liturg.*, II, 10.

opening words: "We, who mystically represent the Cherubim, sing the thrice-holy hymn to the life-giving Trinity. Let us put away all worldly care, so that we may receive the King of all, escorted by the angelic hosts. Alleluia." Finally, there is the *seraphic* hymn, our *Trisagion,* deriving its name from the fact that the Prophet heard it on the lips of Seraphim and from the thrice-repeated ἅγιος (hagios).

The *Trisagion* ends upon a note of triumph: *Hosanna in excelsis! Benedictus qui venit in nomine Domini! Hosanna is excelsis!* The Church acclaims the King of glory who is so soon to be upon our altar in the words with which the crowds welcomed our Lord on the day of His triumphant entry into the Holy City: "The multitude that went before and that followed cried, saying: Hosanna to the Son of David: Blessed is he that cometh in the name of the Lord: Hosanna in the highest."[17]

Our Lord truly comes *in nomine Domini*—that is, by the will of the Father, for "God so loved the world as to give His only begotten Son."[18] The Eucharistic Sacrifice which is even now being offered up, is but the continuation of the work of redemption accomplished by Christ upon the altar of the cross. To His presence upon the altar at Mass we may apply the words which Holy Church puts on our lips in the procession of Palm Sunday: *Hic est qui venturus est in salutem populi.... Salve Rex, fabricator mundi, qui venist redimere nos. Benedictus qui venisti in multitudine misericordiae tuae.*

Hosanna is one of those Hebrew words which have remained untranslated in order that the mind may be the more impressed. It is a cry of hope and yearning, of loyalty and love combined: Save us, save us now! Lord, Thou hast power to save, since Thou art the Master of heaven and earth! The first *Hosanna* may be considered as a cry addressed to the three divine Persons, the last is an acclamation to Jesus Christ. When reciting the first *Hosanna,* the priest remains bowed before the cross as during the *Sanctus.* He stands erect when he recites *Benedictus qui venit* and the last *Hosanna,* making at the same time the sign of the cross.

---

17 Matt., xxi. 9.   18 John, iii. 16.

CHAPTER XV

THE CANON

Historical Origin of the Canon

WE have now come to the central and most important part of the Liturgy of the Mass. All that has gone before has been only a preparation leading up to and preparing the mind for a sublime climax. Strictly speaking, the prayers,, readings, or chants which precede the Canon, might be dropped either wholly or in part; they are no integral part of the Sacrifice; the consecration alone is the continuation of what took place in the Upper Room and upon the Cross of Calvary. However, the rites and prayers which immediately precede and follow this divine act are a worthy accompaniment of the Eucharistic Sacrifice, each of them being, as it were, a precious pearl forming the setting of a priceless gem.

The word canon ($\kappa\alpha\nu\omega\nu$) signifies rule, law, fixed order. Thus, the laws or decrees promulgated by councils are called canons, as when we speak of the *Canones et Decreta Concilii Tridentini*. Then there is the Canon of the Scriptures—that is, the list, authentic and fixed for all time, of the books which Holy Church receives and gives to us as inspired, that is, of divine origin, "for prophecy came not by the will of man at any time: but the holy men of God spoke, inspired by the Holy Ghost."[1]

The Canon of the Mass is the fixed and obligatory order which must be observed in the most important part of the celebration of the Holy Eucharist. It forms that section of the Liturgy of the Eucharist which remains unalterable, save for a very few minor variations

---

[1] II Pet., i, 21.

on certain great feasts of the year.

Another name for the Canon is *Prex* (that is, the "prayer" *par excellence*). It is an expression made use of by St Cyprian, Tertullian, St Gregory. Yet another name is *Actio*. "The Canon is called *Actio*, because in it we have the lawful and regular performance of the Sacrament."[2]

The Canon is not only a fixed rule to which we must inviolably adhere, but it is also the embodiment of the oldest and most primitive prayers and ceremonies. As such it is a rich inheritance, handed down to us from apostolic days. The Council of Trent speaks with great emphasis, of the venerable antiquity and inherent sacredness of our Canon: "Since it is meet that holy things should be holily administered, and since this [the Mass] is of all sacrifices the holiest, the Catholic Church, in order to secure its worthy and reverent oblation and reception, has formed many centuries ago the sacred Canon, so free from all error that naught is found therein that is not supremely redolent of a certain holiness and piety, so that the minds of those that offer, are thereby raised to God. For, indeed, it is made up of the very words of our Lord, the traditions of the Apostles and the devout institutions of holy Pontiffs."[3]

The Council bases this declaration upon a book on the Sacrament attributed to St Ambrose (and now generally acknowledged to be his), upon a letter of St Augustine to Januarius, and on the works of several other ecclesiastical writers. For instance, St Augustine, after quoting I Cor., xi. 20-24, which concludes with the words *caetera cum venero disponam* (the rest I will set in order when I come), says: "Whence we are given to understand (for it would have taken too long to indicate in detail an order which the whole Church observes throughout the world) that he himself had established a practice which is not subject to local changes" [*Unde intelligi datur (quia multum erat ut in epistola totum illum agendi ordinem insinuaret, quem universa per orbem servat Ecclesia) ab ipso ordinatum esse quod nulla morum diversitate variatur*].[4] True, Augustine speaks here only of fasting before Communion, but the in-

---

2 Walafrid Strabo, *De reb, eccl.*, 23,
3 Session XXII, cap. 4, *De Sacrificio Missae*.
4 *Ep. liv. ad Gordian.*, 8.

ference is obvious, and the Council states that St Paul had already laid down some rules—that is, had established some kind of Canon—for the orderly celebration of the Lord's Supper.

Speculation is rife among scholars about the date of the formation and fixation of the Canon of our Latin Mass. Some attribute it to Pope St Damasus. What is certain is that our Canon has undergone no change or alteration since the days of St Gregory the Great. But this great Pope cannot be said to have been the real author of the Canon. All he did was to revise finally the formularies of the Gelasian Sacramentary (end of the fifth century), though even Pope Gelasius must have used material handed down from earlier ages. John the Deacon tells us in his Life of St Gregory that the Pontiff "condensed within the limits of one volume the Gelasian codex of Masses, omitting much, changing little, and adding some (*multa subtrahens, pauca convertens, non nulla vero superadjiciens*); and in the Canon he added the words: *diesque nostros in tua pace disponas, atque ab aeterna damnatione nos eripi, et in electorum tuorum jubeas grege numerari*" (dispose our days in Thy peace, and command us to be delivered from eternal damnation and numbered in the flock of Thine elect).

One of the arguments by which medieval liturgists sought to prove the high antiquity of the Canon is that the list of the Apostles contained therein differs from that which is found in the Vulgate, a version completed towards the end of the fourth century. Again, among the Saints whose names are mentioned in the Canon, there occur only those of martyrs, the *cultus* of confessors being a later development.

Medieval liturgists are wont to divide the Canon into two sections, the Canon of the Consecration and that of the Communion. However, the Canon properly begins with the prayer *Te igitur* and ends before the *Pater noster*. "When the Preface is ended," says the *Ritus Celebrandi Missam*, VIII, 1, "the priest...bowing profoundly, begins the Canon, saying in a very low voice: *Te igitur*." As for the conclusion, St Gregory says that *mox post precem* ("shortly after the prayer," by which he means the Canon, or consecration prayer) the *Pater noster* is recited.

Each of the prayers of the Canon has been attributed to some Pope; for instance, *Te igitur* is said to be St Clement's. However, these assertions are very far from proven. On the other hand, in the book *De Sacramentis,* attributed to St Ambrose, we find the complete text of the prayers *Quam oblationem, Qui pridie quam pateretur, Unde et memores, Supra quae propitio.*

The Solemnity of the Ceremonies

There is an element of secrecy and mysteriousness about the Canon, and an added solemnity arises from the fact that its prayers are recited by the celebrant alone and in silence. The *Gloria* and *Credo,* the *Sanctus* and *Agnus Dei,* are recited by the celebrant and his assistants. But always and under all circumstances the Canon is the prayer of him alone who offers the adorable Sacrifice: *Solus Pontifex, et tacito, intrat in Canonem* (The Pontiff alone and in silence begins the Canon), says the *Ordo Romanus* II. The only exception to this rule is the Mass of Ordination, when the newly ordained priests recite all the prayers aloud with the bishop. When the custom was general for several priests to celebrate together (*concelebratio*), it was obvious that the Canon had to be recited in an audible voice. Liturgists and medieval commentators generally see some wonderful mystical reasons for the silent recitation of the Canon. "The Canon is recited in silence because this immolation pertains to the priest alone" (*Canon secreto agitur eo quod haec immolatio ad solum pertinet sacerdotem*); and again "to show that human reason cannot fully grasp so great a mystery." Thus wrote Sicardus of Cremona at the end of the twelfth or the beginning of the thirteenth century.

The priest at the altar is a mediator between God and man. He speaks and acts in the name and in the person of the one perfect "mediator of God and men, the man Christ Jesus."[5] Our Lord was alone in the garden, alone upon the cross, alone also did He enter the Holy of Holies: "I have trodden the wine-press alone: and of the Gentiles there is not a man with Me."[6] His own loneliness at the altar, and the silence in which he is wrapped as in a garment, should help the priest to a realization of the sublimity of the tremendous action he is about to accomplish. To emphasize yet more the sacredness of this part of

---

5 1 Tim., ii. 5.   6 Is., lxiii. 3.

the Mass, it was customary in the Middle Ages to draw the curtains which were hung on either side of the altar, so as to enfold the priest, and, as it were, wrap the altar, as when "the glory of the Lord filled the temple."[7]

The late Dr A. Fortescue, whose untimely death was an immense loss for liturgical studies, quotes a story which, he says, "were it the true reason for our silent Canon, would fix the date of the rule, because the tale is related by John Moschus, who died in 619." The story is that some boys in Palestine were playing "at church." As is the wont of pious boys, they were "saying Mass," and even repeated the words of consecration, as they heard them said in church, when fire came from heaven, destroyed their altar, and nearly consumed the would-be priests. When they had recovered from their fright, they told the local bishop what had happened. From that time the custom began of saying the consecration prayer silently to shield it from future profanation.[8]

Whatever may have originated the rule of secrecy and silence, no one can question its singular appropriateness. The Mass is not a prayer-meeting—the priest does not merely "lead the people in prayer," to quote our non-Catholic friends' expression; he offers a sacrifice of priceless value to the majesty of God. The holy silence which falls upon the assembly, the solemn hush around the altar, is well calculated to make even the thoughtless realize the awful grandeur of the hour. *Quam terribilis est haec hora!* (How terrible is this hour!), the deacon cries out in the Syrian Liturgy.

The first prayer of the Canon begins with the words, *Te igitur*. A few words may be said here on the way in which the Canon is printed in our Missals. To emphasize its importance (as well as for greater facility in reading it) and to mark its sacredness, the text is printed in larger type than the remainder of the Mass. Moreover, the first letter of the opening prayer naturally lends itself to elaborate illumination or decoration, the nature of which is suggested by the very appearance of the letter T, which is simply a cross—an emblem, therefore, of the sacrifice of Calvary of which the Mass is the continuation and

---

[7] Is., vi. 1. [8] Cfr. Fortescue, *The Mass*, p. 326.

reënactment. One naturally turns to Ezechiel, where we find a symbolic and prophetic allusion to the letter T and the idea of the cross: "And the Lord said: Go through the midst of the city, through the midst of Jerusalem, and mark Tau (T) upon the foreheads of the men that sigh, and mourn...upon whomsoever you shall see Tau, kill him not."[9]

From the configuration of T the custom arose of painting a figure of Christ crucified on the first page of the Canon, the cross being simply the first letter of the *Te igitur*. In course of time these pictures of the Crucified, from being simple miniatures, became of such size as to take up a goodly part of the first page of the consecration prayers. We now have, in our Roman Missal, a full-page picture of the Crucifixion, but the sacred image is no longer part of the printed text, or of the first word of the opening prayer.

Another feature of the Canon is the frequent tracing of the sign of the cross over the elements, both before and after consecration. Twenty-five times is the sign of the cross thus made. Medieval liturgists read many mystical significations into these crosses and blessings. St Thomas gives the best and the obvious explanation, when he says that "the priest in celebrating Mass uses the sign of the cross to express the passion of Christ, which terminated on the cross" (*sacerdos in celebratione Missae utitur crucis signatione ad exprimendam passionem Christi, quae ad crucem est terminata*). The crosses traced over the Sacred Elements after consecration are not, according to the Angelic Doctor, for the purpose of blessing or consecrating, "but only to commemorate the virtue of the cross and the manner of Christ's passion" (*sed solum ad commemorandam virtutem crucis et modum passionis Christi*).[10]

Nothing could be more impressive or dignified than the ceremonies which precede and accompany the opening prayer of the Canon. The *Ritus celebrandi*, placed at the beginning of the Roman Missal, is very precise and definite in its directions. As soon as he has said *Hosanna in excelsis*, the priest, standing erect before the altar, raises his hands and likewise his eyes to God (*ad Deum*, says the rubric). Im-

---

9 Ezech., ix. 4, 6.   10 *Summa Theol.*, III, Q, lxxxiii, a, 5.

mediately afterwards, he devoutly (*devote*) lowers his eyes and folds his hands, places them upon the edge of the altar-table, and, bowing profoundly, he begins the Canon, saying silently *Te igitur*. Such an elaborate ceremony is in itself a supplication. The whole attitude, in fact, of the priest during the Canon is one of humility and supplication. Whenever he is not actually carrying out some ceremony, he stands almost continuously with hands extended, like the figures of the *orantes* which we see in the early Christian paintings on the walls of the Catacombs of Rome. Since the priest officiates in the name and person of Jesus Christ, it is but meet that his very attitude should represent our High Priest pleading, praying, sacrificing Himself upon the altar of the cross.

It should be noted that, according to the best interpretation of the rubric, *Te igitur* should only be begun after the priest has extended his hands, raised his eyes, and bowed before the cross.

The prayers of the Canon are all addressed to God the Father. The three first have one common conclusion. We may consider the three as forming substantially but one prayer; in fact, the whole Canon, to be properly understood, should be looked upon as forming one continuous prayer. Only thus can we understand some of the expressions used *before* the consecration, which speak of the unconsecrated elements in terms which are literally true only *after* it. Scholars have devised many varying theories in their efforts to explain the origin and formation of the Roman Canon. Some say that the two *Mementos* were at first said before the Preface; in like manner the *Te igitur* and the *Nobis quoque peccatoribus*. Be this as it may, let us take the Canon as we find it today. It is surrounded by the halo of venerable antiquity, since it has undergone no change or alteration during more than thirteen centuries. It is an uplifting thought to realize, as we repeat the words of the Canon morning after morning, that we utter the selfsame words which have so often lingered on the lips of martyrs and doctors, of bishops and priests of every race and country where the majesty of the Roman Rite and the stately dignity of the Latin tongue were known and revered.

The Prayers before the Consecration

The opening prayer of the Canon is a humble supplication to our most merciful Father (*Te igitur clementissime Pater*) through His Son Jesus Christ, our Lord, that He would receive and bless our offerings. The conjunction, *igitur*, is not easily explained. It may have been placed here in order to express the intimate connexion of the prayer of consecration with the hymn of praise which we have sung in the Preface and *Sanctus*; it may be here merely for the sake of emphasis.

Let us note in the first place that the priest speaks in the plural. Like the Sacrifice of the Cross, the Eucharistic Sacrifice is a universal one. The Mass is the act of the Church, accomplished on behalf of the Church—that is, for the pastors and the sheep and the lambs entrusted to their care. Hence we make explicit mention of the Pope, the universal shepherd, of the diocesan bishop, and finally of all those who profess the Catholic and Apostolic Faith.

Te igitur ... supplices rogamus ac petimus uti accepta habeas et benedicas haec dona, haec munera, haec sancta sacrificia illibata (Wherefore, we humbly pray and beseech Thee that Thou wouldst vouchsafe to accept and bless these gifts, these presents, these holy unspotted sacrifices). It has been suggested that the plural "we" (*rogamus, petimus*) is to be explained by the ancient practice of concelebration. But, as we have shown already, the silent recitation of the Canon is of great antiquity. Hence it is a more natural explanation of the plural, if we see in these prayers an utterance of the priest in his capacity as official mediator in behalf of the people. The faithful pray with the priest, and he treats with God in their behalf. Moreover, the gifts upon the altar have been offered by the people—their gifts and oblations become truly a spotless sacrifice when the priest changes the bread and wine presented by them into the Sacred Flesh and Blood of the Son of God.

The priest's first request is for the peace of the Church, a peace that springs from external security and internal unity and harmony: *quam pacificare, custodire, adunare et regere digneris* (to which vouchsafe to grant peace, as also protect, unite and govern it).

When he has prayed for the Universal Church and her chief Pastor, the priest passes on to the second prayer of the Canon, the *Memento, Domine, famulorum famularumque tuarum* (Be mindful, O Lord, of Thy servants and handmaids). Here the priest mentions the names of those persons for whom he wishes to pray in a special manner. He makes a short pause and pronounces the names silently or only mentally. In this practice we have a survival of the old-time reading of the diptychs—that is, of the lists or catalogues of persons in communion with the Church, or of such as had died in the profession of the Catholic Faith. The names of the living were read from the diptychs before the Consecration, those of the dead after it. The humility, but assured confidence, of the prayer is most remarkable. *Memento!* We only ask for a remembrance by the Lord of infinite mercy, certain that, if He will but think of us and of our friends, all our wants shall most assuredly be satisfied. It is thus we see the Saints pray in the holy Books: *Memento Domine David, et omnis mansuetudinis ejus* (O Lord, remember David and all his meekness).[11] *Memento mei, Deus meus, in bonum* (Remember me, O my God, unto good).[12] On the cross, likewise, the good thief asked but for a remembrance: *Memento mei, Domine, cum veneris in regnum tuum* (Lord, remember me when Thou shalt have come into Thy kingdom).[13]

The priest goes on to pray for those who are now assisting at Mass, who stand or kneel around the altar (*et omnium circumstantium*), and thus take an immediate part in the sacrifice, by reason also of their having supplied the material elements of our oblation. The words *qui tibi offerunt hoc sacrificium, laudis...tibique reddunt vota sua* (who offer up to Thee this sacrifice of praise...and who pay their vows to Thee), must be understood to refer to the offerings in kind made by the faithful at the Offertory. The sublime nature and efficacy of our Sacrifice is beautifully described in the course of the prayer. The Mass is called *sacrificium laudis,* a sacrifice of perfect praise and acknowledgment of God's excellence, one that is endowed with power to save our souls and to procure everlasting security even for the body. The body shares in the salvation and well-being (*incolumitas*) of the soul in its own way, through a glorious immortality.

11 Ps., cxxxi. 1.
12 II Esd., xiii. 31.
13 Luke, xxiii. 42.

The third prayer of the Canon is headed *Infra actionem* (During the Action). This rubric may, at first sight, appear rather purposeless, since the preceding prayers have also been said *infra actionem*. However, it is easy to account for the origin and position of the rubric. The third prayer is the only one of those found in the Canon which, together with the *Hanc igitur* in Easter and Whit-week, admits of a slight change or addition on certain solemnities. These additions or changes are printed in our Missals immediately after the proper Prefaces of these same feasts; thus, the words *Infra actionem* serve simply as a reminder to the priest to revert to this part of the Missal when he reaches the prayer *Communicantes* which he reads in the unchanging part of the book. In course of time the rubric came to be inserted in the Canon itself. The brief addition to the *Communicantes* invariably contains a reference to the mystery celebrated that day. The prayer begins with two participles: *Communicantes et memoriam venerantes* (Communicating with and venerating the memory). Several explanations have been offered, but the easiest and most natural is to interpret the words as if they were in the indicative: *Communicamus et memoriam veneramur* (We communicate and venerate the memory). In justification of this interpretation we may refer to II Mach., i. 6: *Et nunc hic sumus orantes pro vobis* (And now here we are praying for you), the participle here implying insistence or perseverance in prayer.

Our sacrifice is not only beneficial to the children of Holy Church as yet fighting the battles of this life; it likewise procures honor to those who have already reached the goal of everlasting life, inasmuch as in the Mass we magnify the grace of God in them, a grace that came to them from this universal source of all blessings. Moreover, the Saints are able and willing to help us. We are not strangers to them, because the whole Church is the body of Christ, and our common membership in the mystical body of Jesus Christ gives us a claim to the perpetual intercession of the friends of God whose memory we honor upon earth (*quorum meritis precibusque concedas ut in omnibus protectionis tuae muniamur auxilio*).

The *Communicantes* contains an enumeration of twenty-four Saints—or twenty-five, if we include the special mention of the Queen of all Saints. The terms in which the blessed Mother of God is spoken of are noteworthy, for they bear witness to the unique position which Mary holds in the kingdom of grace, and the peculiar veneration which the Church has bestowed upon her from the beginning. *In primis* (first and foremost) in our remembrance comes the glorious and ever virginal Mary, the Mother of God, our Lord Jesus Christ. The very omissions in the Canon testify to its antiquity, quite as much as do the Saints whose names occur in it. Thus, St Joseph's name is not mentioned for the simple reason that his *cultus* is of comparatively recent date. St Teresa may be said to have been th first apostle of popular devotion to the foster-father of our Lord.

After our blessed Lady, memory is made of the Twelve Apostles, St Paul, however, being mentioned in the place of St Matthias. After the names of the Apostles come those of twelve holy martyrs, five of whom are popes, one a bishop, one a deacon, and five laymen. In this list we see a further proof of the venerable antiquity of the prayers of the Canon, because, in the early centuries of the Church, martyrs alone were the objects of a liturgical *cultus*. All these martyrs with the exception of St Cyprian, either lived or suffered in Rome, or at least were buried there, and thus became objects of special veneration on the part of the local Church of Rome. Hence their admission into the Canon. It must be borne in mind that our Mass and Canon is that of the local Church of Rome. Linus, Cletus and Clement were the immediate successors of St Peter. St Xystus, or Sixtus II, was Pope in the middle of the second century. He was preceded by Cornelius in the chair of St Peter, but, because the feast of that holy Pontiff and that of St Cyprian were kept on the same day, they are mentioned together in the Canon. St Chrysogonus was martyred at Aquileia in 304. Sts John and Paul are famous in ecclesiastical history. They were men of great wealth and held important positions at court. When they saw the envy of Julian the Apostate and his hatred for the Christian religion, they made haste to distribute among the poor of the city the treasures which might otherwise have fallen into the hands of a greedy tyrant. Their memory was very dear to the Roman people. In her Liturgy, Holy Church says of them that they are "two olive trees, and two torches burning before the Lord: they have power to cover the sky with clouds and to open its gates, for their tongues have become the keys of heaven."[14] Sts Cosmas and Damian were brothers; they were born in Arabia, and suffered death for Christ at Cilicia in 297. Their relics have been greatly venerated in Rome since the beginning of the sixth century.

The prayer *Hanc igitur* pleads once more for a favorable acceptance of our offering. By the words *servitutis nostrae* (of *our* servitude), we are to understand the priest and his ministers. But the sacrifice is not theirs only, but *cunctae familiae tuae* (of Thy whole family). The clause *diesque nostros in tua pace disponas*, etc. (dispose our days in Thy peace etc.), was added by St Gregory the Great. While reciting this prayer, the priest spreads his hands over the *oblata*. This ceremony dates from the fifteenth century, and became law in the Missal of St Pius v. During the whole week of Easter and Pentecost the prayer is slightly altered by a reference to the recently baptized catechumens. On Maundy Thursday allusion is made to the institution of the Holy Eucharist on that same day.

The fifth prayer, *Quam oblationem,* is held by some commentators to be the equivalent of the famous *epiclesis* of the Greek Liturgy. However, the Holy Ghost is not invoked in it. Our invocation is addressed to God the Father, since we pray that, by accepting our offering, God would make it the Body and Blood of His most dear Son, our Lord Jesus Christ. The five epithets applied to our oblation (*benedictam, adscriptam, ratam, rationabilem, acceptabilemque*) are not easy to explain. They may be thus translated: "Do Thou, O God, render this our oblation wholly blessed, legitimate, valid, reasonable and acceptable." The Mass is an authentic, lawful and valid sacrifice by reason of its being the faithful carrying out of our Lord's injunction to the Apostles, after He had Himself celebrated the first Mass: "Do this in memory of Me." Through the wondrous change which takes place at the moment of the consecration, our offering becomes most truly, *rationalis* (reasonable), since mere bread and wine are changed into the Flesh and Blood of Him in whom are hidden all the treasures of wisdom and knowledge. Perhaps the words are an allusion to the saying of the Apostle: "I beseech you ... that you present your bodies

---

14 *Antiph. ad Magnif.*, 11 Vesp., June 26.

a living sacrifice, holy, pleasing unto God, your reasonable service."[15] If the spiritual sacrifice whereby we give ourselves to God is a "reasonable service," how much more truly such is the sacrifice in which we offer God's own Son as a saving Victim! Such an offering must be acceptable to God, because of the infinite worth and dignity of the Victim which lies, mystically slain, upon our altar, for it is that beloved Son of His in whom the Father is well pleased.

Ut nobis corpus et sanguis fiat dilectissimi Filii tui (that it may become for us the Body and Blood of Thy most beloved Son), these words are calculated to fill our hearts with joyful confidence. *For us*—for our temporal and eternal well-being—God accomplishes the stupendous miracle of the Mass. On Christmas night the Angels bade the shepherds rejoice because "this day is born to you a Saviour."[16] *Nobis datus, nobis natus* (Given for us, born for us), sings St Thomas. *For us* the daily sacrifice is offered; for us, no less than for the glory of the Father, Christ is mystically sacrificed upon ten thousand altars, as long as the world shall endure.

---

15 Rom., xii. 1. 16 Luke, ii. 11.

CHAPTER XVI

THE CONSECRATION

The Climax of the Mass

WE have now reached the climax of the mystery of the Eucharistic Sacrifice. What has gone before has all been by way of preparation. The preliminary prayers recited at the foot of the altar, the song of praise in the *Gloria*, the selected readings from our Holy Books, the public profession of our faith in the *Credo*, have brought our minds and hearts into harmony with the tremendous thing that is about to take place upon the altar. At the Offertory the faithful people have presented the material elements of the sacrifice, and the priest has received and blessed them and offered them for God's acceptance. A solemn hush has fallen upon the assembly. Since the recitation of the *Sanctus* even the priest's voice has remained dumb. He prays in silence, communing alone with God, as did Moses on the summit of Sinai. And indeed, since the Mass and Calvary are substantially one and the human priest does but act and speak in the name and person of the one perfect High Priest, his silent prayer and his loneliness at the altar are verily reminiscent of the awful loneliness of Jesus upon the altar of the cross.

Without doubt the moment of the consecration is the most wonderful of all those instants of fleeting time which make up the history of our world. In those precious moments there takes place something that can only be compared to the creative act of God, when in the beginning, at His bidding, light burst forth from darkness. In virtue of the words of consecration, what is nothing more than bread and wine—perishable elements—is changed into the Body and Blood of the Incarnate Son of God. *Transubstantiation* is the word by which Catholic theology describes this stupendous change. The substance of bread and wine—that is, the ultimate reality which underlies and sustains the sensible qualities by which we know these elements—is changed into something infinitely precious, something infinitely greater than mere food and drink. It would not be right to say that the substance of bread and wine simply ceases to be, or that it is merely replaced by the substance of the Body and Blood of our Lord. Bread does indeed cease to exist as such, but the words of consecration are not destructive; on the contrary, they are productive of a reality greater than the one that existed until now. There is a change, an alteration, call it what you will, by which bread is converted into the living Flesh of the Son of God. The Fathers generally, and St Thomas in particular, when speaking of the words of consecration, say that the priest makes or produces (*conficit*) the Body and Blood of Jesus Christ. In the prayer of Gregory XIII, which is found at the beginning of our Missal, Holy Church desires priests to direct their intention in this wise: *Ego volo celebrare Missam, et conficere corpus et sanguinem Domini nostri Jesu Christi.*

When we pronounce the words of consecration, we do not draw Christ down from heaven. He is seated at the right hand of God the Father, and shall only rise from His throne of glory upon the last day, when all eyes shall behold Him coming in the clouds of heaven. When the priest stands at the altar morning after morning, he accomplishes an even more stupendous thing, for by the exercise of his divinely-given powers he is able so to change bread and wine that these perishable things become the immortal Flesh and Blood of Jesus Christ. Such is the meaning and import of transubstantiation. Only thus can our Lord begin to be really upon our altars without leaving His place in heaven. But let us hear the Angelic Doctor himself: "There are two ways in which a thing can be conceived as beginning to be where it was not before, that is, either by a local movement, or by a substantial change of that where it is said to be now; as fire is in a house in a new manner, either because it has been taken thither from outside, or because it has been produced within. But it is manifest that Christ's Body does not begin to be in the Sacrament by any kind of local movement, for in that case He would be no longer in heaven, since that which is moved by local motion (that is, from one place to another) does not reach its new location until it has left its former one. Moreover, one and the same movement of one and the same thing cannot have different objectives. Yet Christ begins to exist simultaneously in this Sacrament in several places. It follows, therefore, that Christ's body cannot be said to enter upon a new existence in this Sacrament, except by the change of the substance of bread into Himself."[1]

To the uninitiated these words may seem but a bald and obscure statement of the incomprehensible. To the priest and the theologian they are like a revelation, throwing a flood of light upon one of the deepest of the mysteries of divine wisdom and power. We shall not get a vital hold of the dogma of the Real Presence and the living reality of the Eucharistic Sacrifice, until we think in terms of transubstantiation. "Christ's body and blood are truly contained in the Sacrament of the altar, under the *species* of bread and wine, the bread being transubstantiated into His Body and the wine into His Blood."[2]

Holy Church has always stated the mystery of the Real Presence of our Lord in terms of transubstantiation. We cannot lay too much stress on this cardinal point of the Church's teaching. We are the ministers, and the words we utter at Mass are the instrument by means of which the miracle is brought about. "Before the consecration, we confess it sincerely, there is but bread and wine, formed by nature; but after the consecration, there is the Flesh and Blood of Christ, consecrated by our blessing."[3] "The body assumed by our Lord has not come down from heaven, but the bread and wine are changed into the Body and Blood of Christ."[4] The Fathers of Trent quote these words and identify themselves with them, so that they become an authentic and official expression of the mind of the Church.

The Words of Consecration

Let us now ponder the very words of consecration. *Qui pridie quam pateretur accepit panem* (Who the day before He suffered took bread).

[1] *Summa Theol.*, III, Q. lxxv, a. 2.   [2] *Concil. Trid.*, Sess. XIII, c. 4.
[3] St Augustine, cfr. *Concil. Trid., loc. cit.*
[4] St John Damascene, cfr. *Concil. Trid., loc. cit.*

In all Rites, reference is made, in this part of the Canon, to the scene enacted in the Upper Room on the eve of the Passion. The Mass is essentially a memorial of the Passion (*recolitur memoria Passionis ejus*). On Maundy Thursday there is a slight addition to the first clause of the consecration prayer: "Who the day before He suffered for the salvation of us and all men, that is, on this day, took bread" (*Qui pridie quam pro nostra omniumque salute pateretur, id est, hodie ... accepit panem*). The priest does in his own person what he relates of his Master. Whilst reciting these words, he also takes the host, the Eucharistic bread, into his hands. The hands of Jesus are the hands of omnipotence: they are holy and worthy of all reverence (*sanctas ac venerabiles*). Let us priests see to it that our poor mortal hands be at least free from all stain of sin. For that reason were they blessed and anointed with oil in the solemn hour of our ordination. It is a salutary exercise for priests frequently to recall to mind that great moment of our lives when the Bishop prayed over them: *Consecrare et sanctificare digneris, Domine, manus istas, per istam unctionem et nostram benedictionem, ut quaecumque benedixerint, benedicantur, et quaecumque consecraverint, consecrentur, in nomine Domini nostri Jesu Christi* (Deign to consecrate and sanctify, O Lord, these hands, by this unction and our blessing, that whatsoever they shall have blessed, may be blessed, and whatsoever they shall have consecrated, may be consecrated, in the name of our Lord Jesus Christ). Thus did the bishop pray whilst he anointed and consecrated our hands on the first day of our priesthood.

Et elevatis oculis in coelum ad te Deum, Patrem suum omnipotentem (and with eyes lifted up to heaven unto Thee, God, His almighty Father). The Evangelist does not relate that our Lord raised His eyes to heaven in the act of consecration, but the statement here made is based on apostolic tradition. The clause may have been introduced into the form of consecration through a reminiscence of another great scene in our Lord's life (one that is most clearly prophetic of the Eucharist), namely, the multiplication of the loaves. Every one of the Synoptics relates that Christ looked up to heaven before He blessed the bread with which He fed the multitude which had followed Him into the wilderness. We may gather from this insistence upon the fact of our Lord's raising His eyes to heaven that He was wont to do so whenever He blessed bread or any other object. Hence, He would not have omitted this symbolic act at the moment of performing a miracle, of which the multiplication of the loaves, wonderful as it was, was yet no more than the prophetic shadow. *Tibi gratias agens, benedixit, fregit, deditque discipulis suis, dicens: Accipite et manducate ex hoc omnes* (Giving thanks to Thee, blessed, broke and gave it to His disciples, saying: Take and eat ye all of this). Whilst saying *Tibi gratias agens*, the priest bows the head. At the word *benedixit*, he blesses the host by making the sign of the cross over it. Before uttering the actual words of consecration, the celebrant collects himself yet more earnestly. Silence reigns in the sanctuary. Bending low over the altar and holding the spotless bread in both hands, he pronounces the tremendous words by which the King of Glory becomes present upon the altar. These words must be pronounced distinctly, with reverence and in a whisper (*distincte, reverenter et secreto*).[5] The priest utters them, not *historically* (as one who relates an event which happened long ago), but *effectively*; that is, he intends to do that which the words signify, and what Jesus did and meant when, on the eve of His Passion, He officiated in His capacity of priest according to the order of Melchisedech. Father Faber thus describes that first consecration: "The awful words have been spoken: 'This is My body.' It is the first time earth has heard them. If it were not inanimate, it would have rocked to its very foundations, even as the gates of hell are vehemently shaken by the Sacrifice of the Mass. Our Lord stands, cognizable as Mary's Son, and in the dimensions of mature mortal age. On His face is a light of love. He stands there, body, soul and divinity, holding in His hand, with unutterable thrills of joy, His own very body."[6]

As soon as he has pronounced the words of consecration, the priest genuflects, for he is now in the presence of his Lord and his God. Then he raises the Sacred Host for a moment in such wise as to enable the faithful to see and adore It. In like manner he raises the chalice after consecration.

The consecration of the wine follows immediately upon that of the bread, thus completing the essence of our Sacrifice. *Simili modo,*

---

5 *Rit. cel.*, VIII, 5.   6 *The Blessed Sacrament*, IV, iii.

postquam coenatum est (In like manner, after He had supped, *i.e.,* taken supper). Our Lord consecrated the bread during the course of the Last Supper (*coenantibus illis*). The chalice, however, He consecrated at its close (*postquam coenatum est*). *Accipiens et hunc praeclarum calicem in sanctas ac venerabiles manus suas* (Taking also this glorious chalice into His holy and venerable hands). Holy Church identifies our own chalice with the cup which Jesus Christ took into His holy and venerable hands. Since the Mass is substantially one with the unbloody sacrifice of the High Priest according to the order of Melchisedech, our chalice is verily identical with His, and His chalice was assuredly a glorious one (*praeclarum*). The words are likewise an allusion to Psalm xxii. 5: *Calix meus inebrians, quam praeclarus est* (My chalice which inebriateth me, how glorious it is)!

Item tibi gratias agens, benedixit, deditque discipulis suis, dicens: Accipite et bibite ex eo omnes (again giving thanks to Thee, He blessed and gave to His disciples, saying: Take and drink ye all of this). At the words *gratias agens,* the priest bows his head, and, whilst saying *benedixit,* blesses the chalice by tracing the sign of the cross over it. Then, bending over the altar and holding the chalice with both hands, he pronounces the words of consecration *attente, continuate et secreto* (attentively, without a pause and in a whisper).[7] By this injunction of the rubric priests are warned against habits which are all too readily contracted. It is not uncommon to hear priests utter these awful words with a jerky violence in a manner which is painful to themselves and to the witnesses of their over-anxious scrupulosity.

As soon as he has pronounced the words of consecration, the priest replaces the chalice upon the altar, saying at the same time: *Haec quotiescumque faceritis, in mei memoriam facietis* (As often as ye shall do these things, ye shall do them in remembrance of Me). Only then does he genuflect and raise the chalice, with both hands, slowly and reverently; in such a way that the assistants may see it for a moment.[8]

The words *aeterni testamenti* (of the eternal testament) are not found in the sacred text, nor are those others, *mysterium fidei* (the

---

[7] *Rit. cel.,* VIII, 7. [8] *Rit. cel.,* VIII, 7.

mystery of faith). Fortescue suggests that the latter clause may have been an exclamation or acclamation, at first uttered by someone else, which finally became inserted in the very formula of consecration. In some of the Eastern Liturgies the people say *Amen* after each consecration.[9]

Here we may pause a moment and consider the astonishing ease with which one of the most stupendous of God's mighty deeds is brought about. Only a few fleeting words need be whispered by a validly ordained priest, and all at once bread and wine become the Flesh and Blood of the King of heaven and earth. And not only on some rare or special occasions, or in a few privileged places, is this wonderful thing accomplished, but a thousand times a day, upon countless altars, "from the rising of the sun even to the going down" (Mal., i. 11) and as long as the world shall endure. "When a Saint works miracles, first of all he *is* a Saint, and that is to be remembered, for it tells of long years of prayer and conflict and modest secrets of corporal austerity. So, if long fasting and great learning and much toil and vigils of preliminary ceremony were necessary before consecration, it would seem an easy exercise of power, when we consider the stupendous majesty of the work performed. But no! Five little words, and it is done.... But why all this facility? For the same reason as the great motley crowd of priests—for us, for our sakes, for our convenience."[10]

The Elevation

The elevation of the Eucharistic Elements follows immediately upon the consecration. This ceremonial lifting up and solemn showing of the Host and the chalice is very impressive, and, perhaps more than any other of our ritual observances, excites a sense of wonderment in the breast of the outsider whom curiosity, real interest, or some other motive makes a not infrequent witness of our sacred mysteries. It is possible that sometimes even the faithful may attach excessive importance to the ceremony, and come to look upon it as an essential element of the Eucharistic Sacrifice. No doubt the elevation is a very

---

9 *The Mass*, p. 337.
10 Faber, *The Blessed Sacrament*, pp. 77–78.

beautiful and most appropriate rite, since it enables the whole assembly of worshippers to look upon that which is but a thin veil hiding the Lord of glory, like the cloud which hid the triumphant Saviour from the men of Galilee, who followed Him with their eyes as He ascended into the heights of heaven. None the less, the elevation of the Host is of no great antiquity, and that of the chalice is of even later date.

The practice is not of Roman origin, but began North of the Alps at some time in the twelfth century. Many writers and commentators on the liturgy have long maintained that the ceremonial lifting up and display of the Host was introduced as a protest against the heresy of Berengarius, who denied the doctrine of transubstantiation and the real presence of our Lord in the Holy Eucharist. The late Dr Fortescue, summarizing some remarkable articles by Father Thurston in *The Tablet* (London) of October and November, 1907, gives perhaps the truest account of the origin and motive of the institution of the ceremony. The first beginning of the rite may be seen in the rubric which prescribes that the priest lift the Host from the altar table in the act of consecration. In the twelfth century it was customary to raise it as high as the breast whilst the words of consecration were spoken. Then the priest immediately replaced it upon the altar, and at once went on to consecrate the chalice. There was neither elevation nor genuflection. Apparently it sometimes happened that, while the Host was being consecrated, it was held so high that the assistants could see it, so much so that bishops became anxious lest the people should be led to worship it before consecration. For this cause decrees were issued forbidding the raising of the Host in such a way that the faithful could be misled into worshipping the unconsecrated bread.

The first bishop who formally commanded the ceremonial elevation of the Host is Eudes de Sully, who was Archbishop of Paris from 1196 to 1208. The prelate, by his ordinance, decided a very important point of Catholic dogma. There was, at one time, some division of opinion as to the exact moment when the bread was actually changed into the Body of Christ. Some theologians contended that the change only took place after the chalice had likewise been consecrated. It seems strange that there should ever have been even the slightest hesitation in a matter of such importance. The truth on this point of doctrine is easily gathered from the account which the Evangelist gives of the institution of the Holy Eucharist. At the Last Supper the Apostles partook of the consecrated Bread which our Lord declared to be His Body some time before they drank of the cup which contained His Blood, since He only consecrated the wine towards the end or at the close of the repast (*postquam coenatum est*).

The practice of lifting the Host on high in such wise that all might see it, spread steadily and rapidly. The elevation of the chalice followed more slowly. The reason of the difference is easily perceived. At the first elevation we can see the consecrated Element, whereas in the second we only see the vessel that contains it. This solemn elevation was instituted for the express purpose of presenting the Holy Eucharist for the adoration of the assistants, so much so that in the thirteenth *Ordo Romanus* (published under Gregory X about the year 1275) it is formally stated that "at the elevation of the Body of Christ let them prostrate on the ground and reverently worship upon their faces, and let them thus remain prostrate until the *Pater Noster*." The fourteenth *Ordo Romanus* emphasizes this point yet more. In this document, which belongs to the beginning of the fourteenth century, it is prescribed that the priest shall "reverently and carefully elevate on high the Body of our Lord so that it may be adored by the people." This prescription became part of the rubrics of the Roman Missal, as may be proved by comparing our early Missals with the small *Ordo Missae* compiled by the papal Master of Ceremonies, John Burchard. That document belongs to the end of the fifteenth century, and forms the basis of the *Ritus celebrandi* now found at the beginning of our Missals.[11] The genuflection now made by the priest before and after each consecration and elevation did not become general and strictly obligatory until the publication of the Missal of 1570. To this day the Carthusians do not genuflect, but merely bow to the Blessed Sacrament.

In the estimation of the people the elevation, at any rate of the Sacred Host, became an all-important feature of the Mass, particularly so in England. To assist at Mass was spoken of as "seeing God" or

---

11 Cfr. *The Month* (London, December, 1906).

"seeing Jesus." People imagined they had not heard Mass if they had not witnessed the elevation. In his attacks on the Mass, John Becon describes how at that moment a man would jostle his neighbor, in his eagerness to look at the Holy Sacrament, on the plea that "he could not be blithe until he had seen his Lord God that day." Dan Lydgate speaks thus in his *Vertue of the Masse:*

> First every morrow, or Phoebus shine bright,
> Let pale Aurora conduct you and dress
> To holy church, of Christ to have a sight,
> For chief preservation against all ghostly sickness.

Almost immediately upon her accession, Elizabeth took the occasion of this remarkable devotion of our Catholic forefathers to display her unbelief in what was so dear to their hearts. "The Queen being present at the Bishop of Carlisle's Mass on Christmas morning, while the cantors of her chapel were singing the *Gloria in excelsis Deo* at their lectern, sent a message to his lordship within the sanctuary, peremptorily forbidding him to elevate the Host. But Oglethorpe replied that, as it was the unvarying rule of the Catholic Church for all priests to do so, he must ask her Majesty's permission to allow him to conform. Upon this, before the Gospel, she rose from her faldstool, biting her thin lips in anger, stamped vigorously upon the floor, and so hastily departed."[12]

In order to draw the attention of the people yet more forcibly to the lifting up of the consecrated Elements, the custom arose in the late Middle Ages of ringing a small bell called "the sacring bell." Besides this bell, each church possessed a yet larger one, which was rung at the *Sanctus,* and for that reason was popularly called "sance bell." Very often also the big bell in the steeple would be rung at the elevation, so that those who were engaged in their household work or in the labors of the field, might thus know the supreme moment of the Mass. Our *Ritus celebrandi,* VIII, 6, merely says that "the server rings a little bell with his right hand, three times at each elevation or continuously, until the priest replaces the Host upon the altar; the same is done at the elevation of the chalice."

---

12 F.G. Lee, *The Church and Queen Elizabeth,* I, 12.

There is but little uniformity in this matter, various customs obtaining in different countries. In some countries people are very fond of the sound of a bell, and Mass is often accompanied by a vast amount of bell-ringing, apparently at the discretion—or otherwise—of the altar boys. The present writer well remembers one morning when he said Mass in one of the side chapels of the noble cathedral which is the glory of Rouen. The boy who served him took hold of a handbell from the moment he approached the altar and kept ringing it on the least provocation; in fact, he only put it down when he had to present the cruets or change the book. Such abuses should be ruthlessly suppressed. On the other hand, if a church possesses a big bell, it should always be rung at the *Sanctus* and Consecration, at least of the principal Mass. The sound of the Mass bell is welcome to many of our devout people whose duty and toil keep them from church, and cheers many a sufferer lying on his sick-bed. The priest should urge his people to stop work for a few moments and lift their hearts on high, when the bell warns them that the priest is raising the Body and Blood of Jesus Christ towards heaven in order to draw down the blessing of our heavenly Father.

It has long been the custom of our good people to bend their heads and shoulders during the elevation, or to cover their faces with their hands as an aid to and an outward manifestation of their humble and loving worship. More recently the practice has sprung up of looking at the Host. This seems a very commendable custom, seeing that the priest lifts up the consecrated Elements for the very purpose that the faithful may see them. The practice was much encouraged by the act of Pius x, when that great Pontiff, of holy memory, granted an indulgence of seven years and seven quarantines to all who, whilst looking at the Sacred Host, reëcho the cry of faith and love of St Thomas the Apostle: "My Lord and my God!"[13] The more recent practice can be made to harmonize with the older custom. Let the priest exhort his people first to look at the Host and then to bow in lowly adoration.

Some persons, with more eagerness for gaining indulgences than sound liturgical instinct, have asked the Holy See whether the priest

---

13 Decree of the S. Cong. of Indulg., June 12, 1907.

actually celebrating might say the words *Dominus meus et Deus meus*, and thus gain the indulgence. The answer has been in the negative. The mind of Holy Church is that there should be no innovations or alterations in the Canon. For that very reason Rome has always refused to insert the name of St Joseph in the *Confiteor*, or in the prayers of the Canon. The following lines from Dan Lydgate's *Vertue of the Masse*,[14] which he recommended to devout people to say whilst looking at the Sacred Host, are an admirable expression of the sentiments which should fill the hearts of priests and people alike at this solemn moment:

> Hail, holy Jesu, our health, our ghostly food:
> Hail, blessed Lord, here in form of bread:
> Hail, for mankind offered on the rood
> For our redemption with Thy blood made red,
> Stung to the heart with a spear's head.
> Now, gracious Jesu, for Thy wounds five,
> Grant of Thy mercy, before I be dead,
> Clean shrift [*confession*] and housel [*viaticum*] while
>   I am here alone.

The consecrated Elements are lifted on high primarily for the spiritual comfort of the people. But for the priest, also, the ceremony is full of deep significance. The material raising on high of the Body and Blood of the Saviour of the world forcibly recalls to mind the scene enacted on the heights of Calvary, when, suspended between heaven and earth, our Lord offered Himself to His heavenly Father: "And I, if I be lifted up from the earth, will draw all things to Myself."[15] From the cross, Christ calls down the Father's mercy and forgiveness, whilst at the same time He draws us to Himself, thus raising us to an abiding union with Himself.

In a fine passage in one of his earliest works, Msgr Benson gives a vivid description of the unearthly scenes enacted on the altar at the moment of consecration: "Another space and a tingling silence;

---

14 Cfr. J.H. Matthews, *The Mass and its Folklore* (Catholic Truth Society, London), p. 97.

15 John, xii. 32.

the crowds bow down like the corn before the wind. He comes, He comes! On He moves, treading under foot the laws He has made, yet borne up by them as on the Sea of Galilee; He who inhabits eternity at an instant is made present; He who never leaves the Father's side rests on His white linen carpet, held yet unconfined; in the midst of the little gold things, and embroidery and candle flames and lilies, while the fragrance of the herbs rises about Him. There rests the gracious King, before this bending group...; the rest of the pageant dies into silence and nothingness outside the radiant circle of His Presence. There is His immediate priest-herald, who has marked out this halting place for the Prince, bowing before Him, striving by gestures to interpret and fulfill the silence that words must always leave empty; here behind are the adoring human hearts, each looking with closed eyes into the face of the Fairest of the children of men, each crying silently words of adoration, welcome and utter love."[16]

---

16 *By What Authority?* p. 382.

CHAPTER XVII

THE PRAYERS AFTER THE CONSECRATION

Unde et memores.

WE gather from the Gospel account of the institution of the Holy Eucharist, as well as from St Paul's relation of what he had learned from the Lord Himself, that our divine Saviour bade the Apostles do in their turn what they had just seen Him do: "This do in commemoration of Me."[1] For this reason all Liturgies contain some formal affirmation or assurance that we do indeed bear in mind what our Lord accomplished on the eve of His Passion. In the Greek Liturgy this prayer of remembrance bears the name of ἀνάμνησις (remembrance). It is evident that our Eucharistic Sacrifice is primarily a memorial of the Passion and Death of Jesus Christ: "As often as you shall eat this bread and drink the chalice, you shall show the death of the Lord, until He come."[2] The Roman Liturgy has the equivalent of the Greek ἀνάμνησις in the first prayer which follows the consecration: *Unde et memores, Domine, nos servi tui, sed et plebs tua sancta, ejusdem Christi Filii tui Domini nostri tam beatae passionis, nec non et ab inferis resurrectionis, sed et in coelos gloriosae ascensionis* (Wherefore, O Lord, we Thy servants, as also Thy holy people, calling to mind the blessed passion of the same Christ Thy Son, our Lord, and His resurrection from hell and glorious ascension into heaven). The first word of the prayer (*Unde*, wherefore) closely connects it with our Lord's injunction: "Do this in memory of me." By reason of this command we are bold enough to repeat, day by day, *tempore mortalitatis nostrae* (during the time of our mortal life),[3] what He performed in His own person ere

1 I Cor., xi. 24.   2 II Cor., xi, 26.
3 Postcommunion of Maundy Thursday.

He gave His life for us. But for such a formal command, who would dare to stand at the altar and attempt so divine a thing?

The compiler of the *Liber Pontificalis* ascribes to Pope Alexander I (109–119) the ordering of an express mention of the Passion at Mass (*Hic passionem Domini miscuit in precatione sacerdotum, quando missae eelebrantur*). So it came about that some writers have attributed the whole prayer *Unde et memores* to this holy Pontiff. It may have been so. However, the very nature of the Mass makes it a commemoration, a mystical reënactment of the Passion, so there could never have been a time when the Passion was not remembered in the act of sacrifice.

The priest speaks both for himself and for the faithful: "we Thy servants." It is a great thing to be even a servant or slave of God, for, as St Agatha said to Quintianus, the Governor of Sicily, "it is more glorious to serve Christ in all lowliness than to possess the wealth and honor of kings."[4] We are God's servants, ministering on behalf of the people. The people also belong to God, and as such they deserve to be called holy. The Church, by reason of her being the Bride of Christ, is necessarily "a glorious church, not having spot or wrinkle, or any such thing," but is "holy and without blemish."[5] And the Prince of pastors declares that the children of the Church are "a chosen generation, a kingly priesthood, *a holy nation,* a purchased people."[6]

We remember with love and gratitude the *blessed Passion of our Lord* (*beatae passionis*). How bitter that Passion was to Him; how blessed for us! It was the source of all grace and the efficient cause of everlasting happiness. The epithet "blessed" may seem a strange way of describing the consummation of the career of Him who is spoken of as "the man of sorrows and one acquainted with grief." In reality, the only true view of the Passion is to look upon it, not as a defeat or failure, but as a conquest and triumph. Our Lord on the cross is not defeated, He triumphs; the cross is a sacrificial altar and a kingly throne. For that reason our Christian forefathers in the ages of faith have frequently represented our Lord on the cross as a king crowned, not with a crown of thorns, but with a royal diadem. The insistence upon the physical side of the Passion is comparatively modern, and

---

[4] *Brev. Rom.*, 5 Febr., Noct. II.   [5] Eph., v. 27.
[6] 1 Pet., ii. 9.

harmonizes with modern refinement of sentiment—not to say, modern sentimentality. The early Christian writers, assuredly, were not less tender-hearted than we are. Their souls were full of sympathy with the suffering Redeemer, but they never lost sight of the essential triumph of Calvary. In what noble terms does not St Leo the Great speak of the Passion? "What is there," he asks, "among all the works of God which so wears out the intentness of human admiration, that so delights and overcomes the mind as the contemplation of the Passion of our Saviour? The Lord submitted to that which of a set purpose He had Himself chosen. He permitted the hands of criminal men to vent their fury upon Him; yet these very hands, whilst becoming stained with their own crime, ministered to the Redeemer."[7] Our Lord's personal attitude towards the Passion is described in His own words: "I have a baptism wherewith I am to be baptized: and how am I straitened until it be accomplished?"[8]

Besides the Passion, memory is likewise made of its triumphant sequel in the Resurrection and glorious Ascension.

Offerimus praeclarae Majestati tuae, de tuis donis, ac datis, hostiam puram, hostiam sanctam, hostiam immaculatam: Panem sanctum vitae aeternae et calicem salutis perpetuae (We offer unto Thy glorious Majesty of Thy gifts and grants a pure Host, a holy Host, an immaculate Host, the holy Bread of eternal life and the chalice of everlasting salvation). Sacrifice and oblation are reciprocal terms. By the very act in which the Victim is sacrificed, it is likewise offered. But we cannot express in one phrase all that is suggested to our minds by these concepts of sacrifice and oblation, so that what in itself is accomplished in a moment, is apparently spread out through a number of prayers and ceremonies. The Mass is our Lord's sacrifice, but also very really that of the Church. The Victim upon the altar is indeed pure, holy, and spotless, since it is the Flesh and Blood of the Lamb of God. Again that which we are permitted to offer upon the altar has first been given to us by God (*Nobis datus, nobis natus*). *De tuis donis ac datis* (Of Thy gifts and grants), may be traced back to I Par., xxix. 14: "All things are Thine: and we have given Thee what we have received of Thy

---

[7] II Noct., Palm Sunday.   [8] Luke, xii. 50.

hand." We need not be disturbed by the five signs of the cross which accompany the concluding clauses of the prayer. They are real blessings, called forth by the words, and are made, as it were, in sympathy with their meaning. We must always bear in mind that, essentially, the prayer of consecration is one. The climax is reached at the moment of consecration—at that moment Christ becomes truly present, and rests upon the altar, and the divine Victim is mystically slain. The whole Eucharistic prayer asks of God to work the tremendous change by which bread and wine become the Flesh and Blood of His divine Son. The Greek Church formally asks the Holy Ghost in a solemn invocation (*epiclesis*) to come down from heaven and operate this change. God is above all space and time, whereas they constitute the necessary framework of all our thinking and doing. So we may rightly persist in asking even though we have already been answered, because the grace is granted and the sacrifice effected in view of the whole prayer. The change wrought at the consecration is instantaneous; Holy Church asks for it during the whole of the prayer of the Canon, which necessarily takes time. Thus we must understand the words *hostiam puram,* etc., as we understand those of the Offertory when we call the unconsecrated host *immaculatam hostiam* (spotless host), and again *sacrificium tuo sancto nomini praeparatum* (sacrifice prepared for Thy holy name). In this last instance there is a dramatic *anticipation,* in the former a *retrospect,* emphasizing the essential oneness of the whole act. We have been heard by God, but we still persevere in our request; God has not waited until our prayer be complete. However, His antecedent goodness, which makes Him, as it were, impatient of delay, is no reason why we should not faithfully carry out to the full the prayer and rites which are our share in this truly *admirabile commercium*. We shall readily take this view of a rather difficult prayer, if we consider for a moment the prayers and supplications which Holy Church puts into our mouth during Advent. All through that period the Church sighs and prays for the Saviour in the words used by the patriarchs and prophets of old. *Rorate coeli desuper et nubes pluant justum* (Send down dew, ye heavens, from above, and let the clouds rain on the just), she cries out, although her Lord has been with her those two thousand years! The devout and learned

Dom Guéranger says that these prayers of Holy Church, though subsequent to the wondrous divine event, hastened its realization in time. We are now sending up to heaven prayers which were answered these many centuries ago, but they exercised a positive influence upon the choice of the moment when God sent His Son into the world, and hastened "the fullness of time."

Panem sanctum vitae aeternae et calicem salutis perpetuae (the holy Bread of eternal life and the chalice of everlasting salvation): Jesus Christ is the true bread of life (*Ego sum panis vitae*),[9] and in very deed the Holy One of God, embodying and showing forth in His Humanity the uncreated holiness of God, and sanctifying all those who come in contact with His Flesh in this ineffable mystery of divine and human sanctity. The chalice upon the altar contains that Blood which is shed for the remission of the sins of many. The effect of the outpouring of the Blood of the Lamb of God cannot be merely negative; neither is the justification of the sinner a negative thing; sins are blotted out, and souls are washed in that precious Blood, and made holy precisely because they are dyed with the hues of that crimson flood: "Blessed are they that wash their robes in the Blood of the Lamb: that they may have a right to the tree of life, and may enter in by the gates into the city."[10]

Supra quae propitio

What has been said of the first prayer, applies with equal force to the second, in which we ask that God would look down upon this altar, and the gifts that are upon it, with a favorable and serene countenance (*Supra quae propitio ac sereno vultu respicere digneris*). Assuredly God cannot but look with favor upon our sacrifice, since it is the Flesh and Blood of His beloved Son, in whom He is well pleased. Our prayer, then, is that the Father would accept this holy Sacrifice *as offered by us*, who need His mercy and kindness. In order to make our sacrifice acceptable, we remind God of those other sacrifices which He was pleased to receive, which were typical of this perfect oblation: *et acep-*

---

9 John, vi. 35.   10 Apoc., xxii. 14.

ta habere, sicuti accepta habere dignatus es munera pueri tui justi Abel, et sacrificium Patriarchae nostri Abrahae, et quod tibi obtulit summus sacerdos tuus Melchisedech, sanctum sacrificium, immaculatam hostiam (and accept them, as Thou wert graciously pleased to accept the gifts of Thy just servant Abel, and the sacrifice of our Patriarch Abraham, and that which Thy high-priest Melchisedech offered to Thee, a holy sacrifice, an immaculate host). In these sublime phrases our minds are taken back into the earliest dawn of human history. "Abel by faith offered to God a sacrifice, by which he obtained a testimony that he was just."[11] Abraham is called our father, inasmuch as his faith made him the spiritual head of the vast family of believers. *Pater fidei nostrae, Abraham summus* (Father of our faith, the most distinguished Abraham), is the title Holy Church gives to this most venerable personage, who in his day was the friend and *confidant* of God, so that the Lord said: "Can I hide from Abraham what I am about to do?"[12] At the bidding of God he was prepared to slay his only son, whom he knew to be the heir of the divine promises, "accounting that God is able to raise up even from the dead."[13] The sacrifice of Abraham, though not carried so far as the actual shedding of blood, was accepted by God. It is a perfect figure of our sacrifice, wherein the Victim is not physically slain, because the risen Christ is now beyond the reach of suffering and death.

Melchisedech is the most mysterious figure in the whole of the Old Testament: we know only two things about him, namely, that he was a king and a priest of the most high God. As such, he is the real type or figure of our kingly High Priest. In the Bible he is described as "the priest of the most high God";[14] here he is styled "Thy high priest." The title is bestowed by Holy Church because, in her mind, the personality of the King of Salem is merged in that of Him who is the one High Priest, whom that other did but foreshadow in those far-off ages. In the words of the great Leo: "He [Christ] it is, whose person Melchisedech the high priest (*pontifex*) signified, in that he did not offer to God a sacrifice of Jewish victims, but the elements of that mystery which our Redeemer consecrated in His Flesh and Blood." These and other like sayings of the great Pope of the fifth century

11 Heb., xi. 4,   12 Gen., xviii. 17.
13 Heb., xi. 19.   14 Gen., xiv. 18.

may have been the reason why the prayer itself and its insertion in the Canon have been attributed to him. However, other Liturgies have similar expressions, and the symbolism of Melchisedech is an obvious one. In the Liturgy of the Maronites, allusion is made to yet other Biblical personages and their offerings: "O God, who didst accept the sacrifice of Abel in the field, of Noe in the ark, of Abraham on the mountain-top, of David on the threshing floor, of Ornan the Jebusite, of Elias on Mount Carmel, and that of the widow's mite in the treasury, do Thou, O Lord God accept these offerings which are presented to Thee by my weak and sinful hands."

The mention of three of the outstanding figures of the Old Law serves to show forth the essential oneness of the Old and New Testament. The Old Law was the reign of shadows; we enjoy the blessed reality. But, already in that dim and distant age, divine wisdom (was at work preparing mankind for the glorious inheritance which has fallen to our lot. Here we may appropriately apply the well-known saying of St Augustine: *Novum testamentum in vetere latet; vetus in novo patet* (The New Testament lies concealed in the Old; the Old lies revealed in the New).[15] Through the Mass we, "upon whom have come the ends of the world," are made heirs of all preceding ages. We are at one with all the Saints and Patriarchs of old, and yet far more blessed than they, for "all these died not having received the promises, but beholding them afar off, and saluting them." Abel, Abraham, Melchisedech, though approved by God by reason of their faith, "received not the promise [the realization of the promise]; God providing some better thing for us, that they should not be perfected without us."[16]

The concluding words of our prayer (*sanctum sacrificium, immaculatam hostiam*) refer directly to the sacrifice of bread and wine offered by Melchisedech. However, inasmuch as the prayer practically identifies the King of Salem and our Lord, the words apply to the offering upon our altar, which is the sacrifice of Christ officiating (in the person of His ministers) in His capacity as "priest for ever, according to the order of Melchisedech."[17]

---

15 In Exod., lxxiii.

16 Heb., xi. 39, 40.

17 Ps. cix. 4.

Supplices te rogamus

The third prayer after the consecration is of very great beauty, but it is also extremely difficult to explain. Perhaps this is the prayer which St Gregory had in mind, when he wrote thus in the third book of his *Dialogues:* "Let us think what manner of sacrifice this is which continuously reproduces the Passion of the only-begotten Son for the remission of our sins. For who among the faithful can entertain a doubt that, in the very hour of immolation, at the call of the priest the heavens are opened, the choirs of the Angels are present at this mystery of Jesus Christ, that which is lowest is mingled with what is highest, earth is joined to heaven and the visible and invisible world are merged into but one whole" (*Pensemus quale sit pro nobis hoc sacrificium, quod pro absolutione nostra passionem unigeniti Filii semper imitatur. Quis enim fidelium habere dubium possit in ipsa immolationis hora, ad sacerdotis vocem, coelos aperiri, in illo Jesu Christi mysterio Angelorum choros adesse, summis ima sociari, terrena coelestibus jungi, unum quoque ex visibilibus atque invisibilibus fieri*).[18]

Supplices te rogamus...: "We humbly beseech Thee, Almighty God, to command that these things be borne, by the hands of Thy holy Angel, to Thine altar on high, in the sight of Thy divine Majesty, that as many of us as at this altar shall partake of, and receive, the most holy Body and Blood of Thy Son, may be filled with every heavenly blessing and grace."

Many writers see in this prayer the Roman equivalent of the Greek *epiclesis* (ἐπίκλησις)—that is, a petition to the Holy Ghost that He would change the bread and wine into the Body and Blood of Jesus Christ, even as once, by His overshadowing, He formed and fashioned this same Sacred Humanity out of the most pure substance of the Virgin Mother. Duchesne remarks that our prayer has not the definiteness of the Greek *epiclesis;* none the less it occupies the same place in the sacred rite. Moreover, it is an invocation to God to intervene in the mystery; but, whereas the Eastern Liturgy speaks clearly and precisely, the Latin has recourse to symbolism. It asks that an Angel should carry our offering to the high altar of God in heaven.

---

18 lviii, *sub. init.*

THE PRAYERS AFTER THE CONSECRATION

The Greek Liturgy prays the Holy Ghost to come down upon our offering. Our *Supplices* asks that what is placed upon the altar may be borne up into heaven; but in both cases contact is demanded between God and our offering, that so it may become the Body and Blood of the Son of God.

We need not be troubled by the position of our prayer, for the difficulty is only an apparent one. As we have said repeatedly, we must look upon the whole Canon as forming but one prayer—the consecration prayer. "God," says Fortescue, "answers that one prayer by changing the bread and wine into the Body and Blood of our Lord, and, no doubt, He does so, according to our ideas of time, before the whole prayer has been spoken. Our Baptism service is the obvious parallel case. All through it we ask God to give the child the graces which, as a matter of fact, He gives at once, at the moment when the essential matter and form are complete. So the ordination rite dramatically separates the elements of the priesthood (power of sacrificing, of forgiving sins), which presumably are really conferred at one moment, when the man becomes a priest. In all such cases we say that, at whatever moment of our time God gives the sacramental grace, He gives it in answer to the whole prayer or group of prayers, which of course take time to say."[19]

Supplices te rogamus (literally, "as suppliants we beseech Thee"). In order that he may show his humility even outwardly, the rubric prescribes that the priest should bend low, with hands joined and resting upon the edge of the altar table. Our humble supplication is to an Almighty God (*omnipotens Deus*). *Jube haec perferri* (Command these things to be carried)—*haec* (these things) corresponds to the *Supra quae* (Upon which) of the preceding prayer, and designates the ineffable gifts that Holy Church offers now in the sight of God, namely the spotless Flesh and Blood of His own divine Son.

Per manus sancti Angeli tui (by the hands of Thy holy angel). Who is this Angel? Some have thought he was our Lord Himself, of whom Holy Church sings thus in the Introit of the third Mass of Christmas Day: *vocabitur nomen ejus, magni consilii Angelus* (His name shall be

---

19 *The Mass*, p. 353.

called the Angel of great counsel). Others again see in this Angel the person of the Holy Ghost, who has been called down in the *epiclesis*.

A third interpretation sees in the Angel the prince of the heavenly hosts, St Michael, once the protector of the people of Israel and now the guardian of God's Church on earth. However, it seems more natural to take the phrase as being a petition to God that He would accept our sacrifice through the ministry of the Angels in general. This view appears to us to be the correct one, and our opinion is based on a reading of the prayer which is found in that priceless book, *De sacramentis,* which has long been, and still is, attributed to St Ambrose. There we find the original text of our three prayers after the consecration, which were then merged in one: "After the consecration the priest says: *Ergo memores ... et petimus et precamur ut hanc oblationem suscipias in sublimi altari tuo per manus angelorum tuorum*" (Wherefore, mindful we beseech and pray that Thou wilt accept this oblation on Thine altar on high through the hands of Thy angels).[20]

From the earliest times Holy Church has believed in the presence of the Angels during the celebration of the divine Liturgy. Already in the second century Tertullian asserts that it is irreverent to sit down during divine service: *sub conspectu Dei vivi, angelo adhuc orationis adstante* (in the sight of the living God, while the angel of prayer is still present),[21] a phrase that suggests a belief in the ministry of an Angel specially detailed to assist at the prayers of the Church. St Thomas[22] also says that in our prayer the priest asks that *orationes sacerdotis et populi angelus assistens divinis mysteriis Deo repraesentet, secundum illud:* "*Ascendit fumus incensorum de oblationibus sanctorum de manu angeli*"—"the angel assisting at the divine mysteries will present to God the prayers of the priest and people, in accordance with the saying: 'The smoke of the incense of the prayers of the saints ascended from the hand of the angel.'"[23] St John Chrysostom, in his book on the priesthood, speaks with glowing enthusiasm on this same subject: "Then [during the sacrifice of the Mass] do the Angels assist the priest,

20 *De sacram.,* IV, 6.
21 *De orat.,* xvi.
22 III, Q. lxxxiii, a. 4.
23 Apoc., viii. 4.

and all the orders of the heavenly powers cry out with one voice, and the whole place round the altar, where the Lord is laid, is filled with their presence.... I have heard of a certain wonderful old man, one who was accustomed to receive revelations, that he was favored with the following vision: He beheld all of a sudden a multitude of Angels, arrayed in shining robes, standing round the altar, with their heads bowed, as one might see a band of soldiers surrounding their King."[24]

In sublime altare tuum, in conspectu divinae majestatis tuae (to Thy altar on high; in the sight of Thy divine Majesty). There can be no question of a physical taking up to heaven of the consecrated Elements, nor is there a material altar set up before the Majesty of God on high. Holy Church makes use of terms which are manifestly symbolical and must be symbolically interpreted. The prayer alludes to the scene described in the eighth chapter of the Apocalypse: "And another Angel came and stood before the altar, having a golden censer; and there was given to him much incense, that he should offer of the prayers of all the Saints upon the golden altar, which is before the throne of God. And the smoke of the incense of the prayers of the Saints ascended up before God from the hand of the Angel."[25] In the Apocalypse, ix. 13, there is yet another mention of "the golden altar, which is before the eyes of God."

The purpose of the prayer is, therefore, that the Body and Blood of Jesus Christ, as they are *our sacrifice*, may be united to and offered with that eternal oblation of Himself by which Jesus Christ ratifies for ever the *actual* oblation of Himself which took place but once upon the altar of the cross. The golden altar in heaven is but one more symbolism by which the inspired writer describes the office of Mediator which our merciful Saviour discharges in our behalf. "By faith we draw nigh to that altar, which is likewise a priest and a sacrifice (*Per fidem venitur ad aram quae et sacerdos et sacrificium est*). For all these things are found in Christ: for He is the heavenly altar of the Father... dost thou imagine there is any other altar at which Christ officiates, than His body, by which and on which the prayers and the

---

[24] *De sacerdotio*, VI, 4.
[25] Apoc., viii. 3, 4.

devotion of the faithful are offered up to God the Father?"[26]

This symbolism of the heavenly altar is very definitely adopted by Holy Church in the rite of ordination of a subdeacon. It is true, the words addressed by the Bishop to the candidate do not date back beyond the Middle Ages, but they do not for that reason lose their interest and importance: "The altar of Holy Church is Christ Himself, according as St John bears testimony, when he relates in his Apocalypse how he saw a golden altar, standing before the throne, on which and by which the offerings of the faithful are consecrated to God. The cloths and coverings of this altar are the members of Christ, that is, those who believe in God, who surrounded the Lord like precious vestures."

In the mind of the Church, our earthly altar is a symbol of the heavenly altar. But "the golden altar, that is set up before God," is our Lord Himself. So it becomes abundantly clear that the *Supplices* is a prayer to God, asking Him to accept our sacrifice with the same benevolence with which He accepts the eternal sacrifice of Christ, who, because "He continueth for ever, hath an everlasting priesthood, whereby He is able also to save for ever them that come to God by Him: *always living to make intercession for us.*"[27]

Ut quotquot, ex hac altaris participatione, sacrosanctum Filii tui Corpus et Sanguinem sumpserimus, omni benedictione caelesti et gratia repleamur (that as many of us as, by this participation at the altar, shall receive the most sacred Body and Blood of Thy Son, may be filled with every heavenly blessing and grace). Here we ask for the full supernatural benefit of our sacrifice, of which we are made partakers when we eat the Flesh and drink the Blood of the Son of God.

At the words *ex hac altaris* (at the altar), the priest kisses the altar, as an outward mark of reverence for the holy table on which lies, mystically slain, the Lamb of God "which was slain from the beginning of the world."[28] This kiss is in very truth an act of homage and adoration to Christ Himself, the altar being the symbol of the Lord of glory. "The altar is of stone," says a Greek writer, "because it represents Christ, who is called a rock and a cornerstone, and because

26 Hugh of Langres, eleventh century.
27 Heb., vii. 24, 25.   28 Apoc., xiii. 8.

the rock from which water flowed for the refreshment of the people of Israel was an image of Him."

At the words *Corpus et Sanguinem* (Body and Blood), the priest makes the sign of the cross over the Host and the chalice, and over himself whilst saying *omni benedictione* (every blessing). These signs of the cross, or blessings, are the natural and spontaneous tokens of the favors which we hope to receive at the moment of partaking of the immortal Flesh and Blood of Jesus Christ, who died for us upon the cross in order that we might live for ever.

The prayer is addressed directly to God the Father, but since mention has been made of His only Son, the conclusion is *Per eumdem Christum Dominum nostrum* (Through the same Christ our Lord). All our graces originate in Christ, "of whose fulness we have all received, grace upon grace."[29] Our Eucharistic Sacrifice is acceptable to God, because it is offered, through the hands of Angels, upon the golden altar of heaven—that is, our Lord intervenes in the Church's sacrifice in such wise that, whenever and wherever the holy Mass is offered, He once more exhibits before the Father that act of submission to the divine will which caused Him to immolate Himself upon Calvary.

What a lofty idea of the greatness of our sacrifice we may derive from a devout consideration of this beautiful prayer! It takes us out of ourselves, and lifts our minds and hearts into the heights of heaven. It points out how this identification with and intervention in the Mass, is the chief function of Christ's office as Mediator—an office which He never renounces: "There is one God, and one mediator of God and men, the man Christ Jesus."[30] May we always say the *Supplices* with that interior fervor and humility which is betokened by our exterior attitude! As we go on celebrating day by day and year by year, the danger is that familiarity may lead to thoughtlessness. We should make unto ourselves certain rallying points, as it were, where we collect our wandering thoughts and renew our faith. Surely the *Supplices* is one such phase of the Mass. It will cost but a small effort to recollect ourselves whilst reciting these wonderful words, and it

---

29 John, i. 16.   30 1 Tim., ii. 5,

may come to pass that not unfrequently we shall experience that holy fear and awe which is a necessary disposition in those who draw nigh unto the altar of the Lord: *Pavete ad sanctuarium meum* (Reverence My sanctuary).[31]

---

31 Lev., xxvi, 2.

CHAPTER XVIII

THE MEMENTO OF THE DEAD

THE prayer for the dead comes as a natural sequel to the *Supplices*, in which we have asked that all we who partake of the Victim offered upon the altar, may be filled with heavenly graces and blessings. Now we beseech our Lord to be likewise mindful of those children of Holy Church who have entered into that mysterious land where souls pay the debt they owe to divine justice. They cannot help themselves, but look to us for succor. The Holy Sacrifice has efficacy enough to make good whatever obligations they may have incurred, since it is an oblation of infinite value, rendering to God both the homage due to His Majesty and satisfaction for the sins by which they have offended Him.

Prayer for the dead has always been practised and recommended by Holy Church. We have the assurance of an inspired writer that "it is a holy and wholesome thought to pray for the dead, that they may be loosed from their sins."[1] From the earliest centuries prayers for the dead were offered during the Eucharistic Sacrifice. The *Memento* of the dead is obviously connected with that of the living. Originally, the one followed immediately upon the other. It was the *Oratio super diptycha* (Prayer over the Diptychs, or Lists of the Living and the Deceased), which was recited after the names both of the living and the dead had been read from the lists prepared beforehand. According to St John Chrysostom, the practice is of apostolic institution: "Not in vain did the Apostles decree that during the awful mysteries a commemoration should be made of the departed."[2] Everyone knows the touching request of St Monica: "Lay," she said, "this body anywhere;

---

[1] II Macch., xii. 46.   [2] *Homil. lxix.*

let not the care for that in any way disquiet you: this only I request, that you would remember me at the Lord's altar, wherever you be."[3] And again, when speaking of the burial of his holy mother, the African Doctor says: "And behold, the corpse was carried to the burial; we went, and returned, without tears. For neither in those prayers which we poured forth unto Thee, *when the Sacrifice of our ransom was offered for her,* when now the corpse was by the grave's side, as the manner there is, did I weep...."[4]

In his book *De cura pro mortuis gerenda*, St Augustine bears testimony to the universal practice of the Church of making a remembrance of the departed during the prayers which the priest recites at the altar. And again, in his thirty-second sermon, he says: "The whole Church observes the tradition of the Fathers, according to which prayers are offered for those who have died in the communion of the Body and Blood of Christ, at the moment when their names are commemorated during the sacrifice, and the sacrifice itself is offered in their behalf."

The text of our prayer is impressive in the highest degree. It is redolent of the spirit of the early Christians, whose idea of death and belief in immortality is given so beautiful an expression in the inscriptions found on the walls of the Roman Catacombs. To the Christian death is but a sleep. The body is laid aside for a while: its resting-place is a dormitory (*caemeterium*), where it slumbers during the brief night of time. On the morning of the world's last day all these sleepers shall suddenly be roused by the mighty sound of the Angel's trumpet: "In a moment, in the twinkling of an eye, at the last trumpet: for the trumpet shall sound, and the dead shall rise again incorruptible."[5]

Memento etiam, Domine, famulorum famularumque tuarum qui nos praecesserunt cum signo fidei, et dormiunt in somno pacis (Be mindful, O Lord, of Thy servants and handmaids who are gone before us with the sign of faith and rest in the sleep of peace).

The words *cum signo fidei* (with the sign of faith) restrict the priest's prayer to those who have departed this life in communion with the Catholic Church. However, the charity of the universal Mother of souls cannot but extend itself to all those who rest in Christ, even

---

3 St Augustine, *Confess.*, IX, 11.   4 *Confess.*, IX, 12.
5 1 Cor., XV. 52.

though, in life, they may not have been in visible communion with her. When the priest stands at the altar, he is the representative of the Church, speaking and acting in her name. But, for all that, he does not cease to be a private person, and as such he may include in his prayer even those for whom the Church does not pray officially and publicly. We have no means of knowing who they are who need our suffrages, hence, according to the custom which has obtained from the beginning, we pray for all the departed. "Our suffrages," says St Augustine, "are not beneficial to all those for whom they are offered, but only to such as have taken care, during their lifetime, that they should be so. But, since we have no means of knowing who these may be, it is necessary that suffrages should be made for all who are born again, so that none be neglected who could or should be made partakers of these benefits. For it is better that suffrages should be superfluous to those whom they can neither help nor hurt, than that they should be wanting to those to whom they may be profitable." And again: "Supplications for the spirits of the dead must not be omitted. The Church has indeed undertaken to offer these for all who died whilst sharing in our Christian and Catholic fellowship. But, because their names are not known, she includes them in a general remembrance. Thus, even though some of the departed should be lacking parents or children, relatives or friends, who ought to make these suffrages, they are yet offered by the charity of the common Mother of all...."[6]

Officially, therefore, the priest may pray or offer the holy Sacrifice only for those who departed this life in full membership of the Church. As a private person, however, he may mention the names of any of his friends, whether they were in visible communion with the Church or not. It is, as a matter of fact, our bounden duty not to exclude anyone from our personal, private supplications, though it would not be lawful to mention, at the altar, the name of one who has been under a sentence of excommunication and has died unrepentant or unabsolved.

We do not know and cannot penetrate into the secret dealings of God with the souls of men. Hence, both prudence and charity

---

6 St Augustine, *De cura pro mortuis gerenda;* cfr. II Noct., Office of the Dead, Nov. 2.

demand that we should pray in general for all the departed. Holy Church makes us do this in the concluding paragraph of the *Memento of the dead*: "To these, O Lord, and to all that rest in Christ, grant, we beseech Thee, a place of refreshment, light and peace" (*in Christo quiescentibus, locum refrigerii, lucis et pacis*). There is a fragrance of the Scriptures and Christian antiquity in the words. Death is only a sleep, for did not the Author of life bid the parents of the young maiden dry their tears, saying: "Weep not; the maiden is not dead, but sleepeth?"[7] Death is not extinction; the body is laid aside for a while, waiting for the day when "those that sleep in the dust of the earth shall awake: some unto life everlasting, and others unto reproach, to see it always."[8]

The place of refreshment, light and peace is, properly speaking, Heaven alone. Yet even Purgatory may be thus described, inasmuch as the time of strife is now over. The Holy Souls are no longer in danger of eternal loss. They are in light, because they know with absolute certainty that they are the friends of God. Moreover, by reason of their perfect conformity to His will, they await, with ineffable longing yet with a holy calm, the hour when they shall at long last enter into the joy of their Lord. Our prayer is inspired by what we might well call the ninth beatitude, as thus proclaimed in the book of St John's Revelation: "And I heard a voice from heaven, saying to me: Write: Blessed are the dead, who die in the Lord. From henceforth now, saith the Spirit, that they may rest from their labors: for their works follow them."[9] That they may rest! What music there is in those words for all who labor and toil and grow weary in the struggle! Let us not grow faint, for soon we shall be at rest. "Eternal rest is the rest of the Eternal; as eternal life is the life of the Eternal. It is the repose of the divine activity; the sleep of infinite energizing; the stillness of the All-mover.... As eternal life, so also eternal rest enters into the Saints, even here on earth, with every new access of sanctifying grace. In the midst of all their struggles and labors for their own souls and the souls of others, their heart sleeps like a tranquil lake. While others rise before dawn after a brief slumber, and

[7] Luke, viii. 52. [8] Daniel, xii. 2.
[9] Apoc., xiv. 13.

hurry fretfully through joyless days to restless nights, He giveth His beloved sleep."[10]

The adorable Sacrifice is offered up for the living and the dead. It is by itself the most efficacious intercession on behalf of the Holy Souls, since it is not so much we who plead and pray, as Christ who mystically sacrifices Himself and so presents to God atonement and reparation far exceeding that which may be owing to divine justice. The expiatory efficacy of the Mass is absolutely infinite. In our daily Mass power is given to us to empty Purgatory and to open the gates of the heavenly mansions.

In the *Life* of St Teresa, written by herself, we are told again and again how she beheld the souls of her daughters and those of others rising from the ground and going up to heaven during the time the holy Sacrifice was being offered: "I was once in one of the colleges of the Society... the night before one of the brothers of that house had died in it; and I, as well as I could, was commending his soul to God, and hearing the Mass which another Father of that Society was saying for him, when I became recollected at once, and saw him go up to heaven in great glory, and our Lord with him."[11]

St Gregory declares that the oblation of the Sacred Victim is wont to help the souls of the departed, so that they themselves not unfrequently ask for it. To prove this, he relates the experience of a certain priest who served a church in a place called Tauriana, where there were hot springs. One day, as this priest entered the baths for the sake of his health, he found there a man unknown to him, ready to minister to his wants. The stranger took off the priest's shoes, received his clothes, and, as he came out of the vapor bath, handed him towels, and, in a word, assisted him in every way. After he had been the object of these attentions for a considerable time, the priest bethought himself how he could best reward the man. So he presented him with two loaves which had been offered at the altar. But the man sadly replied: "Why dost thou offer me these things, Father? This bread is sacred, I may not eat it. I, whom thou seest here, was at one time the owner of this establishment, and for my sins I was sent hither

---

10 Tyrell, *Nova et Vetera*, p. 360.   11 *Life*, xxxviii, 39.

after my death. However, if thou art minded to help me, offer this bread to Almighty God in expiation of my sins. Thou shalt know that thou hast been heard, when, on coming to take the waters, thou shalt no longer find me here." Whereupon he vanished, so that it became manifest that he was no living man, but a spirit. The priest prayed with tears for a whole week and daily offered the Holy Sacrifice for that soul. When he next returned to the baths, he no longer found the man who had waited on him. This fact shows how beneficial to the souls of the departed is the immolation of the Sacred Victim, since the dead themselves demand it from the living, and indicate by what signs they may know that their souls have been set free.[12]

The *Memento* is addressed to God the Father, but concludes with an express mention of the Son, "in whom we have boldness and access with confidence by the faith of Him."[13] Whilst saying *Per eumdem* etc., the priest folds his hands and makes a moderate inclination of the head. It is difficult to assign a reason for this inclination. Perhaps the best explanation is to be found in an association of ideas, for we have been praying for the departed: their death reminds us of our Lord's own death upon the cross when, "bowing His head, He gave up the ghost" (*inclinato capite, tradidit spiritum*).[14]

---

12 Cfr. *Dialog.*, IV, 4.
13 Eph., iii. 12.
14 John, xix. 30.

CHAPTER XIX

NOBIS QUOQUE PECCATORIBUS

IN the *Memento* of the living, the priest has discharged his obligation of praying for the Church militant in general and for those who have asked him to offer the Holy Sacrifice, or who assist at it. In the *Memento* of the departed, he has implored God's compassion on behalf of those who are detained in Purgatory, the prison-house of eternal justice, whence there is no escape until full payment has been made, even to the last farthing.[1] Now he offers supplication to God on his own behalf and on behalf of the ministers of the altar. The *Nobis quoque* (And to us) is thus a natural sequel to the prayers for the departed. The first three words are said aloud, in order to draw the attention of the sacred ministers.

The first condition of efficacious prayer is that it be humble. Humility is the acknowledgment of what we are in the sight of God; in other words, humility is truth. God is the God of truth; hence, his love of humility and hatred of pride. "God resisteth the proud, but to the humble He giveth His grace."[2] Already in the Old Law we are told that "the prayer of him that humbleth himself shall pierce the clouds...and the Lord will not be slack."[3]

Then do we walk in truth when we acknowledge ourselves to be sinners: "We are all sinners, even the child whose life upon earth is but one day," says the gloss on Job.[4] On the other hand, no sooner do we acknowledge our guilt than God is ready to wipe away the stains of our souls: "If we confess our sins, he is faithful and just, to forgive us our sins, and to cleanse us from all iniquity."[5] For that reason

1 Matt., v. 26. 2 James, iv. 6.
3 Eccl., xxxv, 21, 22. 4 xiv. 4.
5 1 John, i. 9.

Holy Church bids us imitate the humble publican, who, standing afar off, would not so much as lift up his eyes towards heaven, but struck his breast, saying: "O God, be merciful to me a sinner."[6] So we are bidden by the rubric to strike our breast whilst saying: *Nobis quoque peccatoribus*. At the same time we raise the voice somewhat (*elata aliquantulum voce*), just enough to be heard by those who stand or kneel round the altar, on whose behalf the priest asks for the intercession of the Saints. We are sinners; yet we are also the servants of God and the dispensers of His mysteries, and as such we have a claim upon the liberality of His mercy. In fact, we do not trust in ourselves, or in our merits, or even in the singular dignity vouchsafed to us, which compels men to "account of us as the ministers of Christ, and the dispensers of the mysteries of God."[7] All our hopes are based solely upon the unshakable foundation of divine goodness; *de multitudine miserationum tuarum sperantibus* (hoping in the multitude of Thy mercies), is obviously inspired by the well-known psalm verse: *Et secundum multitudinem miserationum tuarum, dele iniquitatem meam* (And, according to the multitude of Thy mercies, blot out my iniquity). Holy Church for ever keeps reminding her children of the riches of divine compassion. This thought is most admirably developed in the moving prayer which we recite in the Mass of the Eleventh Sunday after Pentecost: "Almighty, eternal God, the plenty of whose compassion exceeds both our merits and our desires, pour out Thy mercy upon us; that so Thou mayest forgive that which fills our conscience with fear, and mayest even grant what we dare not ask for."

Partem aliquam et societatem donare digneris, cum tuis sanctis Apostolis et Martyribus (vouchsafe to grant some part and fellowship with Thy holy apostles and martyrs). We ask for some share in the fellowship of Apostles and Martyrs. It is a demand reminiscent of what we read in the Epistle to the Colossians, wherein St Paul bids us give thanks to God the Father "who hath made us worthy to be partakers of the lot of the Saints in light" (*partem sortis sanctorum in lumine*).[8]

Fellowship with the Saints is one of the chief joys of the abode of bliss. Companionship with the Angels and Saints is necessary to per-

---

6 Luke, xviii. 13.   7 1 Cor., iv. 1.
8 Coloss., i. 12.

fect happiness. Heaven is described to us in Holy Scripture in terms of a life shared with many: "You are come to mount Sion, and to the city of the living God, the heavenly Jerusalem, and to the company of many thousands of angels... and to the spirits of the just made perfect."[9] "Eternal life," says St Thomas, "consists in the sweet companionship of all the Blessed, and this companionship will be most pleasing, for each of the elect will have everything in common with all the others... hence the joy and happiness of each will be great in proportion to the joy of all."[10]

After praying for the blessing of fellowship with all the holy Apostles and Martyrs in general, we now ask for the favor of being admitted into the society of some Saints in particular. Fifteen names are mentioned—*viz.*, those of eight men and seven women Saints, all of them witnesses to Christ, for whom they shed their blood. This list of Saints is supplementary to that found in the *Communicantes*. Saints who were not mentioned before the Consecration, are now honored by having their names uttered in the hearing of their Lord who lies upon the altar, the Lamb which "though sacrificed, remains yet whole and alive."[11] First comes *St John the Baptist*. Some writers have thought St John the Evangelist was meant. But on March 27, 1824, the Sacred Congregation of Rites declared that St John the Baptist was meant, and, though this Decree was rescinded in 1898, we must maintain that the Forerunner is here to be honored, since the list in the *Nobis quoque* is supplementary to that of the *Communicantes* and does not repeat names there mentioned, not even that of Our Lady. *St Stephen* is the first Martyr, one of the seven deacons appointed by the Apostles, "a man full of faith and the Holy Ghost."[12] *Mathias* took the place in the apostolic college left vacant by the traitor Judas. *Barnabas* was one of the seventy-two disciples, "a good man, and full of the Holy Ghost and of faith."[13] *St Ignatius* is said to have been the child whom our Lord one day placed in the midst of His Apostles, setting him before them as a model of humility and simplicity. Later on, he became Bishop of Antioch and died in the Roman Amphitheatre under Tra-

9 Heb., xii. 22, 23.
10 St Thomas, *In symbol.*, xxxix.
11 St Andrew, 11 Noct.
12 Acts, vi. 5.
13 Acts, xi. 24.

jan, in 107. *Alexander* was Pope in the first years of the second century. *Marcellinus* was a priest, and *Peter* an exorcist; both were martyred at Rome under Diocletian. *Felicitas* and *Perpetua* are famous martyrs of Carthage in the year 202. *Agatha* died for the faith at Catania, in Sicily, under Decius in 251. *Lucy* was likewise a Sicilian, one of the last victims of the persecution of Diocletian; she died at Syracuse about the year 304. *Agnes* is one of the greatest glories of Rome, of whom the Liturgy says that "in the thirteenth year of her age she lost death and found life."[14] *St Cecilia* sprang from a most illustrious family, in her tenderest years she consecrated her virginity to God, and to the fragrance of her purity she added the glory of martyrdom (towards the end of the second century). *Anastasia*, a Roman widow, died a martyr's death on the day on which we celebrate the birthday of the King of Martyrs; this was during the persecution of Diocletian, in 304.

These are some of those who "are come out of great tribulation, and have washed their robes, and have made them white in the Blood of the Lamb. Therefore, they are before the throne of God, and they serve Him day and night in His temple... they shall no more hunger nor thirst, neither shall the sun fall on them, nor any heat. For the Lamb... shall lead them to the fountains of life...."[15] In a striking description of the Mass during a time of persecution, Msgr Benson thus speaks of these glorious names: "Again the hands opened and the stately flood of petition poured on, as through open gates, to the boundless sea that awaited it, where the very heart of God was to absorb it in Itself. The great names began to flit past, like palaces on a river-brink, their bases washed by the pouring Liturgy—vast pleasure-houses alight with God, whilst near at hand now gleamed the line of the infinite ocean."[16]

With these and all the Saints we beg to have communion and fellowship. What exquisite humility and trust there is in the concluding words of our prayer! *Intra quorum nos consortium, non aestimator meriti, sed veniae, quaesumus, largitor admitte* (Into whose company we beseech Thee to admit us, not considering our merit, but freely granting us pardon). We have here but another version of the petition of

---

14 Resp., 1 Noct.
15 Apoc., vii. 14 sqq.
16 *The King's Achievement*, p. 314.

the *Te Deum: Aeterna fac cum sanctis tuis in gloria numerari* (Grant that they may be numbered among Thy saints in everlasting glory). For eternal bliss, in the words of Holy Scripture, is the companionship of the elect; hence, on the Last Day, the reprobate shall exclaim with dismay: "We fools esteemed their life [the Saints'] madness, and their end without honor. Behold how they are *numbered among the children of God, and their lot is among the Saints.*"[17] So great a destiny is infinitely beyond our unaided efforts. No doubt, God rewards our good works, and we may merit the bliss of heaven; yet this very possibility of meriting is an effect of God's gratuitous goodness, for "the goodness and kindness of God our Saviour appeared: not by the works of justice, which we have done, but according to His mercy, He saved us."[18]

The priest concludes his supplication to the Heavenly Father with an express mention of His beloved Son (*Per Christum Dominum nostrum*). There is no *Amen*, but the priest goes on praying: "By whom, O Lord, Thou dost always create, sanctify, quicken, bless and give us all these good things." The words, *haec omnia bona* (all these good things), cannot originally have referred to the consecrated Elements upon the altar, for they are not bread and wine any longer. The most natural explanation of the prayer is that of Duchesne, who says that formerly, at this moment, all kinds of fruits were blessed. To this very day, on Maundy Thursday, the oils are consecrated at this moment of the Mass. According to Duchesne, there can be no doubt that the formula, *Per quem haec omnia*, was originally preceded by some prayer for the fruits of the earth. When the blessing of fruits disappeared from the Canon, the prayer remained, and is now "accommodated" to the Eucharistic Victim. The three blessings over the consecrated Elements are attracted, so to speak, by the words *sanctificas, vivificas, benedicis* (sanctify, quicken and bless).

The priest now uncovers the chalice, genuflects, rises, arid, taking the Sacred Host in his right hand, holds it over the chalice and traces three crosses with it; then he makes two crosses between the chalice and himself. Finally, he raises slightly (*parum,* says the rubric) both the chalice and the Host, whilst saying *omnis honor et gloria* (all

17 Wis., v. 4, 5.   18 Tit., iii. 4, 5.

honor and glory). He once more places the Host on the corporal, covers the chalice, and genuflects. The words which accompany this ceremony form a famous doxology: *Per ipsum, et cum ipso, et in ipso est tibi Deo Patri omnipotenti, in unitate Spiritus sancti, omnis honor et gloria* (Through Him, and with Him, and in Him, is to Thee, God the Father Almighty, in the unity of the Holy Ghost, all honor and glory). All this is said silently. Then, raising his voice, the priest says *Per omnia saecula saeculorum* (For ever and ever). All honor and glory belongs to God, world without end. The assistants answer *Amen*, and their acclamation of approval and firm faith marks the conclusion of the Canon.

We might wonder why five crosses are traced with the Sacred Host. The reason is to be found in the fact that the priest has taken It into his hands for the "Little Elevation," during which he pronounces the words *omnis honor et gloria*. Now, since the words that precede suggest or attract a blessing, it is natural to make it with the Sacred Host. In like manner, and for the same reason, the priest makes the sign of the cross with the paten, which he takes up whilst saying the prayer *Libera nos, quaesumus, Domine* (Deliver us, we beseech Thee, O Lord).

There could be no nobler conclusion to the essential part of the Mass, the Canon, than the sublime doxology which accompanies the "Little Elevation." The Mass is by its very nature a sacrifice of praise. It renders infinite glory to God, since it is the continuance of the perfect homage which Jesus Christ rendered to His Father during His life, and above all by His death. May we always associate ourselves interiorly with the action we perform exteriorly, and render to the Blessed Trinity the homage due to its Majesty "through Him, and with Him and in Him, for ever and ever. Amen"!

CHAPTER XX

FROM THE PATER NOSTER TO THE FRACTIO PANIS

Sacrifice and Sacrament

THE most sacred phase of our sacrifice is ended, the "little Elevation" very appropriately marking its close. However, the victim must not merely be immolated; those who offer the sacrifice are bound to partake of its flesh. Holy Communion is the natural termination of the Mass and its consummation. When our divine Lord, the true High Priest of the New Law, instituted the sacrifice of the New Dispensation with Himself acting as priest according to the order of Melchisedech, He immediately added a solemn command to the words whereby He had wrought the tremendous change which takes place in the consecration: "Do this in memory of Me." If the assistants are not compelled to communicate, at least the celebrant is. But in all the prayers of the Mass Holy Church supposes that the faithful shall partake of the Body and Blood of Christ, and never allows an alteration to be made in their wording. St Paul, writing to the Corinthians, speaks of the participation of the assistants in the Eucharistic Sacrifice: he evidently supposes that what is consecrated upon the altar is consumed by the faithful: "The chalice of benediction, which we bless, is it not the communion of the Blood of Christ? And the bread, which we break, is it not the partaking of the Body of the Lord?"[1]

The Angelic Doctor teaches that, "although the use of a sacrament does not belong to the essence, it is nevertheless the complement of the sacrament" (*quamvis Sacramenti usus non sit de essentia sacramenti,*

---

[1] I Cor., x. 16.

est tamen ad complementum esse ipsius); that is, the Sacrament would fail of its chief purpose, unless those in whose behalf it has been instituted, make use of it in Communion. The perfection of the Sacrament is in its actual use (*in quantum pertingit ad hoc, ad quod institutum est*); it has been instituted in order that it may be used.²

The *Pater Noster*

Holy Church opens the last part of the Holy Sacrifice with the solemn recitation or singing of the Lord's Prayer This practice is as old as the Church herself, for there can be no doubt that it goes back to apostolic days. According to St Jerome, Christ Himself commanded the Apostles to recite this prayer during the sacred rites of the Sacrifice of the New Law: [*Christus*] *docuit discipulos suos ut quotidie in corporis illius sacrificio credentes audeant loqui: Pater noster*, etc. (Christ taught His disciples that daily, in that sacrifice of His body, the believers may presume to speak thus: *Pater noster*).³

St Jerome's expression, *audeant loqui* (may presume to say), is noteworthy, for we preface the *Pater noster* with the words, *audemus dicere* (we presume to say). It is scarcely to be believed that, when the Apostles met for the "breaking of bread" or the celebration of the Lord's Supper, they did not accompany the solemn function with prayer. And what prayer of their own invention would they have dared to prefer to that which, at their own request, the Master had taught them with His own divine lips? So we find the Lord's Prayer in all Liturgies, both in the East and the West. In fact the *Pater noster* is simply *the* prayer—the "legitimate and ordinary prayer" (*legitima et ordinaria oratio*)—and, therefore, the obligatory supplication which must needs accompany the Mass. St Augustine bears witness to the use of the Lord's Prayer in his time: "In church, at God's altar, this prayer of the Lord is daily recited and the faithful hear it" (*In ecclesia, ad altare Dei, quotidie dicitur ista dominica oratio, et audiunt illam fideles*).⁴

There is, therefore, no uncertainty about the recitation of the Lord's Prayer; the only difficulty is in tracing the place it originally

2 St Thomas, IV Dist., dist. XIII, q. 2.
3 *Advers. Pelag.*, III, 15.   4 *Sermo lviii*, 12.

occupied in our Latin Liturgy. The difficulty arises from a very obscure passage of a letter of St Gregory the Great to John of Syracuse. "We say the Lord's Prayer immediately after the Canon (*mox post precem*), because it was the custom of the Apostles to consecrate the offering of the sacrifice (*oblationis hostiam*) by this prayer alone (*ad ipsam solummodo orationem*), and it seemed very unseemly to me that we should recite over the oblation a prayer composed by some scholar (*scholasticus*), and that we should not say the very tradition which our Redeemer composed over His body and blood (*ipsam traditionem quam Redemptor noster composuit super ejus corpus et sanguinem non diceremus*)"—that is, should not keep to that which the Redeemer Himself established and originated.

There are several difficulties in this text. What appears fairly certain is that Gregory ordered the *Pater noster* to be said over the Body and Blood of Christ; we may, therefore, infer that prior to his time it was recited before the Consecration. He contrasts the Lord's Prayer and a prayer composed by some scholar or learned man, and rightly asserts that it is not meet that a prayer of human origin should take the place of that which sprang from the Heart of the Son of God. John the Deacon tells us that St Gregory prescribed the Lord's Prayer to be said over the Host at the close of the Canon. When the holy Pontiff says that the Apostles used to consecrate by this prayer alone, he cannot, of course, mean what some Protestants have suggested, namely, that they never used the words which Christ used in the Upper Room. It appears reasonable to explain the text by saying that the Pontiff did away with some prayer which followed immediately upon the Canon, and substituted the Lord's Prayer in its place. That there were such prayers we know, since we find one in the Missal of Stowe, which reads thus: "We believe, O Lord, we believe that we have been redeemed by this breaking of Thy body and the outpouring of Thy blood (*Credimus, Domine, credimus in hac confractione corporis et effusione sanguinis nos esse redemptos*)."

In the Liturgies of East and West the Lord's Prayer is preceded by a short introduction, or preface. In the Roman Liturgy this preface is itself preceded by an exhortation to the people to pray: *Oremus*. The introduction never varies. We find traces of it already in St Cyprian's treatise on the Lord's Prayer: "Among the rest of His salutary admonitions and divine precepts, by which He provides for the wellbeing of His people, He (Christ) also gave them a standard of prayer, He Himself teaching us what we should pray for [*inter caetera salutaria sua monita et praecepta divina, quibus populo suo consulit ad salutem, etiam orandi ipse formam dedit (Christus), ipse quid precaremur, monuit et instruit*]."[5]

Whilst he recites the introductory preface, the priest stands with his hands joined, but, as soon as he begins the first petition of the *Pater*, he extends them crosswise, in the attitude of the *orantes* (praying figures) which we see depicted on the walls of the Roman Catacombs. Though the prayer is directly addressed to God the Father, the rubric bids us look at the Sacred Host (*stans oculis ad Sacramentum intentis*),[6] as if to remind ourselves that, if we dare at all to address ourselves to God's Majesty, it is because we have been thus taught and bidden by Him who is now before our eyes upon the altar. The *Pater noster* should be said with great earnestness and deliberation. If we ponder its various petitions, even superficially, we cannot fail to be struck by their singular beauty and dignity. This should of itself prevent any unseemly haste in their recitation.

The Lord's Prayer has ever been the favorite prayer of Holy Church. The early Fathers and Doctors and the Saints of later centuries have left us commentaries upon this divine masterpiece, of which Tertullian says that the terseness of its wording is matched by its depth of meaning (*Quantum substringitur verbis, tantum diffunditur sensibus*).[7] It seems right to make a few comments upon the seven petitions of the divinely dictated prayer, but it is best to do so, not in one's own words, but in the weighty ones of a great Father of the Church. One of the most admirable treatises upon prayer that have come down to us from the early centuries of Christianity is a letter of St Augustine to a noble lady of the name of Proba. This lady had but recently become a widow, and found herself at the head of a large household. She was still young and her wealth was immense, but, realizing the vanity of all things earthly, she felt but one desire, namely, to serve the Lord

5 *De orat. dom.*
6 *Rit. cel.*, x.
7 *De or.at.*, i.

with all her heart. When Alaric plundered Rome, she narrowly escaped from the violence of his Goths. Fearing their return, she sold her possessions and went to live at Carthage with a number of maidens and young widows of her acquaintance. She consulted the saintly Bishop of Hippo about prayer—how she ought to pray, and what should be the object of her supplication. Augustine's answer is a long and detailed exposition of the necessity and advantages of prayer. In Chapter XI of the treatise, he gives a brief analysis and explanation of the Lord's Prayer, clearly showing that, to his mind, it was the perfect prayer, expressive of all our needs, and all the more powerful in that it is not so much ours as Christ's, who taught it to His disciples. "To us," says the holy Doctor, "words are necessary, that by them we may be assisted in considering and observing what we ask, not as means by which we expect that God is to be either informed or moved to compliance." When, therefore, we say: "Hallowed be Thy name," we admonish ourselves to desire that His name, which is always holy, may be among men also esteemed holy, that is to say, not despised; this is an advantage, not to God, but to men. When we say: "Thy kingdom come," which shall certainly come whether we wish it or not, we do by these words stir up our own desires for that kingdom, that it may come to us, and that we may be found worthy to reign in it. When we say: "Thy will be done on earth as it is in heaven," we pray for ourselves, that He would give us the grace of obedience, that His will may be done by us in the same way as it is done in heavenly places by His Angels. When we say: "Give us this day our daily bread," the words "this day" signify "for the present time," in which we ask either for that competency of temporal blessing which I have spoken of before ("bread" being used to designate the whole of those blessings, because of its constituting so important a part of them), or for the Sacrament of believers, which is in this present time necessary, but necessary in order to obtain the felicity not of the present time, but of eternity. When we say: "Forgive us our debts as we forgive our debtors," we remind ourselves of what we should, ask and what we should do in order that we may be worthy to receive what we ask. When we say: "Lead us not into temptation," we admonish ourselves to seek that we may not, through being deprived of God's help, be either ensnared to consent or compelled to yield to temptation. When we say: "Deliver us from evil," we admonish ourselves to consider that we are not as yet enjoying that good estate in which we shall experience no evil. The last petition, according to the holy Doctor, is so comprehensive that a Christian, in whatsoever affliction he be placed, "may begin with this petition, go on with it, and with it conclude his prayers."

The Lord's Prayer is the truly "legitimate prayer," the model of every prayer; for, whatever form of words we may use, "if we pray rightly and becomingly, we never say but what is found expressed in this prayer of the Lord" (*nihil aliud dicimus quam quod in ista dominica oratione positum est, si recte et congruenter oramus*).[8]

The assistants join in the last petition by saying: *Sed libera nos a malo* (But deliver us from evil), the priest himself adding *Amen* in silence. In the Eastern Liturgies, and the Gallican also, the people recite the whole of the *Pater Noster*; in the Mozarabic the priest alone says it, the people answering *Amen* to each clause.

There is an interesting prescription in the Rule of St Benedict which shows that already in the fifth century the Lord's Prayer was recited by the one who presided, the assistants only saying the concluding petition. The great monastic liturgist orders that Lauds and Vespers must never be terminated without the petitions of the *Pater* being said in order: *Ultimo, per ordinem, Oratio Dominica, omnibus audientibus, dicatur a Priore* (Lastly, let the petitions of the Lord's Prayer be said in order by the Superior, all listening). At the other Canonical Hours, "let only the last part of the same Prayer be said, so that all may answer: But deliver us from evil" (*ultima pars ejus orationis dicatur, ut ab omnibus respondeatur: Sed libera nos a malo*).[9]

The *Libera Nos*

The last petition of the Lord's Prayer is one for deliverance from evil, or from the evil one (*a maligno*). It is the assistant's share in the solemn supplication and is immediately followed by a lengthy prayer, silently

---

8 *Ep. cxxxii*, 11, trans. by J.G. Cunningham, edition of Rev. M. Dods.
9 *Regula S. Benedicti*, XIII.

recited by the priest alone and technically called *embolism* (i.e., a paraphrase, or development). In most Liturgies we meet with some form of development of the last clause of the *Pater*, though in the Liturgy of St John Chrysostom the priest recites only the well-known clause: "For thine is the kingdom, and the power, and the glory, of the Father, and of the Son, and of the Holy Ghost, now, and for ever, and from all ages to all ages." The text of the Roman embolism is probably as old as that of the Canon itself. We already find it almost word for word in the Gregorian and Gelasian Sacramentaries.

Libera nos quaesumus, Domine, ab omnibus malis praeteritis, praesentibus et futuris (Deliver us, we beseech Thee, O Lord, from all evils, past, present and to come). The prayer is most comprehensive and makes no distinction between what we call physical and moral evils. The former are the inevitable consequence and punishment of the latter; hence we are fully justified when we pray to be delivered from them. When Holy Church prays to be delivered from *past evils*, she has not only in mind the sins by which some of her children have offended God, but likewise the consequences and the punishment of these transgressions; for, even though sin is blotted out by repentance, the temporal punishment due to it is not thereby wholly condoned. Even the just are subject to much sorrow and tribulation whilst they dwell in this place of banishment, complete deliverance from pain being reserved for a future state: "Every creature groaneth and travaileth in pain, even till now. And not only it, but ourselves also, who have the first fruits of the Spirit, even we ourselves groan within ourselves, waiting for the adoption of the sons of God, the redemption of our body."[10] And, when we look ahead into the uncertain future, our hearts may justifiably quail at the thought of what awaits us. If we cannot hope to escape the common lot of man, we trust and pray that God will not deal with us according to our deserts, but rather according to His wonted mercy.

Et intercedente beata et gloriosa semper Virgine Dei Genitrice Maria, cum beatis Apostolis tuis Petro et Paulo, atque Andrea, et omnibus Sanctis (and by the intercession of the blessed and glorious Virgin Mary,

---

10 Rom., viii. 22, 23.

etc.). Our prayer will receive additional efficacy if offered through the blessed and glorious Mother of God and in union with the constant supplication of the twin princes of the Church, Sts Peter and Paul. The name of St Andrew, the brother of St Peter, appears to have been added by St Gregory the Great, who had a special devotion to this Apostle, in whose honor he dedicated the monastery into which he converted his own house on the Crelian Hill. In the Middle Ages it was customary to add the names of other Saints, particularly those of the patrons of the church. We now include all the Saints in one common remembrance (*et omnibus Sanctis*).

Da propitius pacem in diebus nostris: ut ope misericordiae tuae adjuti, et a peccato simus semper liberi, et ab omni perturbatione securi (Mercifully grant peace in our days, that by the assistance of Thy mercy we may be always free from sin and secure from all disturbance).

Even the most casual student of the Church's prayers must be struck by the frequency of her petitions for peace. Obviously this demand is not confined to that supernatural peace of which the Apostle speaks: "The peace of God, which surpasseth all understanding, keep your hearts and minds in Christ Jesus."[11] The Church of God cannot grow and develop, at least not normally, unless she enjoys a certain amount of external, social and political tranquillity. There is nothing morbid in the Church's attitude towards evil and suffering: she knows how to accept and endure hardships of every kind, but she does not desire them for their own sake; rather does she pray for deliverance from them. Again and again her Collects ask for freedom from all evils of soul and body. She knows full well, from an experience of many centuries, that her lot must needs be that of the Apostle, "combats without, fears within";[12] but even as God, "who comforteth the humble," comforted Paul by the coming of Titus, so may she lawfully pray to be strengthened from on high, not only where souls are concerned, but likewise in the purely natural order. On this point the prayer to Our Lady, which we say so often in the course of the year, is most illuminating: *Concede nos famulos tuos ... perpetua mentis et corporis sanitate gaudere ... a praesenti liberari tristitia et aeterna perfrui*

---

[11] Philip., iv. 7. [12] II Cor., vii. 5.

laetitia (Grant us, thy servants, to rejoice in continual health of mind and body... and to be freed from present sorrow and enjoy everlasting happiness). There is something eminently wholesome in the attitude of the Church towards suffering. Just as a healthy organism resists and easily repels any deleterious influence from without, and readily overcomes every poisonous germ that may have penetrated within, so are we to look upon evil as an evil, from which good does indeed often result, not however as from a source, but inasmuch as it becomes an occasion of spiritual advantage to us. Some modern exponents of spirituality seem to take a kind of morbid, pessimistic delight in pain, and would have us believe that there can be no sanctity if the would-be Saint be a man or woman of normal physical health. Do what we may, we shall not escape pain (*multae tribulationes justorum*), but the Lord will deliver us from all these, wholly in the world to come, and in part even in this life, if we pray as the Holy Ghost makes us pray in the inspired Liturgy of the Church.

As soon as the priest begins the *Libera nos*, he wipes the paten with the purificator, takes it in his right hand, holds it erect upon the altar until he comes to the words *da propitius pacem in diebus nostris* (mercifully grant peace in our days), when he makes the sign of the cross upon himself with it. Then he slips the paten under the Sacred Host, uncovers the chalice, and genuflects.

The *Fractio Panis* (Breaking of the Host)

The breaking of the Sacred Host is one of the oldest elements of the Eucharistic Sacrifice, and for that reason we find it in all Liturgies. After our Lord had Himself celebrated the first Mass, He bade the Apostles do in their turn what they had just witnessed. The Gospels insist upon the breaking of the bread, previous to its distribution among the disciples: *Accepit panem, et benedixit ac fregit, deditque discipulis suis* (Took bread, and blessed, and broke, and gave to His disciples);[13] *Accepto pane gratias egit, et fregit* (Taking bread, He gave thanks, and broke).[14] "To break bread" speedily became a Eucharistic expression, as may be

---

13 Matt., xxvi. 26.   14 Luke, xxii. 19.

gathered from the Acts of the Apostles. In the pages of that most fascinating book we are given a glimpse of the life of the Early Church at Jerusalem: the believers frequented the temple, we are told, *frangentes circa domos panem* (breaking bread from house to house).[15] Abbot Cabrol justly remarks that though the word *fregit* (broke) occurs in the Sacred Text, it is not mentioned in connection with *corpus* (Body), but only with *panis* (bread). The word, however, passed very soon into the formula of consecration: *Hoc est corpus meum quod pro multis frangitur* (This is My Body which is broken for many);[16] *hoc est corpus meum quod pro vobis frangitur et datur* (This is My Body which is broken and given for you);[17] *hoc est corpus meum quod pro vobis confringitur* (This is My Body which is shattered for you).[18]

These expressions are evidently based upon the well-known text of St Paul: "The bread, which we break, is it not the partaking of the Body of the Lord?"[19] "In the Eucharist," says St John Chrysostom, "we see the Lord's body broken, but not upon the cross; on the contrary, it is written: 'You shall not break a bone of Him'; but what He did not endure upon the cross, that He suffers for thee in the sacrifice, that He may fill all."[20] Clement of Alexandria tells us that, when the Eucharistic bread has been broken according to custom, every one of the assistants is allowed to take a part.[21]

The breaking of the consecrated Bread was for the purpose, primarily, of distribution among those present. St Augustine, in a letter to Paulinus, thus explains the fraction of the Eucharistic bread (*in celebratione Sacramentorum ... illud quod est in Domini mensa ... cum benedicitur et sanctificatur, et ad distribuendum comminuitur*).[22]

In the Latin Rite the Host is divided into three parts, and during the fraction the conclusion of the *Libera nos* is recited. The priest first breaks the Host in two, whilst saying: *Per eumdem Dominum nostrum Jesum Christum, Filium tuum* (Through the same Jesus Christ our Lord, Thy Son) Having placed the half which he holds in his right hand upon the paten, he breaks off a small fragment from the half which

15 Acts, ii. 46.
17 *Liturg. Sti. Jacobi.*
19 1 Cor. x. 16.
21 *Strom.*, 1.
16 *Const. Apost.*, VIII.
18 *Testam. Dni.*
20 *Hom.* xxiv. in 1 *Cor.*, x.
22 *Ep. cxlix*, n. 16.

he holds in his left hand, whilst he says: *qui tecum vivit et regnat, in unitate Spiritus sancti, Deus* (who liveth and reigneth with Thee in the unity of the Holy Ghost, one God). When he has reunited the two halves upon the paten, he holds the small fragment over the chalice saying: *Per omnia saecula saeculorum* (For ever and ever). When the server has answered *Amen,* the priest makes three crosses with the particle over the chalice, saying: *Pax Domini sit semper vobiscum* (May the peace of the Lord be always with you). The server answers: *Et cum spiritu tuo.* Then the priest drops the particle into the chalice, whilst he prays that "this mingling mixture and consecration of the Body and Blood of our Lord Jesus Christ may be unto us that receive them effectual of eternal life."

This ceremonial mixture of the two consecrated Elements is a very old custom. It may have originated in the practice of mixing bread and wine at meals, as our Lord did at the Last Supper: "And when He had *dipped* the bread, He gave it to Judas Iscariot, the son of Simon."[23]

The words which accompany the mixture have been variously interpreted. The two consecrated Elements are united in order to represent the resurrection of our Lord, just as His passion and death are shown forth in their separate consecration. But it is not easy to see how this mingling of the Elements becomes a new *consecration*. It is evident that the wine is not consecrated, or changed into the Blood of our Lord at that moment, and yet Holy Church never uses words at random. We may, therefore, see in this reunion of the two Elements a new and special *consecration* of the *species* under which Christ's Flesh and Blood is upon the altar. This is the opinion of Gihr and others. However, the word can also be taken to signify a final preparation of the sacred Elements for use in the Holy Communion, which is about to take place. This explanation seems the more natural when we remember that during many centuries the laity received Holy Communion under both kinds.

Both fraction and mixture are symbolical acts of the highest significance. The former, at first only a reproduction of the action of our Lord at the Last Supper, soon came to signify His sacrifice upon

---

23 John, xiii. 26.

the cross, as well as to express the faith of the Church in the reality of the Eucharistic Sacrifice. But, if the separate consecration and the breaking of the Host show forth the death of the Lord, the mingling of the Elements declares that He who is mystically slain is now living in the glory of God the Father.

The fraction of the Sacred Host should be accomplished with the utmost reverence. True, we do no injury to the Lord of glory, but merely divide the sensible element which hides Him from our gaze. None the less we shall do well to ponder what Father Faber says at the end of his great book on the Blessed Sacrament. After relating how Blessed Angela of Foligno, when assisting at the Mass of an unworthy priest, at the moment of the fraction of the Host, heard a low, sweet voice complaining: "Alas! how they break Me and make the blood flow from My limbs!" the saintly Oratorian cries out: "Ah! my Fathers and Masters, my Brothers in this intolerable grace! do we not, each of us, know in his own secret soul at least one priest, who, if he had his due, could never break the Host without having his own heart broken also by the lamentable sweetness of that plaintive cry?"[24]

---

24 *Blessed Sacrament*, IV, 6.

CHAPTER XXI

FROM THE AGNUS DEI TO THE DOMINE NON SUM DIGNUS

The *Agnus Dei*

THE Holy Eucharist is the outward symbol and the most efficacious cause of the wonderful union that obtains between our Lord and those who belong to Him, and, again, of the unity and harmony that should reign among those who claim to be, and are in very deed, members of the body of Jesus Christ. Hence it is most appropriate that we should pray that peace may ever reign amongst the children of the Church. This is done by the priest when he makes a triple cross over the chalice, with a fragment of the Host, whilst saying: *Pax Domini sit semper vobiscum* (The peace of the Lord be always with you). He also prays for peace and tranquillity in the last of the three invocations addressed to Jesus Christ under the title of Lamb of God.

The symbolism of the lamb, as applied to our Lord, is based upon some of the noblest passages to be found in our Sacred Books. In the famous prophecy in which he describes the Passion of the Messias with a vividness of detail that might have been expected from an eye-witness, Isaias speaks thus: "He was offered because it was His own will, and He opened not His mouth: He shall be led as a sheep to the slaughter, and shall be dumb as a lamb before His shearer, and He shall not open His mouth."[1] Elsewhere the Lamb is described as a king and lawgiver: "Send forth, O Lord, the lamb, the ruler of the earth... to the mount of the daughter of Sion."[2] In Jeremias our Saviour's voice is heard: "I was as a meek lamb that is carried to be a victim."[3]

1 Is., liii. 7. 2 Is., xvi. 1.
3 Jer., xi. 19.

In the Apocalypse the image recurs again and again: "I beheld, and lo! a Lamb stood upon mount Sion, and with Him an hundred forty-four thousand... these follow the Lamb... the first fruits to God and to the Lamb."[4] But the most impressive picture of the Lamb and of the worship that is rendered to it in the Liturgy of heaven, is found in the fifth chapter, for there the seer describes the Lamb as slain. One might almost say that the Apostle describes the Eucharistic Sacrifice with its accompanying chants and prayers: "And I saw; and behold in the midst of the throne and of the four living creatures, and in the midst of the ancients, a Lamb standing, as it were slain." We are even allowed to hear an echo of the hymns of the great crowd of heavenly worshippers: "The Lamb that was slain is worthy to receive power, and divinity, and wisdom, and strength, and honor, and glory, and benediction.... To Him that sitteth on the throne, and to the Lamb, benediction, and honor, and glory, and power, for ever and ever."[5]

St Peter assures the early Christians that they have been bought "with the precious Blood of Christ, as of a lamb unspotted and undefiled."[6] Even before the Prince of the Apostles, St John the Baptist had pointed out the Saviour from among the crowd that surged around Him: "Behold the Lamb of God, behold Him who taketh away the sin of the world."[7] The old and widely-spread custom of representing our Lord under the form of a lamb arose from this exclamation of the Forerunner. The Council *in Trullo* (692) arrogated to itself the right of prohibiting such representations, but without success, and Rome strenuously opposed these pretensions.

The thrice repeated invocation to the Lamb of God dates back to the end of the seventh century. The *Liber Pontificalis* relates that Sergius I (687–701) ordained that, during the fraction of the bread, clergy and people should sing together: *Agnus Dei qui tollis peccata mundi, miserere nobis*. At first the invocation was only said once, then twice, that is, once by the clergy and once by the people. In the twelfth century we find that it is said three times, the conclusion of the third invocation being our *dona nobis pacem* (grant us peace). However, the Basilica of St John Lateran has retained to this day the primitive cus-

4 Apoc., xiv. 1, 4-
5 Apoc., v.
6 1 Pet., i. 19.
7 John, i. 29.

tom of a triple *miserere nobis*. In Masses for the dead, *miserere nobis* is replaced by *dona eis requiem* (grant them rest), and at the third invocation we add *sempiternam* (everlasting). This custom also was general as far back as the twelfth century.

The habit of "farcing" (or interpolating) liturgical pieces, which was so common in the later centuries of the Middle Ages, did not spare the *Agnus Dei*. Cardinal Bona quotes the most widely known form:

> *Agnus Dei, qui tollis peccata mundi, crimina tollis, aspera mollis, Agnus honoris, miserere nobis.*
>
> *Agnus Dei, qui tollis peccata mundi, vulnera sanas, ardua planas, Agnus amoris, miserere nobis.*
>
> *Agnus Dei, qui tollis peccata mundi, sordida mundas, cuncta fecundos, Agnus odoris, dona nobis pacem.*

> Lamb of God, who takest away the sins of the world, takest away its crimes, and dost soften its harshnesses, O Lamb of honor, have mercy on us.
>
> Lamb of God, who takest away the sins of the world, dost heal its wounds, and level its steep places, O Lamb of love, have mercy on us.
>
> Lamb of God, who takest away the sins of the world, dost cleanse its sordidness, and fructify all things, O Lamb of fragrance, grant us peace.

The Prayers of Preparation for Holy Communion

In the early centuries of the Church, Holy Communion followed immediately after the fraction of the Host. The three prayers which now precede it were at first private devotions only, by which the celebrant prepared his soul for the final act of the Eucharistic Sacrifice. The first prayer is clearly only a development or paraphrase of the last petition of the *Agnus Dei*. It dates as far back as the eleventh century at least, and is mentioned by the author of *Micrologus*. By the fourteenth century it had a place in the Missal of the Roman Church, since we read in the *Ordo Rom.* xiv that the Pope, after the *Pax*, "reverently, with joined hands, says these prayers: *Domine Jesu Christe, Filii Dei vivi*, etc. (Lord Jesus Christ, Son of the living God), and the other prayers to be said before he receives the Host, as they are in the book." As the three prayers are addressed to the Second Person of the Blessed Trinity, the rubric prescribes that the priest should fix his eyes upon the Host, placing his folded hands on the edge of the altar and making a moderate inclination. The first prayer asks for peace and union among the children of the Church. Its purpose, therefore, is not purely personal; on the contrary, the priest prays that our Lord would not regard his sins, but the faith and confidence of His Church.

The second prayer is obviously a prayer of preparation for the celebrant's own Communion as distinct from that of the assistants. It is addressed to Jesus Christ, the Son of the living God, who, with the coöperation of the Holy Ghost, quickened the world by dying for it. We pray to be delivered from all our sins, and from the manifold evils, moral and physical, which are the direct consequence of our transgressions. How simple and childlike is the concluding request: *fac me tuis semper inhaerere mandatis, et a te numquam separari permittas* (make me always adhere to Thy commandments and never suffer me to be separated from Thee)! If we pray thus morning after morning, and correspond with God's preserving grace, what holy, stainless lives ours will be! We shall live in sanctity and justice in His presence all our days (*In sanctitate et justitia coram ipso, omnibus diebus nostris*). The present writer has heard it related, but is not able to verify the story, that St Philip Neri used to say to our Lord, as he held the Sacred Host in his hands: "Keep me, O Lord, today, else I shall betray Thee." May we all reëcho from our hearts the ardent prayer of this wonderful priest!

The coöperation of the Holy Ghost in the work of the redemption consists in this, that He inspired the willing obedience by which the Son of God carried out the will of His heavenly Father: *Christus passus est ex charitate et obedientia, quia et praecepta charitatis ex obedientia implevit, et obediens fuit ex dilectione ad Patrem praecipientem* (Christ suffered from a motive of charity and from obedience, for obedience made Him fulfill the law of charity, and He was obedient because of

His love for the Father who had laid this command on Him).[8] This is made even clearer in the holy Doctor's commentary on Hebrews, ix. 3: *Causa quare Christus sanguinem suum fudit, fuit Spiritus Sanctus, cujus motu et instinctu, scilicet charitate Dei et proximi, hoc fecit* (The motive which urged Christ to shed His blood, was the Holy Ghost, whose motion and prompting, that is, love of God and the neighbor, made Him act in this way).

The Holy Eucharist is the most powerful means of union with Christ: "He that eateth My Flesh and drinketh My Blood, abideth in Me and I in him."[9] Would that we were less forgetful so that we might ever realize our superabundant wealth, when we cling to Christ and possess Him! *Ipsum enim habes, quem totus mundus tibi auferre non potest. Ego sum, cui te totum dare debes, ita ut jam ultra non in te, sed in me absque omni sollicitudine vivas* (For thou possessest Him whom the whole world cannot take from thee. I am He to whom thou must wholly surrender thyself, so that henceforth thou mayest live free from all solicitude, not in thyself, but in Me).[10]

The opening sentence of the third prayer is inspired by the warning of the Apostle: "Let a man prove himself ... for he that eateth and drinketh unworthily, eateth and drinketh judgment to himself, not discerning the Body of the Lord."[11] We are utterly unworthy to feast upon the spotless Flesh of the Lamb of God; if we dare partake of it, it is solely because we are given an express command to do so. To eat of this immortal Flesh of the Son of God and to drink of the priceless cup, is the condition on which alone we can have everlasting life. More than that: Holy Communion is not alone a source of supernatural life, but it is even an efficacious means of refreshment and healing for our body. The Corinthians were punished with physical ills because of the abuses that had crept into their celebration of the Lord's Supper: "Therefore are there many infirm and weak among you, and many sleep."[12] A worthy Communion, therefore, will not fail to contribute to the wellbeing of mind and body. "The Sacraments," says St Thomas, "produce the salutary effect which they sig-

---

8 St Thomas, *Summa Theol.*, III, Q. xlvii, a, 2, ad 3,
9 John, vi. 57.
10 *Imitation of Christ*, IV, 12.
11 I Cor., xi. 28, 29.
12 I Cor., xi. 30.

nify ... and though the body is not the immediate subject of grace, nevertheless grace reaches it as derived from the soul, whilst in this life 'we present our members as instruments of justice unto God,' as St Paul says,[13] and in the world to come the body is destined to take a share in the incorruption and glory of the soul."[14]

Domine non sum dignus

On the conclusion of the third prayer of preparation, the priest genuflects and expresses the eager longing of his soul for its divinely appointed food, in the words of the psalmist: *Panem caelestem accipiam, et nomen Domini invocabo* (I will take the Bread of heaven, and call upon the name of the Lord).[15] *Accipere* here signifies to take, as we take food (*viz.*, to eat). Hence, St Thomas says that, when we read that our Lord took bread, He took it in the same way in which He commanded the Apostles to take it (*accipite et comedite, bibite*); that is, He also partook of it (*intelligendum est quod ipse accipiens comederit et biberit*). Hence, just as at the Last Supper our Lord celebrated the first Mass, so He communicated Himself before He gave His Flesh and Blood to the Apostles (*Se dat suis manibus*).[16]

The priest now takes up the two halves of the Sacred Host between the thumb and first finger of his left hand, holding the paten under the Sacred Element between the first and middle finger of the same hand. Bending slightly over the altar, he three times protests, in a raised voice, his unworthiness to receive the Lord of glory within the house of his soul. The words of the humble Centurion were admired by our Lord Himself: "Jesus hearing this, marvelled; and said to them that followed Him: Amen I say to you, I have not found so great faith in Israel."[17] Holy Church puts this protestation of humility on the lips of priest and people alike at the awful moment of Holy Communion, knowing that, if anything can render us less unworthy of so stupendous a favor, it is the acknowledgment of our sinfulness. Speaking of the Centurion St Augustine says that "by calling himself

13 Rom. vi. 13.
14 *Summa Theol.*, III, Q. lxxix, a. 1, ad 3.
15 Ps. cxv. 4.
16 *Summa Theol.*, III, Q. lxxxi, a. 1, ad 1.
17 Matt., viii. 10.

unworthy, he rendered himself worthy that Christ should enter, not within the walls of his house, but within his heart. Nor would he have spoken with so much faith and humility, if he had not already borne in his heart Him whom he feared to see enter into his house."[18]

We strike our breast whilst saying *Domine, non sum dignus*, thus imitating the conduct of the publican who, "standing afar off, would not so much as lift up his eyes towards heaven, but struck his breast."[19] To strike one's breast is a very old practice which the Church took over from the Synagogue; in fact, it is the almost spontaneous act of one in affliction, or laboring under a sense of shame and guilt. From the sermons of St Augustine we learn that his people struck their breasts when they recited the fifth petition of the Lord's Prayer: *Dimitte nobis debita nostra* (Forgive us our trespasses). It appears that they struck their breasts quite frequently; thus, when Augustine explains the opening words of Psalm cvii (*Confitemini Domino*, etc.), he says: "When the lector pronounced this word [*Confitemini*, literally, 'Confess ye'], there was immediately a pious rumble from the people striking their breasts" (*ubi hoc verbum lectoris ore sonuerit, continuo strepitus pius pectora tundentium sequitur*). Apparently the good people, hearing the word *confitemini*, at once struck their breasts, as was their wont when reminded of their sins, without waiting for the completion of the sentence, when the true meaning of the word would have been apparent. Hence, the holy Doctor hastens to explain its signification in this instance.

We strike our breast, or heart, as being the seat or origin of our sinfulness, according to the words of our Lord: "The things which proceed out of the mouth, come forth from the heart, and those things defile a man. For from the heart come forth evil thoughts."[20]

The verse, *Panem caelestem accipiam*, and the *Domine, non sum dignus*, as an immediate preparation for the priest's Communion, are first found in Sicardus, and shortly afterwards in Durandus (1215 and 1296, respectively), but they were not definitely inserted in the Roman Mass until 1570, when St Pius V carried out the decisions of the Council of Trent by publishing a revised and definitive edition of the Missal

18 *Sermo lxii*, 1.   19 Luke, xviii. 13.
20 Matt., xv. 18, 19.

of the Latin Church. The following prayer is of interest, because it is found in the *Sarum Missal*, where it forms the priest's immediate preparation for Holy Communion: "God our Father, fount and origin of all goodness, whose mercy prompted Thee to send down into this world Thine only Son, to take up our flesh, and whom I, most unworthy, now hold in my hands, I adore Thee, I glorify Thee; with all the strength of my mind and heart I praise Thee, beseeching Thee not to forsake us, Thy servants, but to forgive our sins, so that we may serve Thee, the only living and true God, with a pure heart and a chaste body."

Immediately before his Communion, the priest, according to the Sarum Rite, saluted the Sacred Host in these words: *Ave in aeternum sanctissima caro Christi, mihi ante omnia, et super omnia, summa dulcedo* (Eternal hail, most holy Body of Christ, before all and above all else sovereignly sweet to me)!

Before taking the Precious Blood, the celebrant prayed thus: *Ave in aeternum coelestis potus, mihi ante omnia, et super omnia, summa dulcedo* (Eternal hail, heavenly cup, before all and above all else sovereignly sweet to me)!

CHAPTER XXII

THE COMMUNION OF THE PRIEST

The Consummation of the Mass

THE Communion is the consummation of our sacrifice; it is also the moment of supreme union with the divine Victim: "The chalice of benediction, which we bless, is it not the communion of the Blood of Christ? And the bread, which we break, is it not the partaking of the Body of the Lord?"[1] The purpose of the Eucharistic Sacrifice is to make us to be one with Christ and with one another: "we, being many, are one bread, one body, all that partake of one bread."[2] The word *Communion* is as old as Christianity. St John Chrysostom, commenting on the above text of St Paul, writes: "What is this bread? The Body of Christ. What do they become who partake of it? The body of Christ; not many bodies, but one body. For just as bread is made up of many grains, yet so that these are nowhere seen, and though they indeed remain, their diversity does not appear owing to their union (oneness), even so are we united both to one another and to Christ. For this one is not nourished by one body, and that other one by another, for all are fed by one and the same; hence he says: 'we all partake of one bread.'"[3]

At first, the breaking of the consecrated Bread took place immediately before its distribution at the moment of the Communion. To break bread is a consecrated phrase, and the eating of it is a normal and necessary sequel: "After the president has given thanks (made the Eucharist), and all the people have uttered the usual acclamation (*Amen*), those who are called by us deacons give to each one present

---

1 1 Cor., x. 16. 2 *Ibid.*, 17.
3 *Hom. xxiv. in Ep.* 1 *ad Cor.*, x.

to share the Eucharistic bread and wine and water, and carry them to those not present.... We do not receive these things as common bread, or common drink, but even as Jesus Christ our Saviour, having been made flesh by the word of God, had flesh and blood of our salvation, so we have learned that the food, made a Eucharist by the word of prayer that comes from Him, from which our blood and flesh are nourished, by change are the Flesh and Blood of the incarnate Jesus."[4]

This text, to which many others might be added, establishes the fact that in the early days of the Church assistance at Mass always implied the reception of the Holy Eucharist. All partook of what was offered in the name of all. There was likewise a very strict order of precedence in the reception of the consecrated Elements. The celebrant (that is, the Bishop) communicated first; then the priests who *concelebrated* with him, the deacons and the rest of the clergy, and finally the entire people, including even little children.

One of the chief preoccupations of the authors of the Roman Liturgy seems to have been to lay stress upon the fact that the Eucharist is a symbol and efficient cause of the oneness of Christ and the faithful. This was done in a very striking manner by means of the so-called *fermentum*. The Pope, or officiating bishop, broke off a piece of the consecrated bread and communicated himself—another fragment of the same Host was dropped into the chalice—the clergy partook of the remainder of the consecrated Host and of the chalice from which the celebrant had drunk. For the Communion of the people, the Pope and other priests (or bishops) distributed the Eucharistic Bread, placing a fragment into the open right hand of each communicant (the men's hand being bare, that of the women covered with a veil). The chalice, or chalices, used for the Communion of the laity differed from that of the Pope and clergy, but to emphasize the unity of the sacrifice and that of the Church, a few drops from the chalice of the celebrant were poured into that from which the deacons made the people drink of the Precious Blood. That the distribution of the Precious Blood was one of the offices of the deacons (their chief duty

---

[4] Justin Martyr, cfr. Fortescue, *The Mass*, pp. 18, 19.

and privilege, in fact), we learn from the Acts of St Lawrence: *Experire utrum idoneum ministrum elegeris, cui commisisti Dominici sanguinis dispensationem* (Try whether thou didst choose a fit minister when thou didst commit to me the dispensation of the Blood of the Lord).[5]

According to the "Apostolic Constitutions," when giving Holy Communion under the form of bread, the celebrant said to each communicant: "The Body of Christ"; and the deacon, whilst giving him to drink from the chalice, said: "The Blood of Christ, the cup of life." The answer was in each case: "Amen." "All over the world," says St Augustine, "we say *Amen*, when we receive the price of our redemption."[6] And again: *Habet magnam vocem Christi sanguis in terra, quum eo accepto ab omnibus gentibus respondetur, Amen* (The blood of Christ speaks with a loud voice all over the earth when, at the moment of receiving it, all the nations answer: *Amen*).[7] The *Amen* of the communicant was his outward profession of faith that what was given him was the Body and Blood of Jesus Christ. Gradually this formula was expanded, and already in the time of St Gregory the Great it has become: *Corpus Domini nostri Jesu Christi conservet animam tuam* (May the Body of Our Lord Jesus Christ preserve thy soul) This is almost our own: *Corpus Domini nostri Jesu Christi custodiat animam tuam in vitam aeternam* (May the Body of our Lord Jesus Christ preserve thy soul to life everlasting). However, *Amen* is now said by the one who gives, not by him who receives Holy Communion, except at the Mass of ordination of priests, in which the candidates say the *Amen*.

The Priest's Communion

When the priest has concluded the threefold *Domine non sum dignus*, he takes the two fragments of the Host into his right hand, and, whilst tracing a cross with them over himself, he says: *Corpus Domini nostri Jesu Christi custodiat animam meam in vitam aeternam. Amen.* According to an answer of the Sacred Congregation of Rites, he bows his head as usual at the words *Jesu Christi*. After consuming the Sacred Host, he folds his hands before his face and remains for a while in contemplation

---

5 Cfr. *Brev. Rom.*, Aug. 10.   6 *Enarr. in Ps. cxxv.* 9.
7 *Contra Faust.*, XII, 10.

of the great mystery (*quiescit in meditatione sanctissimi Sacramenti*).[8] It is not opportune then to pray vocally, nor should the silent meditation be unduly prolonged; *aliquantulum* must be taken in relation to the entire duration of the Eucharistic Sacrifice.

Then the priest uncovers the chalice and genuflects, saying in the meantime: *Quid retribuam Domino pro omnibus quae retribuit mihi?* (What shall I render to the Lord for all He hath rendered unto me?) According to the *Ritus celebrandi*, x, it is only after he has gathered the fragments and wiped the paten that the priest says: *Calicem salutaris accipiam, et nomen Domini invocabo* (I will take the chalice of salvation, and call on the name of the Lord), taking at the same time the cup into his right hand. The rubric in the Canon seems to be at variance with this prescription, when it says: *extergit patenam super calicem, interim dicens: Quid retribuam* (he wipes the paten over the chalice, saying meanwhile: "What shall I render, etc."); then he blesses himself with the chalice. Both ways would appear legitimate; in fact, the general practice of priests seems to be to recite the entire prayer whilst gathering the fragments that may be on the corporal, and wiping the paten. The rubric, speaking of the particles, says "if there are any" (*si quae sint*); there may be none at all, if the Host has been carefully divided over the chalice. In any case, there is no cause for scraping almost the whole corporal, as some priests do, but only that part where the Host lay, and the places nearest to it. The words at the reception of the Precious Blood are identical with those said at the Communion of the Host, except for the change of *Corpus* to *Sanguis*. The Precious Blood should be taken *reverenter*, according to the rubric—that is, with a sense of awe, and at the same time with outward dignity. The cup should not be removed from the lips, nor raised too high, and the Precious Blood should be taken in one or two, or at the utmost in three draughts.

On removing the chalice from his lips, the priest immediately holds it out to the server, who pours into it at first only wine for the purification of the chalice and the lips of the priest. There is nothing in the rubrics to justify the pause which some think themselves at

---

8 *Rit. cel.*, x.

THE COMMUNION OF THE PRIEST

liberty to make before they take the purification. Whilst purifying the Chalice the priest says: *Quod ore sumpsimus, Domine, pura mente capiamus; et de munere temporali fiat nobis remedium sempiternum* (Grant, O Lord, that what we have taken with our mouth, we may receive with a pure mind; and of a temporal gift may it become for us an eternal remedy). The text of this prayer is already found in the Gelasian and in the Gregorian Sacramentary, but as a *Postcommunion*. We eat with our mouth, but only in a clean heart can we receive and retain the fruit of the altar of God. In those far-off days the faithful offered the material elements *(munus temporale)*, which, when changed into the Flesh and Blood of the Son of God, became a means of eternal life. We may also interpret the prayer as signifying that the offering of the Eucharistic Sacrifice, which we make in the days of this temporal life, will become for us an enduring remedy against the evils which now beset us. Holy Church prays thus in the Postcommunion of Maundy Thursday: *Quaesumus Domine Deus noster, ut, quod tempore nostrae mortalitatis exsequimur, immortalitatis tuae munere consequamur* (We beseech Thee, O Lord our God, that what we pursue in the time of our mortality may be ours through the gift of Thine immortality).

After the first purification, the priest places his thumbs and two first fingers over the mouth of the chalice and the server pours wine and water over them. In the meantime the celebrant prays: *Corpus tuum, Domine, quad sumpsi, et Sanguis quem potavi, adhaereat visceribus meis, et praesta ut in me non remaneat scelerum macula, quem pura et sancta refecerunt Sacramenta* (May Thy Body, O Lord, which I have received, and Thy Blood which I have drunk, cleave to my heart; and grant that no stain of sin may remain in me, who have been refreshed with pure and holy sacraments). Then he drinks the wine and water of the ablutions.

The last prayer is in the singular, and would appear to be a more recent addition. However, the ideas which it expresses are already found in a Postcommunion of the Sacramentary of St Leo: *Sacrosancti corporis et sanguinis Domini nostri Jesu Christi refectione vegetati, supplices Te rogamus, Deus, ut hoc remedio singulari, et ab omnium peccatorum nos contagione purifices, et a periculorum munias incursione cunctorum* (Refreshed by partaking of the most sacred Body and Blood of our Lord Jesus Christ, we humbly beseech Thee, O God, that by this unique remedy Thou wouldst purify us from the contagion of all sins, and preserve us from all manner of perils).

We pray that the Body and Blood of our Lord may cleave to our hearts (*visceribus*). In Biblical language the bowels (*viscera*) are described as the seat, or organ, of the feelings and emotions, even of the will itself. As we regard the heart as the seat of the emotions, "heart" is a more accurate and pleasing translation of *viscera* in this sense. Thus, Zachary sings of "the heart of God's mercy."[9] And St Paul tells the Philippians that "God is my witness, how I long after you all in the *heart* of Jesus Christ."[10] To the Corinthians he complains that, whereas "you are not straitened in us, but in your own heart you are straitened."[11] The presence of the infinite Majesty of the Holy One of God within our *hearts* should blot out the stains of our sins and dispel our spiritual darkness, for "what fellowship hath light with darkness... and what agreement hath the temple of God with idols? For you are the temple of the living God; as God saith: I will dwell in them, and walk among them."[12]

Quem pura et sancta refecerunt Sacramenta is used with reference solely to the sensible elements of the Eucharist. Though received under two material elements, it is but one Sacrament, giving to us the Flesh and Blood of the Son of the God of glory. The brief moment of the priest's Communion is among the most precious of his day. If the eyes of the Lord are upon the just and His ears unto their prayers,[13] how much more willingly will He not listen to the prayers and supplications of those with whom He deigns to share His own ineffable priesthood, at the very moment when He dwells within our breast?

The Antiphon of the Communion

After he has taken the ablutions and covered the chalice, the priest turns to the Missal and reads the *Communion*. This Antiphon is an abbreviated survival of the chants that formerly *accompanied* the distribu-

---

9 Luke, i. 78.
11 II Cor., vi. 12.
13 Ps. xxxiii. 16.
10 Philip., i. 8.
12 II Cor., vi. 14, 16.

tion of Holy Communion; in fact, it is the Antiphon of the Psalm, or Psalms, that were then sung. We still see traces of this custom in the Communion of the Mass for the Dead, which remains responsorial to this day. St Augustine tells us that he introduced into the African Church the practice of singing Psalms both at the Offertory and at the Communion. The "Apostolic Constitutions" prescribe the singing of Psalm xxxiii at the Communion. From the fourth century onwards, this Psalm furnished the Communion chants on all days of the year: "Every day, when we have been filled with the bread of heaven, we say: *Gustate et videte quam suavis est Dominus* (Taste and see that the Lord is sweet)."[14] Cassiodorus, in his commentary on Psalm xxxiii, leads us to think that such was the ordinary practice of the sixth century. On verse 6 (*Accedite ad eum et illuminamini*), he says: *Prius laudes praemisit, choros ordinavit; nunc in secunda parte, et ad ipsam communicationem populus hortatur accedere, ut Ecclesiae futurae ritum monitor spiritualis infunderet* (First he ordered hymns of praise and set up choirs of singers; the people are then encouraged to draw nigh, in order that the ritual of the Church to come might thus be foreshadowed). St Augustine looks upon Psalm xxxiii as a Eucharistic one. His commentaries on it make that point very clear; thus, on verse 9 he says: *Aperte modo de ipso Sacramento vult dicere.... Gustate et videte quoniam suavis est Dominus. Nonne aperit se psalmus?* (The psalmist now speaks plainly of the Sacrament itself.... Taste and see how the Lord is sweet. Is not the psalm made plain?)[15]

Later on various other chants were introduced, one of the most popular being the well-known hymn of the Antiphonary of Bangor, which begins thus:

> *Sancti, venite, Christi corpus sumite,*
> *Sanctum libantes quo redempti sanguinem.*
> *Salvati Christi corpore et sanguine,*
> *A quo refecti laudes dicamus Deo....*
>
> Come, ye Saints, take the Body of Christ,

---

14 St Jerome, *Comment. in Is.*, 11, 2.
15 *Enarr. ii in Ps. xxxiii*.

> *Drink the Blood by which you have been redeemed*
> *We were saved by the Body and Blood of Christ,*
> *Refreshed by Him, let us give praise to God.*[16]

The Antiphon of the Communion is generally taken from the Psalms or from some other book of Holy Scripture. However, some few have been composed or adapted by Holy Church; for example, that of the feast of St Ignatius of Antioch is the exclamation of the holy Martyr when he heard the roaring of the wild beasts: *Frumentum Christi sum, dentibus bestiarum molar, ut panis mundus inveniar* (I am the wheat of Christ: let me be ground by the teeth of wild beasts, that I may become pure bread).[17]

The Communion is generally in keeping with the character of the particular Mass, or with the spirit of the feast and the liturgical season. Very often it is taken from the same Psalm from which the Introit or the Gradual and Offertory have been drawn. Thus, the Mass generally ends on the same note as that on which it began.

The Antiphon of the Communion on Easter-day sums up the whole mystery and the peculiar spirit of the greatest of Christian festivals. It proclaims the triumphant victory of Christ, and inculcates once more the lesson which the Apostle teaches in the Epistle of the day: *Pascha nostrum immolatus est Christus, alleluia: itaque epulemur in azymis sinceritatis et veritatis, alleluia, alleluia, alleluia* (Christ our Pasch is immolated, alleluia: therefore, let us feast with the unleavened bread of sincerity and truth. Alleluia, alleluia, alleluia).

---

16 Cfr. an article by Dom Leclercq in *Dictionnaire d'archéol. chrét. et de liturgie*, III, col. 2437.

17 *Missale Rom.*, 1 Feb.

CHAPTER XXIII

THE CONCLUSION OF THE MASS

The Postcommunion

AFTER reading the Antiphon of the Communion, the priest turns towards the assistants and greets them with the words which precede nearly all the Collects of the Church: *Dominus vobiscum*. Whilst the server answers *Et cum spiritu tuo*, the celebrant turns to the Missal to read the Postcommunion. This is a prayer of thanksgiving for the Body and Blood of Jesus Christ, of which the priest and presumably the assistants have partaken at the moment of the Communion. The prayer is already given the name of Postcommunion in the Gelasian Missal, though in the Gregorian it is called *Complenda* (or *Oratio ad complendum*), because it marks the completion or conclusion of the Eucharistic Sacrifice. It is a thanksgiving, but a prayer also for the fullest realization on our part of the blessings we have received. The prayer is invariably in the plural. It is taken for granted that all the assistants have taken a full share in the sacrifice by the reception of Holy Communion.

The structure of the Postcommunion does not differ from that of the ordinary Collects, except that in most of them there is an explicit allusion to Holy Communion. Very frequently the prayer is inspired by the character of the Mass, the spirit of the feast, or the period of the year. Thus, for instance the Postcommunion of Easter Sunday contains an allusion both to the Holy Eucharist and to the solemnity of the day: *Spiritum nobis, Domine, tuae charitatis infunde; ut, quos sacramentis paschalibus satiasti, tua facias pietate concordes* (Pour forth into us, O Lord, the spirit of Thy charity: that those whom Thou hast fed with the Paschal sacraments, Thou mayest through Thy loving-kindness make of one mind).

On all the weekdays of Lent we say an additional Prayer at the Communion, entitled *Oratio super populum*. Many explanations have been given of the origin of this Collect. *Micrologus* gives the following: "The Prayer *super populum* is said during Lent, because the Prayer after Communion is generally only for those who have communicated. However, though the people come together every day of Lent, they do not communicate daily, as they should. Therefore, lest they be deprived of prayer as well as of Communion, this Collect has been added, in which thanksgiving is not made to God, but supplication in behalf of the people."[1] Another reason is given by Honorius of Autun, who says that this Prayer takes the place of the *eulogiae*, or blessed bread, which was distributed to the faithful after or in place of Holy Communion. During Lent these *eulogiae* were not handed round because of the fast.[2] This is very plausible, but a much more likely explanation may be found in the fact that the *Oratio super populum* is invariably the Collect of Vespers. In Lent and on all fast days Mass was said after None; therefore, the next Office to follow would be Vespers. So it seems likely enough that the Vesper Office was joined to the Mass and completed before the final dismissal of the people. This is the case to this day on Holy Saturday, when the Postcommunion is also the Collect of the abbreviated Vesper Office of that day. The invitation to the people: *Humiliate capita vestra Deo*, is not found in old manuscripts, and was evidently added when the Prayer became an exclusive feature of the Lenten Mass.

The Postcommunion is the common and official thanksgiving after Communion. In the account which St Augustine gives to Paulinus of the mode of celebration in the African churches of his day, the holy Doctor says: *Participato tanto sacramento, gratiarum actio cuncta concludit* (After participating in so great a sacrament, we conclude everything with thanksgiving).[3] The note of thanksgiving is always struck in this concluding prayer, but it invariably includes a petition also. On the first Sunday after Pentecost we pray thus: *Tantis, Domine, repleti muneribus, praesta quaesumus, ut et salutaria dona capiamus, et a*

1 *Microlog.*, 51.   2 Cfr. Bona, *Rer. Liturg.*, II, 20.
3 *Ep. ad Paulin.*, 149, in Migne, no. 16.

THE CONCLUSION OF THE MASS

tua numquam laude cessemus (Grant, we beseech Thee, O Lord, to us who have been filled with such great favors, that we may lay hold upon Thy salutary gifts and never cease to praise Thee). Whilst we return thanks to God for having allowed us to partake of so precious a gift as the Flesh and Blood of His beloved Son, it is natural that we should beseech Him to preserve in us and bring to full maturity the grace of holiness of which the Eucharist is the source and token. We give thanks to God whenever we turn to Him, even if we make no formal acts of gratitude, for every prayer and supplication implies a confession on our part that of ourselves we can do nothing and that all our sufficiency is from Him. Prayer is necessarily a glorification of the Majesty of God, for we should not send up supplications to Him, did we not know and confess that "every best and every perfect gift is from above, coming down from the Father of lights."[4]

On the conclusion of the last prayer, the celebrant returns to the middle of the altar, kisses it, and turning towards the people, says *Dominus vobiscum*. After the server's reply, the priest says: *Ite, Missa est* (Go, the Mass is ended). On ferial days he says instead: *Benedicamus Domino:* and at Requiem Masses: *Requiescant in pace,* turned in these last two cases, not towards the people, but towards the altar. Up till the middle of the eleventh century, *Ite, Missa est,* was the invariable conclusion of the Roman Mass.

There has been much and long discussion about the meaning of the word *Missa*, which has given its name to the whole of the Liturgical Sacrifice. The word signifies a formal dismissal. From the earliest days of the Church we find traces of some such ceremonial declaration that the assistants may depart. Even the pagans had such formulas. At the conclusion of a Roman funeral, the leader of the hired mourners cried out: *Ilicet (i.e., ire licet,* you may go)! Whilst the *lex arcani* was enforced, the Catechumens were bidden to leave the assembly of the faithful before the beginning of the Eucharistic celebration. There can be little doubt that this was done in words which closely resemble our present form of dismissal; hence the word *Missa* came to be connected, in the minds of both Catechumens and faithful, with the most sacred part of

---

4 James, i. 17.

the Liturgy, that is, the Mass. Thus, in a sermon of St Augustine we read: "After the sermon the dismissal of the Catechumens takes place: the faithful alone will remain" (*Ecce post sermonem fit missa Catechumenis; manebunt fideles*).[5] Here the word *missa* obviously signifies dismissal. By a transition which it is easy to understand, the word was retained to describe the chief liturgical function of the Church.

We find a form of dismissal already in Tertullian. The oldest *Ordo Romanus* prescribes that, at the end of the service, one of the deacons shall say to the people: *Ite, missa est*. Before that time, St John Chrysostom had warned Christians not to leave the assembly of the faithful until bidden to do so: "Hast thou entered into a church, do not leave before the dismissal" (*Ingressus es in Ecclesiam, O homo; ne exeas nisi dimittaris*).[6]

Micrologus gives the reason why *Ite Missa est* is omitted on certain days: "It is right that on festival days *Ite Missa est* should be said, because on such days there is a larger concourse of people, and they are wont to receive leave to depart in these words. But on ordinary days there is no such attendance of the people at Mass, but only on the part of Religious, who give more attention to spiritual than to worldly matters, and who also assist at the other offices. Hence, it is meet that these should not be bidden to depart immediately after Mass, but rather that they bless God." As for Advent and Lent, the reason why *Benedicamus Domino* replaces *Ite Missa est* is the desire to express the sadness of those days (*pro tristitia temporis insinuanda*). A simpler, but truer explanation is that the faithful are asked to stay for the remainder of the Canonical Office—that is, Vespers, as we have seen above.

Placeat

Since the twelfth century the formal dismissal of the people no longer marks the conclusion of the Mass. Up till that time, the clergy withdrew from the altar and the Pontiff blessed the people whilst returning to the sacristy. In the eleventh century simple priests began to bless the people as they were about to leave the sanctuary. The

5 *Sermo xlix*, 8. 6 Cfr. Bona, *Rer. Liturg.*, II, 20.

blessing is preceded by the prayer *Placeat tibi, sancta Trinitas*. This was only a private prayer which the priest recited as he left the altar. "Everything having been finished, the priest kisses the altar, saying: 'O Holy Trinity, let the performance of my homage be pleasing to Thee'" (*Finitis omnibus, osculatur sacerdos altare, dicens: Placeat tibi, sancta Trinitas*).[7] This prayer is addressed directly to the adorable Trinity. In it the priest expresses, as it were for the last time, the dispositions which have animated and upheld him during the Holy Sacrifice, as well as the motives for which he has offered it. The Mass is the most perfect acknowledgment of our obligations towards the Majesty of the three divine Persons (*obsequium servitutis meae*). *Obsequium* signifies divine worship, or such homage as may be offered to God alone: *venit hora ut omnis qui interficit vos arbitretur obsequium se praestare Deo* (the hour cometh that whosoever killeth you, will think that he doth a service to God).[8] We pray that what we have offered may be, our unworthiness notwithstanding, acceptable to God and beneficial to those in whose behalf we have offered it.

In the Liturgy of St John Chrysostom there is also a final prayer for those who have assisted at the Holy Sacrifice: "O Lord, who blessest those who bless Thee and sanctifiest those that put their trust in Thee, save Thy people and bless Thine inheritance; protect the whole body of Thy Church and sanctify those who love the beauty of Thy house. Do Thou endow them with Thy divine power, and forsake not us who set our hope in Thee ... to Thee we ascribe glory and thanks and worship, to the Father, and to the Son, and to the Holy Ghost, now, and for ever, and from all ages to all ages."

The Liturgy of the Maronites has a touching prayer, which is the priest's farewell to the altar of sacrifice and is recited at the end of Mass: "Abide in peace, holy altar, I shall return to thee in peace. May the oblation which I have taken from thee be unto me for a propitiation and remission of my debts and sins, so that I may stand before the throne of Christ without condemnation and confusion. I know not whether or not I shall return to offer sacrifice again upon thee."[9]

---

7 *Micrologus*, 22.   8 John, xvi, 2.
9 Bona, *loc. cit.*

The Blessing

During the prayer *Placeat*, the priest places his joined hands upon the edge of the altar, and bows his head (*capite inclinato*). At its conclusion he kisses the altar, raises his eyes and extended hands to heaven, folds his hands again and bows to the cross, saying in the meantime: *Benedicat vos omnipotens Deus*. Then he turns towards the people and blesses them by tracing the sign of the cross over them whilst he says: *Pater, et Filius, et Spiritus Sanctus*. The server answers: *Amen*.

A final blessing of the assistants is found in most Liturgies. The power to bless belongs to the priesthood, and has always been exercised by it. Even the priests of the Old Law blessed the people, though their blessing was more by way of supplication to obtain God's goodwill towards His people. God Himself deigned to prescribe the form of that blessing: "Thus shall you bless the children of Israel, and you shall say to them: The Lord bless thee, and keep thee. The Lord show His face to thee, and have mercy on thee. The Lord turn His countenance to thee and give thee peace."[10] The concluding verse of the chapter shows the nature of the Levitical blessing: "They shall invoke My name upon the children of Israel; *and I will bless them*."

The priesthood of the New Law is endowed with a direct and real power to bless things and persons, and this power flows directly from the priestly *character*. In the hour of his ordination, the priest's hands are anointed with oil, whilst the bishop prays that God would "consecrate and sanctify these hands, through our unction and Thy blessing, that whatsoever things they shall bless, may be blessed; and whatsoever things they shall consecrate, may be consecrated and made holy in the name of our Lord Jesus Christ." By his blessing, therefore, the priest bestows a special sanctity upon the object blessed. The efficacy of the priestly blessing is akin to the virtue of the Sacraments in the sense that, as in the Sacraments the external rite signifies and actually causes an inward grace, so the external rite of blessing bestows upon the soul certain special helps called *actual* graces. Sanctifying grace is not *directly* increased by the priest's blessing, but this blessing disposes the soul for such an increase even as all *actual* graces do. The bless-

---

[10] Num., vi. 23–26.

ing is always given by tracing a cross over the objects or persons to whom it is imparted. In the Eastern Liturgies this is often done with a two- or three-branched candle. At the conclusion of the Liturgy of St John Chrysostom, the priest says: "May the blessing of the Lord and His mercy always come upon you, through His divine favor and compassion, now, and for ever, and from all ages to all ages. Glory to Thee, O Christ, our God and our Hope, glory to Thee."

St Augustine alludes several times to the custom of blessing the people. Speaking of the dissensions brought about by the Pelagians, he says: *benedictionibus nostris resistitur, quando super populum dicimus, optantes ei et poscentes a Domino.*[11] Before him Tertullian thus rebukes a pagan: "Whereas with us every blessing pronounced in the name of the God of goodness and kindness is a thing of the highest sacredness... thou sayest as readily as any Christian need: 'God bless thee.'"[12]

The blessing of the priest has a marvellous efficacy, because it is not merely a prayer or a mark of kindliness on his part, but an exercise of the mysterious powers with which he is invested. He blesses the people as the minister and representative of God, and hence, with obvious limitations, to his blessing also may be applied what St Augustine says of the blessing of God: *Deus, cum benedicit, facit quod dicit* (When God blesses, He does what the words signify).[13] The point of Augustine's saying is in the antithesis: *benedicere* and *benefacere* (to speak well and to do well). God does not merely wish us well, He bestows good things upon us; for He is the source of all good.

The Last Gospel

The magnificent revelation of the splendor and glory of God's eternal life, which we are given in the first fourteen verses of the first chapter of the Gospel of St John, has always secured a special reverence and devotion for this portion of the inspired text. The custom of reciting this section of the Fourth Gospel at the end of Mass is, however, one of the very last additions to the Liturgy. The first mention of such a recitation is found in Durandus, who says that some priests, desirous

11 *Ep. clxxix*, 30.   12 Tertullian, *De testim. animae*, 2.
13 *Enarr. in Ps. cviii*, 30.

of reciting at the end of Mass the Gospel of St John, or some other Gospel, make first a sign of the cross upon the altar, and afterwards upon their forehead (*quidam volentes dicere, finita Missa, evangelium Sancti Joannis, vel aliud, imprimunt primo signum crucis super altare, et postea in fronte*).[14] However, the custom was for the priest to say this Gospel, not at the altar, but on his way to the sacristy, by way of thanksgiving. Such is, for instance, the prescription of the Sarum Missal. It finally became an integral part of the Mass in the Missal of St Pius V in 1570. But to this day a bishop, when celebrating pontifically, only says the beginning of the Gospel at the altar (*Dominus vobiscum* and *Initium Sancti Evangelii secundum Joannem*); the Gospel itself he recites whilst returning to the throne.

The priest bends the knee at the words: *Et Verbum caro factum est*, as an act of homage to the Incarnate Word, whom the Angels worshipped upon His entrance into this world.[15] On certain days the Gospel of St John is replaced by another, but, as the *Ordo* invariably warns the priest of such a change, there is no need to enumerate those days.

The first chapter of St John's Gospel has always been an object of wonder and admiration. St Augustine relates that a certain philosopher of the school of Plato was wont to say that the beginning of the Gospel of St John should be written in letters of gold and set up in a prominent place in all the churches of the world.[16]

St John has spoken of the divinity of our Lord as no other Evangelist has done. *Hoc ructabat quod biberat*, says St Augustine in an untranslatable phrase. It is not without cause that it is said of him that, at the Last Supper, he rested his head upon the breast of the Lord. "He drank in secret from that breast, but what he had drunk secretly, he published openly (*De illo ergo pectore in secreto bibebat, sed quod in secreto bibit, in manifesto eructavit*), so that all nations should hear, not only of the Incarnation, Passion and Resurrection of the Son of God, but likewise that, ere He became incarnate, He was the Only Begotten, the Word of the Father."[17]

At the end of the Last Gospel, the server says *Deo Gratias*, and thus

---

14 Durandus, *Rationale div. off.*, IV, 24,
15 Heb. i. 6.
16 *De civ. Dei*, X, 29.
17 *Tract. in Ioan.*, xxxvi.

the Mass comes to an end. After a private Mass we are now bound to recite three Hail Marys, the Hail Holy Queen, and the two prayers first prescribed by Leo XIII, whose command has been maintained by successive Popes ever since. The threefold invocation of the Sacred Heart is strongly recommended. These prayers are in no sense part of the Mass. The Holy Sacrifice ends with the final *Deo Gratias*, which suggests to the priest the all-important duty of returning thanks to God for the wonderful favors he has received.

CHAPTER XXIV

THANKSGIVING AFTER MASS

THE rubric of the Missal says: *Finito Evangelia Sancti Joannis, discedens ab altari, pro gratiarum actione dicit Antiphonam 'Trium Puerorum,' cum reliquis.*... The Canticle of the Three Young Men in the furnace and Psalm cl, with its versicles, and the three short prayers that follow, are the very minimum of the priest's thanksgiving. Since the rubric is so explicit in prescribing this thanksgiving, it appears that it could not be omitted without a real disobedience to the will of Holy Church, and, as a consequence, without incurring the guilt of venial sin. Moreover, the *Codex juris canonici* emphatically enjoins both a private preparation before and a personal thanksgiving after Mass, so that it would appear that the priest has not fulfilled all his obligations even when he has recited the *Benedicite* whilst returning to the sacristy. The following is the injunction of Canon 810: *Sacerdos ne omittat ad Eucharistici Sacrificii oblationem sese piis precibus disponere, eoque expleto gratias Deo pro tanto beneficio agere* (Let the priest not neglect to prepare himself by devout prayers for the oblation of the Eucharistic Sacrifice, and, at its termination, to return thanks to God for so great a benefit). This personal thanksgiving should be prolonged according to one's strength and grace. Spiritual writers tell us unanimously that the priest should not allow it to dwindle down to less than a quarter of an hour. No doubt, his prayer must not be measured by the length of time he spends on his knees. Its value depends chiefly upon the fervor and intensity of his interior acts. But there is a virtue even in mere material faithfulness to a period of prayer which one has laid down as a law unto oneself and from which one does not permit either coldness or distractions to make one swerve. A priest's thanksgiving can be greatly helped if he recites, more with the heart than with the lips, slowly and deliberately, the prayers suggested by Holy Church in the official thanksgiving to be found in the Missal or Breviary. Moreover, the attentive and prayerful reading of and meditation on a chapter of the Fourth Book of *The Imitation,* or a chapter of the New Testament or any spiritual book, will help him to make at least some return to the Author of every best and perfect gift. Let the priest speak to his Lord in the glowing words of the great Benedictine mystic, St Gertrude: "O Jesus, full of love, Thou sweetest Guest of my soul, may Thine exquisite and ravishing union with me be to me today the remission of all my sins, the satisfaction of all my negligences, and my return to the life I had lost. May it be my everlasting salvation, the healing of my soul and of my body, the enlargement of my love, my renewal in virtue, and the establishment of my life in Thee for evermore! May it be within me the source of all virtues, the end of all sin, the increase of all good and the everlasting covenant of Thy love, so that my body alone may linger in this place of exile, and the whole energy of my soul be there, where Thou art, my heritage beyond all price."[1]

Gratias misericordiae ipsius, gratias gratiae ipsius. Nos enim gratias agimus, non damus, nec reddimus, nec referimus, nec rependimus; gratias verbis agimus, rem tenemus [Thanks to His mercy, thanks to His grace. We express our thanks: we do not give them, nor return them, nor repay them: we express our thanks in words, while we retain possession of the (unrequited) benefit].[2]

After the institution of the Holy Eucharist, which was also the celebration of the first Mass, at the conclusion of which the Apostles made their first Communion, Jesus Christ, together with His disciples, sang hymns of praise and thanksgiving: *Hymno dicto, exierunt in montem Oliveti.*[3] Holy Church would have her children make of thanksgiving a constant and lifelong task. More than one Postcommunion concludes with some such phrase: *da quaesumus ut in gratiarum semper actione maneamus.* Such is the prayer we address to God on the Feast of St Aloysius Gonzaga, of whom it is related that, as the custom then was, he received Holy Communion on the Sunday,

---

1 *Exercises of St Gertrude,* 1.
2 St Augustine, *Enarrat. in Ps. lxxxviii,* sub fine.
3 Matt., xxvi. 30.

giving the three preceding days to preparation and spending the three following days in thanksgiving.

The priest's thanksgiving should be made before the Blessed Sacrament—before the altar still redolent with the sweet fragrance of the Eucharistic Sacrifice. Let us beware of telescoping our thanksgiving and the recitation of some part of the Office into the small compass of this most precious quarter of an hour. If the priest's occupations be manifold and pressing, they are a reason, not for shortening, but rather for lingering over his thanksgiving. We can only fulfill our priestly duties worthily and profitably, if prayer is like an atmosphere that surrounds us and clings to us. When the faithful shall see their pastor on his knees before his Lord, they will feel impelled to follow where he leads, and we shall less frequently behold the sorry spectacle of people leaving church almost before the conclusion of a Mass at which they have communicated.

By way of concluding our brief study of the adorable Sacrifice of the Mass, it will be interesting to quote one or two passages from the writings of men differing widely in their ideas on religion, who yet speak of the Eucharistic Sacrifice in terms of such glowing eloquence that they bear repeated quotation.

Mr Augustine Birrell is not a Catholic (if we are not mistaken, he is a Baptist), but he is far from blind to the beauty and solemnity of Catholic belief and worship. In a paper contributed to *The Nineteenth Century*, entitled "What happened at the Reformation?" Mr Birrell coined the oft-repeated dictum: "It is the Mass that matters!" "The Mass," the writer says, "is a mystery so tremendous, so profoundly attractive, so intimately associated with the keystone of the Christan faith, so vouched for by the testimony of Saints.... If the Incarnation be indeed the one divine event to which the whole creation moves, the miracle of the altar may well seem its restful shadow cast over a dry and thirsty land, for the help of man who is apt to be discouraged if perpetually told that everything really important and interesting happened once for all, long ago, in a chill, historic past. *It is the Mass that matters*. It is the Mass that makes the difference, so hard to define—so subtle is it, yet so perceptible—between a Catholic country and a Protestant one, between Dublin and Edinburgh, between

Havre and Cromer."[4]

In *Loss and Gain,* Cardinal Newman puts into the mouth of one of the characters of the story (which is obviously autobiographical) words describing the Mass in a way in which only this great master of style could have depicted it: "To me nothing is so consoling, so piercing, so thrilling, so overcoming as the Mass, said as it is among us. I could attend Masses for ever, and not be tired. It is not a mere form of words: it is a great action, the greatest action that can be on earth. It is not the invocation merely, but, if I dare use the word, the evocation of the Eternal. He becomes present on the altar in flesh and blood, before whom Angels bow and devils tremble. This is that awful event which is the end, and is the interpretation, of every part of the solemnity. Words are necessary, but as a means, not as ends: they are not mere addresses to the throne of grace; they are instruments of what is far higher—of consecration, of sacrifice. They hurry on as if impatient to fulfill their mission. Quickly they go, the whole is quick; for they are all parts of one integral action. Quickly they go; for they are awful words of sacrifice, they are a work too great to delay upon; as when it was said in the beginning: 'What thou doest, do quickly.' Quickly they pass; for the Lord Jesus goes with them, as He passed along the lake in the days of His flesh, quickly calling first one and then another. Quickly they pass; because as the lightning which shineth from one part of the heaven unto the other, so is the coming of the Son of Man. Quickly they pass; for they are as the words of Moses, when the Lord came down in the cloud, calling on the name of the Lord as he passed by: 'The Lord, the Lord God, merciful and gracious, long-suffering, and abundant in goodness and truth.' And as Moses on the mountain, so we too 'make haste and bow our heads to the earth, and adore.' So we, all around, each in his place, look out for the great Advent, 'waiting for the moving of the water.' Each in his place, with his own heart, with his own wants, with his own thoughts, with his own intentions, with his own prayers, separate but concordant, watching what is going on, watching its progress, uniting in its consummation—not painfully and hopelessly following a hard form

---

4 Augustine Birrell in *The Nineteenth Century,* April, 1896.

of prayer from beginning to end, but like a concert of musical instruments, each different, but concurring in a sweet harmony, we take our part with God's priest, supporting him, yet guided by him. There are little children there, and old men, and simple laborers, and students in seminaries, priests preparing for Mass, priests making their thanksgiving; there are innocent maidens, and there are penitents; but out of these many minds rises one Eucharistic hymn, and the great Action is the measure and the scope of it."[5]

Let us conclude with a quotation from a book which enjoyed immense popularity during the centuries which immediately preceded the Reformation, *viz.*, *The Lay Folk's Mass Book:*

> The worthiest thing, most of goodness,
> In all this world, it is the Mass.
> If a thousand clerks did nought else,
> (According to Saint Jerome tells)
> But told the virtue of Mass-singing,
> And the profit of Mass-hearing,
> Yet should they never the fifth part,
> For all their wit and all their art,
> Tell the virtue, meeds, and pardon
> To them that with devotion,
> In cleanness and with good intent
> Do worship to this Sacrament.

---

[5] *Loss and Gain*, xx.

APPENDIX

THE ORDINARY OF THE MASS

As some of the explanations in the body of this work have been based on the Mass for Easter-day, the variable parts of the Mass have been taken from that feast.

When the priest has vested, he goes to the altar, preceded by the server, bows before the altar (or genuflects, if the Blessed Sacrament is in the tabernacle), makes the sign of the cross, and says aloud:

In nomine Patris, et Filii, et Spiritus Sancti. Amen.

In the name of the Father, and of the Son, and of the Holy Ghost. Amen.

Then he joins his hands before his breast and begins the Antiphon:

℣. Introibo ad altare Dei.
℟. Ad Deum qui laetificat juventutem meam.

℣. I will go unto the altar of God.
℟. To God, who giveth joy to my youth.

Then he says the following Psalm xlii *alternately with the server:*

℣. Judica me Deus, et discerne causam meam de gente non sancta: ab homine iniquo et doloso erue me.
℟. Quia tu es Deus fortitudo mea: quare me repulisti, et quare tristis incedo, dum affligit me inimicus?
℣. Emitte lucem tuam, et veri-

℣. Judge me, O God, and distinguish my cause from the nation that is not holy; deliver me from the unjust and deceitful man.
℟. For Thou, O God, art my strength: why hast Thou cast me off? and why go I sorrowful whilst the enemy afflicteth me?
℣. Send forth Thy light and Thy

tatem tuam: ipsa me deduxerunt, et adduxerunt in montem sanctum tuum et in tabernacula tua.
℟. Et introibo ad altare Dei; ad Deum qui laetificat juventutem meam.
℣. Confitebor tibi in cithara Deus, Deus meus: quare tristis es anima mea, et quare conturbas me?

℟. Spera in Deo, quoniam adhuc confitebor illi: salutare vultus mei, et Deus meus.
℣. Gloria Patri, et Filio, et Spiritui Sancto.
℟. Sicut erat in principio et nunc, et semper, et in saecula saeculorum. Amen.

truth: they have led me and brought me unto Thy holy hill, and into Thy tabernacles.
℟. And I will go unto the altar of God: to God who giveth joy to my youth.
℣. To Thee, O God, my God, I will give praise on the harp: why art thou sad, O my soul? and why dost thou disquiet me?

℟. Hope in God, for I will still give praise to Him: the salvation of my countenance, and my God.
℣. Glory be to the Father, etc.

℟. As it was in the beginning, is now, and ever shall be, world without end. Amen.

He now repeats the Antiphon:

℣. Introibo ad altare Dei.
℟. Ad Deum qui laetificat juventutem meam.

℣. I will go unto the altar of God.
℟. To God, who giveth joy to my youth.

Making the sign of the cross on himself, the priest then says:

℣. Adjutorium nostrum in nomine Domini.
℟. Qui fecit coelum et terram.

℣. Our help is in the name of the Lord.
℟. Who made heaven and earth.

Then, joining his hands and bowing profoundly, he says the Confiteor:

℣. Confiteor Deo omnipotenti, etc.
℟. Misereatur tui omnipotens Deus, et dimissis peccatis tuis, perducat te ad vitam aeternam.
℣. Amen.

℣. I confess to Almighty God, etc.
℟. May almighty God have mercy upon thee, forgive thee thy sins, and bring thee to life everlasting.
℣. Amen.

℞. Confiteor Deo omnipotenti, beatae Mariae semper virgini, beato Michaeli archangelo, beato Joanni Baptistae, sanctis Apostolis Petro et Paulo, omnibus Sanctis, et tibi, Pater, quia peccavi nimis cogitatione, verbo et opere: mea culpa, mea culpa, mea maxima culpa. Ideo precor beatam Mariam semper virginem, beatum Michaelem archangelum, beatum Joannem Baptistam, sanctos Apostolos Petrum et Paulum, omnes Sanctos, et te, Pater, orare pro me ad Dominum Deum nostrum.

℞. I confess to almighty God, to blessed Mary ever virgin, to blessed Michael the Archangel, to blessed John the Baptist, to the holy apostles Peter and Paul, to all the saints, and to you, Father, that I have sinned exceedingly in thought, word, and deed, [*he here strikes his breast thrice*] through my fault, through my fault, through my most grievous fault. Therefore, I beseech the blessed Mary ever virgin, blessed Michael the Archangel, blessed John the Baptist, the holy apostles Peter and Paul, all the saints, and you, Father, to pray to the Lord our God for me.

Then the priest, with his hands joined, gives the Absolution, *saying:*

℣. Misereatur vestri omnipotens Deus, et dimissis peccatis vestris, perducat vos ad vitam aeternam.
℞. Amen.

℣. May almighty God have mercy upon you, forgive you your sins, and bring you to life everlasting.
℞. Amen.

Signing himself with the sign of the cross, he says:

℣. Indulgentiam, absolutionem et remissionem peccatorum nostrorum, tribuat nobis omnipotens et misericors Dominus.
℞. Amen.

℣. May the almighty and merciful Lord grant us pardon, absolution, and remission of our sins.
℞. Amen.

Then, bowing down, he continues:

℣. Deus tu conversus vivificabis nos.
℞. Et plebs tua laetabitur in te.

℣. Thou wilt turn again, O God, and quicken us.
℞. And Thy people shall rejoice

℣. Ostende nobis, Domine, misericordiam tuam.
℟. Et salutare tuum da nobis.
℣. Domine exaudi orationem meam.
℟. Et clamor meus ad te veniat.
℣. Dominus vobiscum.
℟. Et cum spiritu tuo.

℣. Show us, O Lord, Thy mercy.
℟. And grant us Thy salvation.
℣. O Lord, hear my prayer.
℟. And let my cry come unto Thee.
℣. The Lord be with you.
℟. And with thy spirit.

Extending and joining his hands, he says aloud Oremus; *then, while ascending to the altar, he says in a low voice:*

Aufer a nobis, quaesumus Domine, iniquitates nostras: ut ad Sancta Sanctorum puris mereamur mentibus introire. Per Christum Dominum nostrum. Amen.

Take away from us our iniquities, we beseech Thee, O Lord: that we may be worthy to enter with pure minds into the Holy of Holies. Through Christ our Lord. Amen.

Bowing down over the altar with joined hands, he says:

Oramus te, Domine, per merita sanctorum tuorum, quorum reliquiae hic sunt, et omnium sanctorum: ut indulgere digneris omnia peccata mea. Amen.

We beseech Thee, O Lord, by the merits of Thy saints whose relics are here [*here he kisses the altar*], and of all the saints, that Thou wouldst vouchsafe to forgive me all my sins. Amen.

Then the priest, signing himself with the sign of the cross, reads the Introit.

Station at St Mary Major

Introitus. Ps. 138.
Resurrexi, et adhuc tecum sum, alleluia: posuisti super me manum tuam, alleluia: mirabilis facta est scientia tua, alleluia, alleluia. *Ps.*

Introit. Ps. 138.
I have arisen, and am still with Thee, alleluia: Thou hast laid Thy hand upon Me, alleluia: Thy knowledge is become wonderful,

THE ORDINARY OF THE MASS

Domine, probasti me, et cognovisti me: tu cognovisti sessionem meam, et resurrectionem meam. ℣. Gloria Patri.

alleluia, alleluia. *Ps.* Lord, Thou hast proved Me, and known Me: Thou hast known My sitting down, and My rising up. ℣. Glory be to the Father, etc.

Then, with joined hands, the priest says alternately with the server:

Kyrie eleison. Kyrie eleison. Kyrie eleison.

Lord, have mercy upon us [*thrice*].

Christe eleison. Christe eleison. Christe eleison.

Christ, have mercy upon us [*thrice*].

Kyrie eleison. Kyrie eleison. Kyrie eleison.

Lord, have mercy upon us [*thrice*].

Afterwards, standing at the middle of the altar, extending and then joining his hands, he says the Gloria in excelsis:

Gloria in excelsis Deo, et in terra pax hominibus bonae voluntatis. Laudamus te, benedicimus te, adoramus te, glorificamus te. Gratias agimus tibi propter magnam gloriam tuam. Domine Deus Rex coelestis, Deus Pater omnipotens. Domine Fili Unigenite, Jesu Christe. Domine Deus, Agnus Dei, Filius Patris. Qui tollis peccata mundi, miserere nobis. Qui tollis peccata mundi, suscipe deprecationem nostram. Qui sedes ad dexteram Patris, miserere nobis. Quoniam tu solus sanctus, tu solus Dominus, tu solus altissimus, Jesu Christe, cum Sancto Spiritu, in gloria Dei Patris. Amen.

Glory be to God on high [*inclining his head*], and on earth peace to men of good will. We praise Thee; we bless Thee; we adore Thee [*inclining his head*]; we glorify Thee. We give Thee thanks [*inclining his head*] for Thy great glory, O Lord God, heavenly King, God the Father almighty: O Lord Jesus Christ [*inclining his head*], the only-begotten Son: O Lord God, Lamb of God, Son of the Father, who takest away the sins of the world, have mercy on us; Thou who takest away the sins of the world, receive our prayer [*inclining his head*]: Thou who sittest at the right hand of the Father, have mercy on us. For Thou only art holy: Thou only art Lord: Thou only, O Jesus Christ [*inclining his head*], with the Holy Ghost [*signing himself with the sign of the cross*], art most high in the glory of God the Father. Amen.

The priest kisses the altar, and, turning to the people, says:

℣. Dominus vobiscum.
℟. Et cum spiritu tuo.

℣. The Lord be with you.
℟. And with thy spirit.

He then says Oremus, *and reads the* Collect *or* Collects *of the day or feast, the* Epistle, Gradual, Tract *(or* Alleluia*) with* Verse, *and* Sequence *(if one is prescribed for the feast).*

Oratio

Deus, qui hodierna die per Unigenitum tuum, aeternitatis nobis aditum devicta morte reserasti: vota nostra, quae praeveniendo aspiras, etiam adjuvando prosequere. Per eumdem Dominum nostrum, etc.

Collect

O God, who through Thine only-begotten Son didst on this day overcome death and open unto us the gates of everlasting life: to our good resolutions which Thou didst anticipate with Thy holy inspirations, grant furtherance also by Thy gracious aid. Through the same, etc.

Lectio Epistolae beati Pauli Apostoli ad Corinthios, 1, c. 5.

Fratres: Expurgate vetus fermentum, ut sitis nova conspersio, sicut estis azymi. Etenim Pascha nostrum immolatus est Christus. Itaque epulemur: non in fermento veteri, neque in fermento malitiae et nequitiae: sed in azymis sinceritatis, et veritatis.

℟. Deo gratias.

Lesson from the Epistle of St Paul the Apostle to the Corinthians, 1, c. 5.

Brethren: Purge out the old leaven, that you may be a new paste, as you are unleavened: for Christ our Pasch is sacrificed. Therefore let us feast, not with the old leaven, nor with the leaven of malice and wickedness, but with the unleavened bread of sincerity and truth.

℟. Thanks be to God.

Graduale. Ps. 117.
Haec dies, quam fecit Dominus: exsultemus, et laetemur in ea. ℣. Confitemini Domino, quoniam bonus: quoniam in saeculum misericordia ejus. Alleluia, alleluia. ℣. Pascha nostrum immolatus est Christus.

Sequentia
Victimae paschali laudes immolent Christiani.

Agnus redemit oves: Christus innocens Patri reconciliavit peccatores.

Mors et vita duello conflixere mirando: dux vitae mortuus, regnat vivus.

Dic nobis, Maria, quid vidisti in via?
Sepulchrum Christi viventis: et gloriam vidi resurgentis:
Angelicos testes, sudarium et vestes.

Surrexit Christus spes mea: praecedet vos in Galilaeam.
Scimus Christum surrexisse a mortuis vere: tu nobis, victor Rex, miserere. Amen. Alleluia.

Gradual. Ps. 117.
This is the day which the Lord hath made: let us be glad and rejoice therein. ℣. Give praise to the Lord, for He is good: for His mercy endureth for ever. Alleluia, alleluia. ℣. Christ our Pasch is immolated.

Sequence
Let Christian men their voices raise
And sing the Paschal Victim's praise
This solemn festival to keep.
Christ, innocent and undefiled,
Sinners to God hath reconciled,
The Lamb redeemed the Father's sheep.

In this great triumph death and life
Together met in wondrous strife,
The Prince of Life, once dead, doth reign.

Say what thou sawest, Mary, say,
Upon thy road at break of day?
"Christ's glory as He rose again.
"I saw the tomb where He did lie,
"And angel witnesses hard by,
"The winding cloths were there to see.
"Christ, my hope, is risen, and He
"Awaiteth you in Galilee."
We know that Christ is risen indeed,
And, Victor King, before Thee plead,

Have pity, Lord, and clemency.
Amen. Alleluia.

Bowing before the middle of the altar and with hands joined, the priest says:

Munda cor meum, ac labia mea, omnipotens Deus, qui labia Isaiae Prophetae calculo mundasti ignito: ita me tua grata miseratione dignare mundare, ut sanctum Evangelium tuum digne valeam nuntiare. Per Christum Dominum nostrum. Amen.
Jube Domine benedicere. Dominus sit in corde meo, et in labiis meis: ut digne et competenter annuntiem Evangelium suum. Amen.

Cleanse my heart and my lips, O almighty God, who didst cleanse the lips of the prophet Isaias with a burning coal, and vouchsafe, through Thy gracious mercy, so to purify me, that I may worthily announce Thy holy Gospel. Through Christ, our Lord. Amen.
Give me Thy blessing, O Lord. The Lord be in my heart and on my lips, that I may worthily and becomingly proclaim His holy Gospel. Amen.

Then, proceeding to the missal, he says with joined hands:

℣. Dominus vobiscum.
℟. Et cum spiritu tuo.

℣. The Lord be with you.
℟. And with thy spirit.

While making the sign of the cross with his right thumb on the missal, then on his forehead, mouth and breast, he continues:

℣. Sequentia sancti Evangelii secundum Marcum.
℟. Gloria tibi Domine.

℣. The continuation of the holy Gospel according to St Mark.
℟. Glory be to Thee, O Lord.

With joined hands, the priest then reads the Gospel.

In illo tempore: Maria Magdalene, et Maria Jacobi, et Salome emerunt aromata, ut venientes ungerent Jesum. Et valde mane una sabbatorum, veniunt ad monumentum, orto jam sole. Et

At that time: Mary Magdalen, and Mary the mother of James, and Salome bought sweet spices, that, coming, they might anoint Jesus. And very early in the morning, the first day of the week, they

dicebant ad invicem: Quis revolvet nobis lapidem ab ostio monumenti? Et respicientes viderunt revolutum lapidem. Erat quippe magnus valde. Et introëuntes in monumentum viderunt juvenem sedentem in dextris, coopertum stola candida, et obstupuerunt. Qui dicit illis: Nolite expavescere: Jesum quaeritis Nazarenum, crucifixum: surrexit, non est hic, ecce locus ubi posuerunt eum. Sed ite, dicite discipulis ejus, et Petro, quia praecedit vos in Galilaeam: ibi eum videbitis, sicut dixit vobis.

come to the sepulchre, the sun being now risen: and they said one to another: Who shall roll us back the stone from the door of the sepulchre? And looking, they saw the stone rolled back, for it was very great. And entering into the sepulchre, they saw a young man sitting on the right side, clothed with a white robe, and they were astonished; who saith to them: Be not affrighted; you seek Jesus of Nazareth, who was crucified: He is risen, He is not here; behold the place where they laid Him. But go, tell His disciples and Peter, that He goeth before you into Galilee: there you shall see Him, as He told you.

℟. Laus tibi, Christe.

℟. Praise be to Thee, O Christ.

The priest then kisses the missal, saying:

Per evangelica dicta deleantur nostra delicta.

May our sins be blotted out by the words of the Gospel.

Now (or at the end of the homily or sermon) standing at the middle of the altar, he extends, raises and then rejoins his hands, and begins the Credo.

The Nicene Creed.

Credo in unum Deum, Patrem omnipotentem, factorem coeli et terrae, visibilium omnium et invisibilium.
Et in unum Dominum Jesum Christum, Filium Dei unigen-

I believe in one God [*inclining his head*], the Father almighty, Maker of heaven and earth, and of all things visible and invisible.
And in one Lord Jesus Christ [*inclining his head*], the only-be-

itum. Et ex Patre natum ante omnia saecula. Deum de Deo, lumen de lumine, Deum verum de Deo vero. Genitum, not factum, consubstantialem Patri: per quem omnia facta sunt. Qui propter nos homines, et propter nostram salutem descendit de coelis. Et incarnatus est de Spiritu Sancto ex Maria Virgine: (Hic genuflectitur) ET HOMO FACTUS EST. Crucifixus etiam pro nobis: sub Pontio Pilato passus, et sepultus est. Et resurrexit tertia die, secundum Scripturas. Et ascendit in coelum: sedet ad dexteram Patris. Et iterum venturus est cum gloria, judicare vivos et mortuos: cujus regni non erit finis.

Et in Spiritum Sanctum, Dominum et vivificantem: qui ex Patre Filioque procedit. Qui cum Patre et Filio simul adoratur et conglorificatur: qui locutus est per prophetas. Et unam, sanctam, Catholicam et Apostolicam Ecclesiam. Confiteor unum baptisma in remissionem peccatorum. Et exspecto resurrectionem mortuorum. Et vitam venturi saeculi. Amen.

gotten Son of God, born of the Father before all ages; God of God, Light of Light, true God of true God; begotten not made; consubstantial with the Father, by whom all things were made. Who for us men, and for our salvation, came down from heaven, [*here the priest and people genuflect*] and was incarnate by the Holy Ghost of the Virgin Mary, AND WAS MADE MAN. [*Standing erect again, he continues.*] He was crucified also for us, suffered under Pontius Pilate, and was buried. The third day He rose again, according to the Scriptures; and ascended into heaven, and sitteth at the right hand of the Father: and He shall come again with glory to judge both the living and the dead: of whose kingdom there shall be no end.
And I believe in the Holy Ghost, the Lord and Lifegiver, who proceedeth from the Father and the Son: who together with the Father and the Son is adored [*inclining his head*] and glorified: who spoke by the prophets. And one holy, Catholic, and Apostolic Church. I confess one baptism for the remission of sins. And I look for the resurrection of the dead, and [*making on himself the sign of the cross*] the life of the world to come. Amen.

THE ORDINARY OF THE MASS

Kissing the altar and turning towards the people, the priest says:

℣. Dominus vobiscum.
℟. Et cum spiritu tuo.

℣. The Lord be with you.
℟. And with thy spirit.

Turning again towards the altar, he says Oremus
and reads the Offertory:

Offertorium. Ps. 75.
Terra tremuit, et quievit, dum resurgeret in judicio Deus, alleluia.

Offertory. Ps. 75.
The earth trembled and was still, when God arose in judgment. Alleluia.

Taking the paten with the host, the priest offers it to God, saying:

Suscipe sancte Pater omnipotens aeterne Deus, hanc immaculatam hostiam, quam ego indignus famulus tuus offero tibi Deo meo vivo et vero, pro innumerabilibus peccatis et offensionibus, et negligentiis meis, et pro omnibus circumstantibus, sed et pro omnibus fidelibus Christianis vivis atque defunctis: ut mihi et illis proficiat ad salutem in vitam aeternam. Amen.

Accept, O holy Father, almighty, eternal God, this immaculate host, which I, Thy unworthy servant, offer unto Thee, my living and true God, for my innumerable sins, offenses, and negligences, and for all here present; as also for all faithful Christians, both living and dead, that it may avail me and them for salvation unto life eternal. Amen.

After making the sign of the cross with the paten, the priest lets the host glide from the paten to the purificator, and partly conceals the paten under the purificator. He then pours wine and water into the chalice, first blessing the water, as he says:

Deus, qui humanae substantiae dignitatem mirabiliter condidisti, et mirabilius reformasti: da nobis per hujus aquae et vini mysterium, ejus divinitatis esse consortes, qui humanitatis nostrae fieri dig-

O God, who, in creating human nature didst wonderfully dignify it, and hast still more wonderfully reformed it: grant that, by the mystery of this water and wine, we made be made partakers of

natus est particeps, Jesus Christus, Filius tuus, Dominus noster: Qui tecum vivit et regnat in unitate Spiritus Sancti, Deus; per omnia saecula saeculorum. Amen.

His divinity who vouchsafed to become partaker of our humanity, Jesus Christ, Thy Son, our Lord; who liveth and reigneth with Thee in the unity of the Holy Ghost, world without end. Amen.

Taking the chalice, he offers it up saying:

Offerimus tibi Domine, calicem salutaris, tuam deprecantes clementiam: ut in conspectu divinae majestatis tuae, pro nostra et totius mundi salute cum odore suavitatis ascendat. Amen.

We offer unto Thee, O Lord, the chalice of salvation, beseeching Thy clemency that it may ascend before Thy Divine Majesty, as an odor of sweetness, for our salvation and for that of the whole world. Amen.

After making the sign of the cross with the chalice, he places it on the altar and covers it. Then, bowing before the altar with joined hands, he says:

In spiritu humilitatis, et in animo contrito suscipiamur a te Domine: et sic fiat sacrificium nostrum in conspectu tuo hodie, ut placeat tibi Domine Deus.

In the spirit of humility, and with a contrite heart, may we be accepted by Thee, O Lord; and grant that the sacrifice we offer this day in Thy sight may be pleasing to Thee, O Lord God.

Standing erect, elevating his eyes, and stretching out and then rejoining his hands, he continues:

Veni sanctificator omnipotens aeterne Deus: et bene✠dic hoc sacrificium tuo sancto nomini praeparatum.

Come, O Sanctifier, almighty, eternal God, and bless ✠ this sacrifice [*making a sign of the cross over the chalice and host*], prepared to Thy holy Name.

Washing his fingers at the Epistle side of the altar, he recites the following:

THE ORDINARY OF THE MASS

Lavabo inter innocentes manus meas: et circumdabo altare tuum Domine. Ut audiam vocem laudis: et enarrem universa mirabilia tua. Domine dilexi decorem domus tuae, et locum habitationis gloriae tuae. Ne perdas cum impiis Deus animam meam: et cum viris sanguinum vitam meam. In quorum manibus iniquitates sunt: dextera eorum repleta est muneribus. Ego autem in innocentia mea ingressus sum: redime me, et miserere mei. Pes meus stetit in directo: in ecclesiis benedicam te, Domine. Gloria Patri, et Filio, et Spiritui Sancto. Sicut erat, etc.

I will wash my hands among the innocent: and will encompass Thy altar, O Lord. That I may hear the voice of Thy praise, and tell of all Thy marvellous works. I have loved, O Lord, the beauty of Thy house, and the place where Thy glory dwelleth. Take not away my soul, O God, with the wicked, nor my life with bloody men. In whose hands are iniquities; their right hand is filled with gifts. As for me, I have walked in my innocence: redeem me, and have mercy upon me. My foot hath stood in the right path: in the churches I will bless Thee, O Lord. Glory be to the Father, to the Son and to the Holy Ghost. As it was, etc.

Bowing before the middle of the altar with joined hands, he says:

Suscipe sancta Trinitas hanc oblationem, quam tibi offerimus ob memoriam passionis resurrectionis et ascensionis Jesu Christi Domini nostri: et in honorem beatae Mariae semper virginis, et beati Joannis Baptistae, et sanctorum Apostolorum Petri et Pauli, et istorum, et omnium Sanctorum: ut illis proficiat ad honorem, nobis autem ad salutem: et illi pro nobis intercedere dignentur in coelis, quorum memoriam agimus in terris. Per eumdem Christum Dominum nostrum. Amen.

Receive, O Holy Trinity, this oblation which we make to Thee in memory of the Passion, Resurrection, and Ascension of our Lord Jesus Christ, and in honor of the blessed Mary ever Virgin, of blessed John the Baptist, of the holy Apostles Peter and Paul, and of these and of all the saints: that it may be available to their honor and our salvation: and may they vouchsafe to intercede for us in heaven, whose memory we celebrate on earth. Through the same Christ our Lord. Amen.

THE PRIEST AT THE ALTAR

*Kissing the altar and turning to the people,
he extends and joins his hands, saying:*

Orate, fratres, ut meum ac vestrum sacrificium acceptabile fiat apud Deum Patrem omnipotentem.

℟. Suscipiat Dominus sacrificium de manibus tuis ad laudem et gloriam nominis sui, ad utilitatem quoque nostram, totiusque Ecclesiae suae sanctae.

Brethren, pray that my sacrifice and yours may be acceptable to God the Father Almighty.

℟. May the Lord receive the sacrifice at thy hands, to the praise and glory of His name, to our own benefit, and to that of all His holy Church.

Adding Amen *in a low voice, the priest with
extended hands now reads the* Secret:

Secreta.
Suscipe, quaesumus, Domine, preces populi tui cum oblationibus hostiarum: ut paschalibus initiata mysteriis, ad aeternitatis nobis medelam, te operante, proficiant. Per Dominum.

Secret.
Receive, we beseech thee, O Lord, the prayers and sacrifices of Thy people: and grant that what we have begun at these Paschal mysteries may by Thy power avail us as a healing remedy unto everlasting life. Through our Lord.

*On reaching the end of the Secret, the priest rests his hands on the altar
(one on each side of the purificator), and says in an audible voice:*

℣. Per omnia saecula saeculorum.
℟. Amen.
℣. Dominus vobiscum.
℟. Et cum spiritu tuo.
℣. Sursum corda.

℟. Habemus ad Dominum.

℣. Gratias agamus Domino Deo nostro.

℣. World without end.
℟. Amen.
℣. The Lord be with you.
℟. And with thy spirit.
℣. Lift up your hearts [*raising his hands a little*].
℟. We have lifted them up unto the Lord.
℣. Let us give thanks to the Lord our God [*meanwhile joining his*

THE ORDINARY OF THE MASS

	hands and bowing his head].
℟. Dignum et justum est.	℟. It is meet and just.

Extending his hands, he says:

Vere dignum et justum est, aequum et salutare: Te quidem, Domine, omni tempore, sed in hac potissimum die gloriosius praedicare, cum Pascha nostrum immolatus est Christus. Ipse enim verus est Agnus, qui abstulit peccata mundi. Qui mortem nostram moriendo destruxit, et vitam resurgendo reparavit. Et ideo cum Angelis et Archangelis, cum Thronis et Dominationibus, cumque omni militia caelestis exercitus, hymnum gloriae tuae canimus, sine fine dicentes:

It is truly meet and just, right and salutary, that we should proclaim Thy glory incessantly, but most especially in this day when Christ our Pasch was immolated. For He is the true lamb that hath taken away the sins of the world; who by dying hath overcome our death, and by rising again hath restored our life. And therefore with the angels and archangels, the thrones and dominions, and the whole host of the heavenly army we sing a hymn to Thy glory, saying again and again:

Joining his hands, he bows while reciting the Sanctus. *At the word* Benedictus *he stands erect, and makes on himself the sign of the cross.*

Sanctus, Sanctus, Sanctus, Dominus Deus Sabaoth. Pleni sunt coeli, et terra gloria tua. Hosanna in excelsis. Benedictus qui venit in nomine Domini. Hosanna in excelsis.

Holy, holy, holy, Lord God of hosts. The heavens and the earth are full of Thy glory. Hosanna in the highest. Blessed is He that cometh in the name of the Lord. Hosanna in the highest.

THE CANON OF THE MASS

Extending and raising his hands, the priest also raises his eyes to heaven. Immediately rejoining his hands and lowering his eyes, he bows profoundly before the altar, and, resting his hands on the edge of the table, says:

Te igitur, clementissime Pater, | Wherefore, we humbly pray and

per Jesum Christum Filium tuum Dominum nostrum, supplices rogamus ac petimus, uti accepta habeas, et benedicas, haec ✠ dona, haec ✠ munera, haec ✠ sancta sacrificia illibata, in primis quae tibi offerimus pro Ecclesia tua sancta Catholica; quam pacificare, custodire, adunare, et regere digneris toto orbe terrarum: una cum famulo tuo Papa nostro N., et Antistite nostro N., et omnibus orthodoxis, atque Catholicae et Apostolicae fidei cultoribus.

beseech Thee, most merciful Father, through Jesus Christ Thy Son, our Lord [*he kisses the altar*], that Thou wouldst vouchsafe to accept and bless [*first joining his hands together and then making three signs of the cross over the host and chalice*] these ✠ gifts, these ✠ presents, these ✠ holy unspotted sacrifices which, in the first place, we offer Thee for Thy holy Catholic Church, to which vouchsafe to grant peace, as also to protect, unite, and govern it throughout the world, together with Thy servant N., our Pope, N., our bishop, as also all orthodox believers and professors of the Catholic and Apostolic Faith.

Memento of the Living

Memento Domine famulorum, famularumque tuarum N. et N. et omnium circumstantium, quorum tibi fides cognita est, et nota devotio, pro quibus tibi offerimus: vel qui tibi offerunt hoc sacrificium laudis pro se, suisque omnibus: pro redemptione animarum suarum, pro spe salutis et incolumitatis suae: tibique reddunt vota sua aeterno Deo vivo et vero.

Be mindful, O Lord, of Thy servants and handmaids, N. and N. [*He pauses, joins his hands, prays silently for those he intends to pray for, and then proceeds with extended hands*]. And of all here present, whose faith and devotion are known unto Thee; for whom we offer, or who offer up to Thee, this sacrifice of praise for themselves, their families and friends, for the redemption of their souls, for the hope of their safety and salvation, and who pay their vows to Thee, the eternal, living, and

true God.

| *Infra actionem.* | *Within the action.* |

Communicantes, et diem sacratissimum celebrantes Resurrectionis Domini nostri Jesu Christi secundum carnem: sed et memoriam venerantes, in primis gloriosae semper Virginis Mariae, Genitricis ejusdem Dei et Domini nostri Jesu Christi: sed et beatorum Apostolorum, ac Martyrum tuorum, Petri et Pauli, Andreae, Jacobi, Joannis, Thomae, Jacobi, Philippi, Bartholomaei, Matthaei, Simonis et Thaddaei: Lini, Cleti, Clementis, Xysti, Cornelii, Cypriani, Laurentii, Chrysogoni, Joannis et Pauli, Cosmae et Damiani: et omnium Sanctorum tuorum; quorum meritis, precibusque concedas, ut in omnibus protectionis tuae muniamur auxilio. Per eumdem Christum Dominum nostrum. Amen.

Communicating, and celebrating the most holy day of the resurrection of our Lord Jesus Christ according to the flesh; and also venerating the memory, first, of the glorious Mary ever a virgin, Mother of the same our God and Lord Jesus Christ; likewise of Thy blessed apostles and martyrs, Peter and Paul, Andrew, James, John, Thomas, James, Philip, Bartholomew, Matthew, Simon and Thaddeus; of Linus, Cletus, Clement, Sixtus, Cornelius, Cyprian, Lawrence, Chrysogonus, John and Paul, Cosmas and Damian, and of all Thy saints; for the sake of their merits and prayers grant that we may in all things be guarded by the help of Thy protection. *[Joining his hands together.]* Through the same Christ our Lord. Amen.

Spreading his hands over the offerings, he says:

Hanc igitur oblationem servitutis nostrae, sed et cunctae familiae tuae, quam tibi offerimus pro his quoque, quos regenerare dignatus es ex aqua, et Spiritu Sancto, tribuens eis remissionem omnium peccatorum, quaesumus, Domine, ut placatus acci-

We, therefore, beseech Thee, O Lord, graciously to accept this oblation of servitude of ourselves and Thy whole family, which we make unto Thee on behalf of these to whom Thou hast vouchsafed to bring to a new birth by water and the Holy Ghost, giving

pias: diesque nostros in tua pace disponas, atque ab aeterna damnatione nos eripi, et in electorum tuorum jubeas grege numerari. Per Christum Dominum nostrum. Amen.

Quam oblationem tu, Deus, in omnibus, quaesumus, bene✠dictam, adscri✠ptam, ra✠tam, rationabilem, acceptabilemque facere digneris: ut nobis Cor✠pus, et San✠guis fiat dilectissimi Filii tui Domini nostri Jesu Christi.

Qui pridie quam pateretur, accepit panem in sanctas ac venerabiles manus suas: et elevatis oculis in coelum, ad te Deum Patrem suum omnipotentem, tibi gratias agens, bene✠dixit, fregit, diditque discipulis suis, dicens: Accipite et manducate ex hoc omnes: HOC EST ENIM CORPUS MEUM.

them remission of all their sins; dispose our days in Thy peace, command us to be delivered from eternal damnation and to be numbered in the flock of Thy elect. [*Joining his hands together.*] Through Christ our Lord. Amen. Which oblation do Thou, O God, vouchsafe in all things to make ✠ blessed, ap✠proved, rati✠fied [*making the sign of the cross thrice over the offerings*], reasonable, and acceptable, that it may become for us the Bo✠dy and Blood ✠ [*making a sign of the cross first over the host and then over the chalice*] of Thy most beloved Son, Jesus Christ our Lord. Who the day before He suffered took bread [*he takes the host*] into His holy and venerable hands and [*he raises his eyes to heaven*] with eyes lifted up towards heaven, unto Thee, God, His Almighty Father, giving thanks to Thee, blessed ✠ [*making a sign of the cross over the host*], broke, and gave to His disciples, saying: Take, and eat ye all of this. [*Holding the host between the thumbs and first fingers of both hands, he continues:*] FOR THIS IS MY BODY.

After pronouncing the words of consecration the priest genuflects in adoration, and then elevates the Sacred Host so that it may be seen by the people, and genuflects again. At the Elevation the bell is rung thrice.

THE ORDINARY OF THE MASS

Simili modo postquam coenatum est, accipiens et hunc praeclarum Calicem in sanctas ac venerabiles manus suas: item tibi gratias agens, bene✠dixit, deditque discipulis suis, dicens: Accepite et bibite ex eo omnes: HIC EST ENIM CALIX SANGUINIS MEI, NOVI ET AETERNI TESTAMENTI: MYSTERIUM FIDEI, QUI PRO VOBIS ET PRO MULTIS EFFUNDETUR IN REMISSIONEM PECCATORUM.

In like manner, after He had supped [*he takes the chalice in both hands*], taking also this glorious chalice into His holy and venerable hands, and again giving thanks to Thee, He blessed ✠ [*holding the chalice with his left hand, he makes the sign of the cross over it with his right*] and gave to His disciples, saying : Take, and drink ye all of this. [*Raising the chalice a little from the altar-table, he continues:*] FOR THIS IS THE CHALICE OF MY BLOOD, OF THE NEW AND ETERNAL TESTAMENT, THE MYSTERY OF FAITH, WHICH SHALL BE SHED FOR YOU AND FOR MANY UNTO THE REMISSION OF SINS. [*Replacing the chalice on the altar, he says:*]

Haec quotiescumque feceritis, in mei memoriam facietis.

As often as ye shall do these things, ye shall do them in remembrance of Me.

Genuflecting, he adores, and rising elevates the chalice. After a second genuflection, he continues with extended hands:

Unde et memores Domine, nos servi tui, sed et plebs tua sancta, ejusdem Christi Filii tui Domini nostri tam beatae passionis, nec non et ab inferis resurrectionis, sed et in coelos gloriosae ascensionis: offerimus praeclarae majestati tuae de tuis donis ac datis, Hostiam ✠ puram, Hostiam ✠ sanctam, Hostiam ✠ immaculatam, Panem ✠ sanctum vitae

Wherefore, O Lord, we Thy servants, as also Thy holy people, calling to mind the blessed passion of the same Christ Thy Son our Lord, His resurrection from hell, and glorious ascension into heaven, offer unto Thy glorious Majesty, of Thy gifts and grants [*he joins his hands and makes three signs of the cross over the Host and chalice*] a pure ✠ Host, a holy

aeternae, et calicem ✠ salutis perpetuae.

✠ Host, an immaculate ✠ Host [*and then a sign of the cross, first over the Host and then over the chalice*], the holy ✠ Bread of eternal life, and the chalice ✠ of everlasting salvation.

Extending his hands, he continues:

Supra quae propitio ac sereno vultu respicere digneris: et accepta habere, sicuti accepta habere dignatus es munera pueri tui justi Abel, et sacrificium patriarchae nostri Abrahae: et quod tibi obtulit summus sacerdos tuus Melchisedech, sanctum sacrificium, immaculatam hostiam.

Upon which vouchsafe to look with a propitious and serene countenance, and to accept them, as Thou wert graciously pleased to accept the gifts of Thy just servant Abel, and the sacrifice of our Patriarch Abraham, and that which Thy high-priest Melchisedech offered to Thee, a holy sacrifice, an immaculate host.

Bowing down and resting his joined hands on the altar, he says:

Supplices te rogamus, omnipotens Deus; jube haec perferri per manus sancti Angeli tui in sublime altare tuum, in conspectu divinae majestatis tuae: ut quoquot ex hac altaris participatione, sacrosanctum Filii tui Cor✠pus et San✠guinem sumpserimus omni benedictione coelesti et gratia repleamur. Per eumdem Christum Dominum nostrum. Amen.

We most humbly beseech Thee, Almighty God, command these things to be carried by the hands of Thy holy angel to Thy altar on high, in the sight of Thy Divine Majesty, that as many of us as, [*he kisses the altar*] by participation at this altar, shall receive the most sacred [*joining his hands, he makes a sign of the cross over the Host and then the chalice*] Body ✠ and Blood ✠ of Thy Son, may be filled with [*he makes the sign of the cross on himself*] every heavenly benediction and grace. [*He joins his hands.*] Through the same Christ, etc, Amen.

Memento of the Dead.

Memento etiam, Domine, famulorum famularumque tuarum N. et N. qui nos praecesserunt cum signo fidei, et dormiunt in somno pacis.	Be mindful, O Lord, of Thy servants and handmaids N. and N., who are gone before us with the sign of faith, and rest in the sleep of peace.

Joining his hands, he prays for such of the dead as he intends to pray for. Then extending his hands, he continues:

Ipsis Domine, et omnibus in Christo quiescentibus, locum refrigerii, lucis et pacis, ut indulgeas, deprecamur. Per eumdem Christum Dominum nostrum. Amen.	To these, O Lord, and to all that rest in Christ, grant, we beseech Thee, a place of refreshment, light, and peace. [*He joins his hands, and bows his head.*] Through the same Christ our Lord. Amen.

Here, striking his breast and slightly raising his voice, he says:

Nobis quoque peccatoribus famulis tuis, de multitudine miserationum tuarum sperantibus, partem aliquam et societatem donare digneris, cum tuis sanctis Apostolis et Martyribus: cum Joanne, Stephano, Matthia, Barnaba, Ignatio, Alexandro, Marcellino, Petro, Felicitate, Perpetua, Agatha, Lucia, Agnete, Caecilia, Anastasia, et omnibus sanctis tuis: intra quorum nos consortium, non aestimator meriti, sed veniae, quaesumus, largitor admitte. Per Christum Dominum nostrum.	And to us sinners, Thy servants, hoping in the multitude of Thy mercies, vouchsafe to grant some part and fellowship with Thy holy apostles and martyrs: with John, Stephen, Matthias, Barnabas, Ignatius, Alexander, Marcellinus, Peter, Felicitas, Perpetua, Agatha, Lucy, Agnes, Cecily, Anastasia, and with all Thy saints: into whose company we beseech Thee to admit us, not considering our merit, but freely granting us pardon. [*He joins his hands.*] Through Christ our Lord.
Per quem haec omnia, Domine, semper bona creas, sancti✠ficas,	By whom, O Lord, Thou dost always create, ✠ sanctify, ✠ quick-

vivi✠ficas, bene✠dicis et praestas nobis.

en, ✠ bless [*making three signs of the cross over the Host and chalice*], and give us all these good things.

Uncovering the chalice, he genuflects, takes the Host in his right hand and the chalice in his left, and makes three signs of the cross with the Host over the bowl of the chalice, saying:

Per ip✠sum, et cum ip✠so, et in ipso ✠, est tibi Deo Patri ✠ omnipotenti, in unitate Spiritus ✠ Sancti, omnis honor et gloria.

Through ✠ Him, and with ✠ Him, and in ✠ Him, is to Thee, [*making two signs of the cross between the chalice and his breast*] God the Father ✠ Almighty, in the unity of the Holy ✠ Ghost, [*raising slightly the chalice and Host*] all honor and glory.

Replacing the Host and chalice on the altar, he covers the chalice, genuflects, and on rising says:

℣. Per omnia saecula saeculorum.
℟. Amen.

℣. For ever and ever.
℟. Amen

He joins his hands until he begins the Pater noster, which he recites with extended hands:

Praeceptis salutaribus moniti, et divina institutione formati, audemus dicere:
Pater noster, qui es in coelis: sanctificetur nomen tuum: adveniat regnum tuum: fiat voluntas tua sicut in coelo et in terra. Panem nostrum quotidianum da nobis hodie: et dimitte nobis debita nostra, sicut et nos dimittimus debitoribus nostris. Et ne nos inducas in tentationem.
℟. Sed libera nos a malo.

Instructed by Thy saving precepts, and following Thy divine institution, we presume to say:
Our Father, who art in heaven, hallowed be Thy name; Thy kingdom come; Thy will be done on earth as it is in heaven. Give us this day our daily bread; and forgive us our trespasses, as we forgive those who trespass against us. And lead us not into temptation.

℟. But deliver us from evil.

THE ORDINARY OF THE MASS

He then says in a low voice Amen, *and, taking the paten between the first and middle fingers of his right hand, continues:*

Libera nos, quaesumus Domine, ab omnibus malis praeteritis, praesentibus, et futuris: et intercedente beata et gloriosa semper Virgine Dei Genitrice Maria, cum beatis Apostolis tuis Petro et Paulo, atque Andrea, et omnibus sanctis, da propitius pacem in diebus nostris: ut ope misericordiae tuae adjuti, et a peccato simus semper liberi, et ab omni perturbatione securi.

Deliver us, we beseech Thee, O Lord, from all evils, past, present, and to come; and by the intercession of the blessed and glorious Virgin Mary, Mother of God, together with Thy blessed Apostles Peter and Paul, and Andrew, and all the Saints [*making the sign of the cross on himself with the paten, he kisses it, and says*], mercifully grant peace in our days: that by the assistance of Thy mercy we may be always free from sin, and secure from all disturbance.

Inserting the paten under the Host he uncovers the chalice, genuflects, rises, takes the Host, and, holding it over the chalice, breaks it in the middle, saying:

Per eumdem Dominum nostrum Jesum Christum Filium tuum.

Through the same Jesus Christ, Thy Son, our Lord.

Placing on the paten the part of the Host which he holds in his right hand, he breaks a particle off the part which he holds in his left, saying:

Qui tecum vivit et regnat in unitate Spiritus Sanctis Deus.

Who liveth and reigneth with Thee in the unity of the Holy Ghost, one God.

Placing on the paten the part of the Host which he holds in his left hand, and holding the particle over the chalice with his right hand, he takes the chalice with his left, and says:

℣. Per omnia saecula saeculorum.
℟. Amen.

℣. World without end.
℟. Amen.

As he makes three signs of the cross with the particle over the chalice, he continues:

℣. Pax ✠ Domini sit ✠ semper vobis✠cum.
℟. Et cum spiritu tuo.

℣. May the peace ✠ of the Lord be ✠ always with ✠ you.
℟. And with thy spirit.

Placing the particle in the chalice, he says in a low voice:

Haec commixtio et consecratio Corporis et Sanguinis Domini nostri Jesu Christi fiat accipientibus nobis in vitam aeternam. Amen.

May this mingling and consecration of the Body and Blood of our Lord Jesus Christ be unto us that receive them effectual to eternal life. Amen.

He covers the chalice, genuflects, bows towards the Blessed Sacrament, and, striking his breast three times, says:

Agnus Dei, qui tollis peccata mundi, misere nobis [*twice*]. Agnus Dei, qui tollis peccata mundi, dona nobis pacem.

Lamb of God, who takest away the sins of the world, have mercy upon us [*twice*]. Lamb of God, who takest away the sins of the world, grant us peace.

Bowing and resting his joined hands on the altar, he says the following prayers:

Domine Jesu Christe, qui dixisti Apostolis tuis: pacem relinquo vobis, pacem meam do vobis: ne respicias peccata mea, sed fidem Ecclesiae tuae; eamque secundum voluntatem tuam pacificare et coadunare digneris. Qui vivis et regnas Deus, per omnia saecula saeculorum. Amen.

Lord Jesus Christ, who saidst to Thy Apostles, "Peace I leave with you, My peace I give unto you," regard not my sins, but the faith of Thy Church; and vouchsafe to it that peace and unity which is agreeable to Thy will; who livest and reignest God for ever and ever. Amen.

Domine Jesu Christe, Fili Dei vivi, qui ex voluntate Patris cooperante Spiritu Sancto, per mortem

Lord Jesus Christ, Son of the living God, who, according to the will of the Father, through the

tuam mundum vivificasti: libera me per hoc sacrosanctum Corpus et Sanguinem tuum ab omnibus iniquitatibus meis et universis malis: et fac me tuis semper inhaerere mandatis: et a te numquam separari permittas: qui cum eodem Deo Patre et Spiritu Sancto vivis et regnas Deus in saecula saeculorum. Amen.

Perceptio Corporis tui, Domine Jesu Christe, quod ego indignus sumere praesumo, non mihi proveniat in judicium et condemnationem: sed pro tua pietate prosit mihi ad tutamentum mentis et corporis, et ad medelam percipiendam. Qui vivis et regnas cum Deo Patre in unitate Spiritus Sancti Deus, per omnia saecula saeculorum. Amen.

coöperation of the Holy Ghost, hast by Thy death given life to the world, deliver me by this, Thy most sacred Body and Blood, from all my iniquities and from all evils; and make me always adhere to Thy commandments and never suffer me to be separated from Thee; who with the same God the Father and Holy Ghost, livest and reignest God, for ever and ever. Amen.

Let not the reception of Thy Body, O Lord Jesus Christ, which I unworthy presume to receive, turn to my judgment and condemnation: but through Thy goodness may it be to me a safe guard and remedy, both of soul and body. Who with God the Father, in the unity of the Holy Ghost, livest and reignest God for ever and ever. Amen.

Making a genuflection, the priest rises and says:

Panem coelestem accipiam et nomen Domini invocabo.

I will take the Bread of heaven, and call upon the name of the Lord.

Then taking the two parts of the Host between the thumb and first finger of his left hand, and holding the paten between the first and middle fingers, he strikes his breast with the right, and, raising his voice a little, says three times:

Domine, non sum dignus ut intres sub tectum meum: sed tantum dic verbo, et sanabitur anima mea.

Lord, I am not worthy that Thou shouldst enter under my roof; but only say the word, and my soul

shall be healed.

Making the sign of the cross over himself with the Host, he says:

Corpus Domini nostri Jesu Christi custodiat animam meam in vitam aeternam. Amen.	May the Body of our Lord Jesus Christ preserve my soul to life everlasting. Amen.

He then reverently receives the Sacred Host, and, after a short pause for meditation, uncovers the chalice, genuflects, and gathers the fragments with the paten and wipes the later over the chalice, saying:

Quid retribuam Domino pro omnibus quae retribuit mihi? Calicem salutaris accipiam, et nomen Domini invocabo. Laudans invocabo Dominum, et ab inimicis meis salvus ero.	What shall I render to the Lord for all He hath rendered unto me? I will take the chalice of salvation, and call upon the name of the Lord. Praising I will call upon the Lord, and I shall be saved from my enemies.

Taking the chalice in his right hand and with it making on himself the sign of the cross, he says:

Sanguis Domini nostri Jesu Christi custiodiat animam meam in vitam aeternam. Amen.	May the Blood of our Lord Jesus Christ preserve my soul unto life everlasting. Amen.

Those who are to communicate go up to the Sanctuary at the Domine, non sum dignus, *when the bell rings: the server spreads a cloth before them, and says the* Confiteor.

Then the priest, turning to the communicants, pronounces the Absolution.

Misereatur vestri, etc. Indulgentiam, absolutionem, etc.	May Almighty God have mercy, etc. May the almighty and merciful Lord, etc.

Elevating a particle of the Blessed Sacrament, and turning towards the people, he says:

Ecce Agnus Dei, ecce qui tollit peccata mundi.	Behold the Lamb of God, behold Him who taketh away the sins of the world.

And then repeats three times, Domine, non sum dignus, *etc.*

He then administers the Holy Communion, saying to each:

Corpus Domini nostri Jesu ✠ Christi custodiat animam tuam in vitam aeternam. Amen.	May the Body of our Lord Jesus ✠ Christ [*making the sign of the cross with the Host*] preserve thy soul to life everlasting. Amen.

Having reverently received the Sacred Blood with the particle, the priest takes the first ablution, saying:

Quod ore sumpsimus Domine, pura mente capiamus: et de munere temporali fiat nobis remedium sempiternum.	Grant, O Lord, that what we have taken with our mouth, we may receive with a pure mind; and of a temporal gift may it become to us an everlasting remedy.

Taking the second ablution of wine and water, he says:

Corpus tuum, Domine, quod sumpsi, et Sanguis, quem potavi, adhaereat visceribus meis: et praesta, ut in me non remaneat scelerum macula, quem pura et sancta refecerunt sacramenta. Qui vivis et regnas in saecula saeculorum. Amen.	May Thy Body, O Lord, which I have received, and Thy Blood which I have drunk cleave to my inmost being, and do Thou grant that no stain of sin remain in me, who have been fed with this pure and holy sacrament. Who livest, etc. Amen.

He then wipes the chalice, covers it, and having folded the corporal, arranges the chalice as at the beginning of Mass. He then reads the Communion.

Communio. 1 Cor. 5.	*Communion. 1 Cor. 5.*
Pascha nostrum immolatus est Christus, alleluia: itaque epulemur	Christ our Pasch is immolated, alleluia: therefore let us feast with

in azymis sinceritatis, et veritatis, alleluia, alleluia, alleluia.

the unleavened bread of sincerity and truth. Alleluia, alleluia, alleluia.

Then, kissing the altar, he turns towards the people and says:

℣. Dominus vobiscum.
℟. Et cum spiritu tuo.

℣. The Lord be with you.
℟. And with thy spirit.

Returning to the missal, he reads the Postcommunion:

Postcommunio.
Spiritum nobis, Domine, tuae caritatis infunde: ut, quos sacramentis paschalibus satiasti, tua facias pietate concordes. Per Dominum.

Postcommunion.
Pour forth upon us, O Lord, the spirit of Thy charity: that those whom Thou hast fed with the Paschal sacraments thou mayest, by Thy loving-kindness, make of one mind. Through our Lord.

Afterwards he turns again towards the people, and says:

℣. Dominus vobiscum.
℟. Et cum spiritu tuo.
℣. Ite, Missa est, alleluia, alleluia.

℟. Deo gratias, alleluia, alleluia.

℣. The Lord be with you.
℟. And with thy spirit.
℣. Go, the Mass is ended, alleluia, alleluia.
℟. Thanks be to God, alleluia, alleluia.

Bowing down before the altar with joined hands, he says:

Placeat tibi sancta Trinitas, obsequium servitutis meae; et praesta, ut sacrificium, quod oculis tuae majestatis indignus obtuli, tibi sit acceptabile, mihique et omnibus, pro quibus illud obtuli, sit, te miserante, propitiabile. Per Christum Dominum nostrum. Amen.

O Holy Trinity, let the performance of my homage be pleasing to Thee; and grant that the sacrifice which I, unworthy, have offered up in the sight of Thy Majesty, may be acceptable to Thee, and through Thy mercy be a propitiation for me, and all those for whom I have offered it. Through Christ our Lord. Amen.

THE ORDINARY OF THE MASS

Then he kisses the altar, and, raising his eyes, extending, raising, and joining his hands, he bows his head to the crucifix, and says:

Benedicat vos omnipotens Deus,   May almighty God,

Turning towards the people, he makes the sign of the cross over them, saying:

Pater, et Filius, ✠ et Spiritus Sanctus. Amen.	the Father, the Son, ✠ and Holy Ghost, bless you. Amen.

Then turning to the gospel side of the altar, he says:

℣. Dominus vobiscum.   ℣. The Lord be with you.
℟. Et cum spiritu tuo.   ℟. And with thy spirit.

Making the sign of the cross, first on the altar table, and then on his forehead, mouth and breast, he continues:

℣. Initium sancti Evangelii secundum Joannem.
℟. Gloria tibi Domine.
In prinicipio erat Verbum, et Verbum erat apud Deum, et Deus erat Verbum. Hoc erat in principio apud Deum. Omnia per ipsum facta sunt: et sine ipso factum est nihil, quod factum est: in ipso vita erat, et vita erat lux hominum: et lux in tenebris lucet, et tenebrae eam non comprehenderunt.

Fuit homo missus a Deo, cui nomen erat Joannes. Hic venit in testimonium, ut testimonium perhiberet de lumine, ut omnes crederent per illum. Non erat ille lux, sed ut testimonium perhiberet de

℣. The beginning of the holy Gospel according to Saint John.
℟. Glory be to Thee, O Lord.
In the beginning was the Word, and the Word was with God, and the Word was God: the same was in the beginning with God. All things were made by Him, and without Him was made nothing that was made: in Him was life, and the life was the light of men; and the light shineth in darkness, and the darkness did not comprehend it.

There was a man sent from God, whose name was John, This man came for a witness to give testimony of the light, that all men might believe through him. He was not the light, but came to

lumine. Erat lux vera, quae illuminat omnem hominem venientem in hunc mundum.

In mundo erat, et mundus per ipsum factus est, et mundus eum non cognovit. In propria venit, et sui eum non receperunt. Quotquot autem receperunt eum, dedit eis potestatem filios Dei fieri, his qui credunt in nomine ejus, qui non ex sanguinibus, neque ex voluntate carnis, neque ex voluntate viri, sed ex Deo nati sunt. ET VERBUM CARO FACTUM EST, et habitavit in nobis: et vidimus gloriam ejus, gloriam quasi Unigeniti a Patre, plenum gratiae et veritatis.

℟. Deo gratias.

give testimony of the light. That was the true light, which enlighteneth every man that cometh into this world. He was in the world, and the world was made by Him, and the world knew Him not. He came unto His own, and His own received Him not. But as many as received Him, to them He gave power to become the sons of God: to them that believe in His name, who are born, not of blood, nor of the will of the flesh, nor of the will of man, but of God. AND THE WORD WAS MADE FLESH [*here all genuflect*], and dwelt among us; and we saw His glory, as it were the glory of the Only-begotten of the Father, full of grace and truth.

℟. Thanks be to God.

Descending to the foot of the altar, the priest now recites the prescribed prayers in the vernacular with the server and people. On their conclusion, he bows before the altar (or genuflects before the Blessed Sacrament) and follows the server to the sacristy, reciting the Antiphon *"Trium puerorum."*

About The Cenacle Press at Silverstream Priory

An apostolate of the Benedictine monastery of Silverstream Priory in Ireland, the mission of The Cenacle Press can be summed up in four words: *Quis ostendit nobis bona*—who will show us good things (Psalm 4:6)? In an age of confusion, ugliness, and sin, our aim is to show something of the Highest Good to every reader who picks up our books. More specifically, we believe that the treasury of the centuries-old Benedictine tradition and the beauty of holiness which has characterised so many of its followers through the ages has something beneficial, worthwhile, and encouraging in it for every believer.

cenaclepress.com

Also Available:

Blessed Columba Marmion, OSB
Christ the Ideal of the Monk

Blessed Columba Marmion, OSB
Words of Life on the Margin of the Missal

Dom Pius de Hemptinne, OSB
A Benedictine Soul: Biography, Letters, and Spiritual Writings of Dom Pius de Hemptinne

Robert Hugh Benson
The King's Achievement

Robert Hugh Benson
By What Authority

Robert Hugh Benson
The Friendship of Christ

Robert Hugh Benson
Confessions of a Convert

Dom Hubert van Zeller, OSB
Approach to Prayer

Dom Hubert van Zeller, OSB
Sanctity in Other Words

Fr Ryan T. Sliwa
New Nazareths in Us

St John Henry Newman (ed. Melinda Nielsen)
Festivals of Faith: Sermons for the Liturgical Year

Fr Willie Doyle, SJ
Pamphlets for the Faithful

Visit cenaclepress.com for our full catalogue.

www.ingramcontent.com/pod-product-compliance
Lightning Source LLC
Chambersburg PA
CBHW030035100526
44590CB00011B/206